Bias to the Poor

Bias to the Poor

David Sheppard

HODDER AND STOUGHTON
LONDON SYDNEY AUCKLAND TORONTO

British Library Cataloguing in Publication Data

Sheppard, David
  Bias to the poor.
  1. Church and social problems—Great
  Britain
  I. Title
  261.3′ 0941   HN390

  ISBN 0-340-32484-8
  ISBN 0-340-32370-1 Pbk

Hodder and Stoughton Editorial Office: 47 Bedford Square, London WC1B 3DP.

Preface

It is not easy for a working bishop to make time for extended study, or to spend unhurried time meeting poor people in a great city. The material for *Bias to the Poor* has been built up over four years and with the help and advice of many friends.

In 1978 I was invited by the Trustees of the William Barclay Lectures to deliver four lectures in Glasgow entitled 'The Divine Bias for the Losers'. Sister Norma Nelson, Church Army, kindly gave me two months of research, before I wrote the lectures and delivered them in 1979. In 1980 I followed this with four lectures on the same subject in Liverpool University Extra-Mural Studies Department. A series of seminars based on the lectures followed, which I attended. Subsequently there was a two-day seminar on the lectures at our home. In 1981 I delivered the Charles Gore Memorial Lecture at Westminster Abbey on 'The Black Experience in Britain'. This was published by Christian Action. In 1982 I delivered the Chavasse Lectures in Oxford on 'Bias to the Poor'. The book has been developing throughout the period of these lectures and seminars. In 1981 I took a study leave, during which I wrote the first draft of the book.

For twenty years I lived and worked in inner city London; my experience of inner city people is constantly being refreshed by both Church and secular engagements in and around Liverpool. I am most grateful to those many friends in Liverpool, who have helped me to interpret the life of inner city people, whether they live in the inner city itself or on the corporation estates round the edge of the city. I have acknowledged their help at various points in the notes at the end of the book. I owe a particular debt of gratitude to those who have read the first draft of the book and made detailed comments; these enduring friends are my wife Grace, Archbishop Derek Worlock, Archdeacon Wilfred Wood and Dr Durstan McDonald. And I am most grateful to Miss Joyce Tweedle and Mrs Ann Latter, who typed the manuscript, and Mrs Vere Cotton, who read the proofs.

DAVID SHEPPARD
Liverpool 1982

Contents

CHAPTER ONE

The Divine Bias

To argue that there should be a bias in favour of one group rather than another risks conflict. The moment one set of people is said to be poor and needy, others will claim that they have similar needs. There is no argument about having a bias for widows, orphans, the aged, the physically or mentally handicapped, the hungry—though that could not always have been assumed. In ancient and modern times there have been societies which have acted on the belief that only the fittest within the human race should survive.

Aid for the poor nations of the Third World is not a subject to win votes in the countries of Europe and North America. Similarly the shifting of trade arrangements in favour of Third World countries very quickly brings protests from the communities within the richer countries who lose jobs as a result. The Churches in wealthy countries have spoken up for the needs of the Third World; they have not so readily gone on to acknowledge that there are definable groups both within the nations of the Third World and in their own countries, which clearly have greater needs than others. To say that aid needs to be well aimed is another way of saying that there should be a bias in the way in which it is directed.

World Development is inclined to assume that whole nations are rich or poor. But the giving of aid or trade to a poor country provides no guarantee that the increased wealth and opportunity will reach the poor. The economic development of a poorer nation will not inevitably lead to a 'trickle down' or increased opportunity for the poorest. And suppose that Britain's trading position weakens in relation to Third World countries; Britain will not then become less affluent in some evenly distributed way. The burdens resulting from changes in trade or from new technology fall unequally on individuals and areas, and they will most frequently fall on those who are already in the weakest positions. In a developed industrial country like Britain the greatest poverty will be found in the major cities.

In the United States poverty has frequently been looked at in ethnic terms. Being black removes a great many opportunities. Britain is slowly facing that reality. You find yourself up against both general and particular disadvantages if you have a black skin; black skins have also revealed what was already going on in urban communities. Mark Bonham Carter described black people as the barium meal in British society. Barium meal introduces nothing into the body except colour; it reveals what is already going on in the body. The handicaps which black people face have revealed other definable groups in urban communities, who do not share the opportunities which are open to many. When we come to believe that such deprivation exists, it becomes clear that all do not set off in life from the same starting line. It will not then seem strange to argue for a bias in favour of such groups to correct their inequality of opportunity.

Bias to the poor sounds like a statement of political preference. My experience has been that some of the most central teachings of orthodox Christianity lead me to this position. I shall argue from Jesus's theme of the Kingdom of God, the calling to the Church to be Catholic, reaching across all human divisions and the doctrine of the Incarnation; they lead me to claim that there is a divine bias to the poor, which should be reflected both in the Church and in the secular world.

The dominant philosophy in countries like Britain and the United States is that you will naturally want to 'make it', to go up in the world to give your children a better chance of success. The effects of such a philosophy on the community from which you come is compounded by housing policies which segregate owner-occupiers from council tenants in huge one-class quarters. The bigger the city, the more this process has taken place, with the assumption that those who are successful will always choose to move away from the communities in which they grew up. This has happened for generations; it inevitably tends towards creating communities of the left behind.

For many years hopes were expressed that the divisions of class were becoming less real in Britain. They were unreal hopes. Today the divisions are as real as ever. An analysis of class in Britain is a complex matter. It is no longer tied to birth and blood. It is influenced by factors such as income, status at work and attitudes to society which neighbours hold. Some like to call themselves working-class who are home owners, earning high wages. Their approaches to life are very different from other working-class people who see life very strongly in terms of the group to which they belong, for example, on a council estate and on the shop floor. It has been helpfully suggested that different attitudes may be distinguished within those who see themselves as working-class. These are described as deferential, proletarian and privatised.[1] The deferential attitude expects others to be the leaders in society; deferential workers expect to fit into what their leaders expect of them. The proletarian attitude feels a strong sense of solidarity, especially in the fellowship of work; it expects working-class people to have their own insight and to take their own decisions. The worker with a privatised attitude sees work as a means to an end; the end is the development of his private life and that of his family.

The return of large-scale unemployment has highlighted what was already the case in some urban areas. It has become more appropriate to talk again about the poor; in Merseyside there are many areas where unemployment on a large scale has been present for years. There are areas where half the working population is out of work. Side by side with working-class families who may be earning large wages will be those who are properly described as poor. As you walk down a street two cars may stand outside No. 12, where three good incomes are coming in. No. 14 has two incomes. In No. 16 a single-parent family is on Family Income Supplement. The pain of relative deprivation is made sharper by advertising and the media. They shout the same message into each of those homes, that the opportunities of the consumer society are available to all of them.

For many years it was assumed that society is shaped like a pyramid, with the majority at the base of the pyramid being the poor. The logic then argued that one man—one vote would enable the interests of the poor to mobilise decisive political power. But for a long time society in a developed country like Britain has been shaped not like a pyramid, but like a diamond. In other words the majority and their votes are to be found somewhere in the middle, with a stake in keeping things as they are.

Christianity seems to be saying that poverty is blessed, and that at the same time we should try to get rid of it. I was among the leaders of the Churches in Liverpool, who led a pilgrimage of some fifty-five young adults—Roman Catholics, Methodists, United Reformed and Church of England—to the Ecumenical Community at Taizé in France. The Prior, Brother Roger, spoke to them about poverty, as though it was a good thing. Some of the Liverpool young people wouldn't accept that. They regarded poverty as an evil thing. St Francis was able to choose poverty and a simpler life style. The poverty which the young people had seen and objected to robbed the urban poor of any choices.

God the Creator made people in His own image: that includes His purpose that all of us should be able in some sense to put our stamp on the world and to know that we have the power to make choices which will affect our destiny and that of others. We must look hard at the difference between a kind of development which offers a higher cash standard of living but keeps large groups of people dependent and without a voice, and a genuine effort to create what the World Council of Churches have called 'a just, participatory and sustainable society.'

The way people feel about their experience of life is very relevant to a debate about what constitutes poverty. My years since ordination (twenty years living in the East End of London and South East London, followed since 1975 by being Bishop of Liverpool) have given me a very special opportunity of trying to enter into how people feel whose whole life is lived outside those circles of power where effective decisions are made. For example, a young black man from New Cross, London, said,

'Some of us look up from where we are, and see a network which exists, where decisions are taken which affect our lives. We should like to have some part in that network.'[2]

While I was away on study leave, writing this book, the Toxteth riots exploded in July 1981. British society was shocked at the violence used against the police and at the destruction of a community's own property and shopping facilities. The violence underlines both the level of alienation of substantial parts of the community in Liverpool and the urgency of action.

This book deliberately includes a number of attempts to express how people feel both about their powerlessness and about what they believe needs to be done. A group largely of black people in inner city Pittsburgh told me that a survey was attempted in the United States asking what black people said they needed and what white people said that black people needed. There was a total difference; when a similar enquiry was made fifteen years later, there was still the same difference. A priest living in a small community in Liverpool 8 wrote to me, 'I wonder whether one could launch a listening campaign for the whole Church.' The results of my listening I regard as at least as important as any authorities or statistics I may quote.

As it does its listening, the Church is called to commit itself to action on behalf of the poor. We start to feel uneasy at this point; 'Is there enough evidence to convict the Church of being on the side of the poor?' asked a black Christian in Philadelphia.[3] Many of us have a nagging sense that the urban poor do not see enough evidence of this kind. Professor A. H. Halscy describes his thoughts as a child at Evensong in a Northamptonshire Church in the 1930s. They were chanting the Magnificat:

> My soul doth magnify the Lord . . .
> He hath put down the mighty from their seat
>   and hath exalted the humble and meek.
> He hath filled the hungry with good things:
>   and the rich He hath sent empty away.[4]

'I vaguely assumed that the archaic language of my elders had led them to essential truth, but with wrong tenses, just as they appeared to be confused as to the geographical location of Jerusalem.'[5]

Many Christians have spiritualised those words, together with Jesus's words about the poor and about the rich, understanding their meaning to be about those who see or don't see their need of God. Certainly St Matthew records Him as saying, 'Blessed are the poor in spirit', but there are several texts where the plain meaning is that Jesus is talking about those who are materially poor.[6] But some people have taken those words in earnest. The message of the Magnificat was right at the heart of the move of one Indian away from the Parsee faith of his parents to become a Christian. He feels angry and betrayed when he sees the Church failing to reflect the divine bias for the poor.

Those who belong to more affluent suburbs sometimes resent the claim that there is a Divine Bias for the poor. They point to particular needs of individuals in their community; are they not also the needy Christ cares for? Yes, He does indeed care for every individual—widow, orphan, handicapped; but it is one of the realities of life, emphasised by urbanisation, that we are all influenced heavily by the group to which we belong. Some whole groups find themselves shut out from the circles in which decisions are taken and where many opportunities exist. Does God not have a word for those who have advantages? He does indeed have a word for all men; it is not always the same word. 'Where a man has been given much, much will be expected of him.'[7] Sometimes His word to the advantaged is that they must surrender their advantage for the sake of the poor.

There is ample evidence to convict the Church of being charitable and paternalistic to the poor. These actions should not be lightly discounted. Very large resources in money and in lifetimes of devoted service have been given by many Christians who had the deepest commitment to people. In many situations these have been the only ways in which badly needed resources have got through. There has been such a thing as genuine paternalism, which in the short term perhaps really has done better than self help efforts. Yet both charity and paternalism are concepts which are rightly criticised; both offer help, but frequently retain control in the fatherly or charitable hands of someone else, and therefore may then be said to strengthen rather than weaken dependence. That dependence is the enemy of a true sense of responsibility and self worth. It should be said that some voluntary and government bodies which give money have learned a great deal about giving without attaching the kind of strings which keep control away from groups who want to help themselves.

The call for justice jars on many ears. To those who broadly believed the status quo to be a just one it seems more wounding than the demand for charity or welfare. There is an honest argument here between people who truly care for the poor. To defend the status quo is not necessarily an attitude to be condemned. Those who do so believe that they are realistic about channelling actual resources to the poor; and about the practical difficulties of sustaining any kind of just society in an increasingly violent and libertarian world. They fear that hard-won ground, for example, in respect for authority, in disciplines at work, and in the pursuit of excellence is being put at risk by the call for more equal opportunity for all people to control their own destiny. Such people feel that the call for justice is somehow a personal attack on themselves or on those, whom they admire, who have gone before them. It says that poverty is not inevitable; that those who are better off could actually do something about it if they would try. It feels as though they are being blamed, and they resent that as unfair; they feel they are prisoners of history.

I hope it will be recognised that I do not wish to belittle genuine achievements, nor to suggest there are unworthy motives in those who want to conserve good bastions in our society. But I want to press the points about justice and about more equal opportunities for all to make real choices about their destiny. That will mean the shift of power and resources.

Such a debate, conducted inevitably with some passion, but always with respect for those with whom we disagree, is greatly needed in countries where the Christian tradition is much bound up with the history of the established structures. The debate needs some rules: I suggest four.

1. We must not assume that the others have unworthy

motives; words like reactionary, Dark Ages, authoritarian, affluent intelligentsia, trendy, elitist, racist, Marxist (unless someone claims to be such), should all switch on amber lights, warning that someone is about to be smeared in order to stop us listening to what he is actually saying.

2. We must not claim a hot line to God, when we know that Christians disagree about a subject.

3. We must not disqualify others from taking part in an honest debate about God's world (the charge that 'interventionist Bishops' should stick to their spiritual task). The Urban Bishops' Coalition of the Episcopal Church in the USA held a series of seven public hearings in urban centres in the United States and the Caribbean. There was heard repeatedly an almost wistful plea from poor people and those who work on their behalf that the Church might be present with its influence and involvement even more than with its money. 'Honest words, candid words, sometimes angry words, often words far too restrained and gentle were spoken, but in every instance the words were pleading, "Be our advocate!" '[8]

4. We must not withdraw from the debate when there seems no easy answer. It's too easy to say that since none of us has clean hands, we will give up speaking to one another about what is most important to us.[9] Then we talk only to those who agree with us, read only the newspapers which feed us what we think already and become victims of our own propaganda.

I believe that there is a divine bias to the disadvantaged, and that the Church needs to be much more faithful in reflecting it. In arguing this, I've been told that I am working out my feelings of guilt at having been given a privileged start. That may have some truth in it. While none of us is detached enough to be sure of his deepest motives, I can only say that I'm not aware of such a sense of guilt. I took it as a compliment, when I was told that in four lectures that I gave on 'The Divine Bias for the Losers' there was nothing that rejected my Cambridge University, Evangelical, Anglican background.[10] There is bound to be conflict within the mind of a Christian when he is confronted by the urban problem. It is easy to make all the evidence fit in to our starting base, or to reject all that it stands for. To be a bridge person means holding different views of life in some tension. That's not the same as sitting on the fence; there are times when the Christian who wants to offer a commentary on society needs to take sides.

I am aware of four motives which make me continue the argument within Church and society. In a book like this, the first is the compulsion to pass on what I have seen and heard. Society in cities like Liverpool and London is deeply divided. Many are unaware of the experiences of life which others face in the same city. One of the callings of the Christian Church is to be a bridge on which different experiences of life can be given a hearing. I want to show how blocking to God-given talents are some of those experiences of urban life; and to share some of the flickers of hope I see, which help to keep me a believer.

The second motive is to show how false it is to suggest, as is so often done, that two proper Christian callings are posed as opposites—that either you are for changing individuals or you are for changing the structures of society.

When I was first ordained and went to serve in inner city London, I would have said that people are the same wherever they live. I believed that if you could change individuals, that was the only way to change the world. I expected broadly to see the same response to the Gospel, to educational and career opportunities, whatever the context in which people lived. I've learned that there are massive blocks in the way of such responses for inner city people, whether they live in the inner city itself or in vast corporation estates on the perimeter of a city. The Gospel needs to proclaim the need and the possibility for God *both* to change people from inside out *and* to change the course of events to set people free to make such choices.

The third motive is to do with people's response to the Gospel. In my book, *Built as a City*[11] I showed that in London visible response to the Churches is dramatically smaller in urban working-class areas than in middle-class or professional areas. The same is true in Liverpool with the exception of the Roman Catholic Church; I will look at some of the reasons for that exception later on. It matters urgently how those who are at a disadvantage see the Church, because their experience of the Church often makes them say that this Christ of the Churches is not for them.

The fourth motive is that the Church is called to reflect God's character in the world. Whether anyone will respond or not, God loves things like mercy, justice and truth, and hates things like greed and oppression. Reflecting this character of God will mean that the Church must risk losing its innocence by becoming involved in the corporate life of cities. It must sometimes take sides, even if that leads to great unpopularity rather than growth in the number of worshippers.

CHAPTER TWO

Losers in the Urban Race

In countries like Britain, the United States and Australia many cling to the assumption that anyone can 'make it', if only he works hard. My experience in London and Liverpool is that this is not true. Liverpool was built on the basis of the energy and enterprise of private merchants. Unskilled labourers came in very large numbers to live in extremely poor conditions in an erratic economy. During 150 years many attempts have been made to pull together what was from the beginning a polarised society.

Some of those attempts were made by private enterprise; business life, fee-paying and selective schools offered the opportunity to some to climb through the openings which led to home ownership and the greater choices which affluence brings. Other attempts were by more socialist means; public ownership of industries like the docks, public housing developments on corporation estates, and comprehensive schools sought to build more equal foundations on which all could enter into the life of a full citizen.

In spite of many honestly conceived efforts, the polarised society is still with us. Winning and losing in the urban race leads to massively different opportunities for generations. This chapter is an attempt to understand what the urban experience in one city is like for the losers in the urban race. I have seen comparable experiences in other cities—the East End of London, South East London, Glasgow, the South Bronx, Harlem, the Lower East Side in New York, Pittsburgh's inner city, Redfern and Glebe in Sydney. The details will be different: my hope is that by using my own experience and the help of Church and secular interpreters in one city, which I know well, a human picture may emerge. The intention is to try to make it more possible to stand in the shoes of the poor.

New housing estates—a dream smashed

Around the perimeter of Liverpool huge public developments of corporation housing estates have been built since 1945. The great dream was that families would be given a flying start if they could get away from crowded inner city streets into spacious estates on green field sites. Perhaps as many as one in three of the million and a half people of Merseyside live on these estates.[1]

When I first visited one large outer estate, I brought with me the eyes of a Londoner. There we used to feel that, if only the suburbs would allow land for building, the housing problems of a crowded city would be solved. Now I was seeing plenty of space; yet every empty house or flat has all its windows broken. In several streets empty houses have their roofs smashed in. Most shops don't go in for glass, but have metal shutters. Blocks of maisonettes, built within the last twelve years, stand boarded up and totally empty. Some of the walk-up blocks have been demolished. In some other estates four-storey blocks have had the top two floors removed, to make smaller houses again; some very large blocks, also built within the last twelve years, are to be demolished. The dream of the green fields development seems in a number of instances to have been smashed.

There is a high crime rate. Mugging is talked about a lot. Police relations with the community are poor. In this almost entirely white area many of the same allegations are made— about police brutality, planting evidence, picking on young people—which may be heard in the black community in Liverpool or London. Police/community relations are claimed to have improved since the police for this district were recruited from Merseyside rather than from Lancashire. Police officers who have themselves grown up in the urban environment of a major city are more likely to understand attitudes of mind and community life than those who come from the industrial towns or villages of Lancashire.

A brief digression may be useful to make the distinction between a big city like Liverpool and Lancashire industrial towns like St Helen's and Wigan, which are also in the Diocese of Liverpool. The Lancashire towns continue to have strong family networks, based on the continuing life of many generations. In that context Church life often flourishes. Hard times have been faced with resilience, which draws much of its toughness from these enduring networks. When poor people from rural areas were sucked into the big cities in the nineteenth century this fabric of family networks and traditions was ripped up. They were torn apart again when so many of the terraced streets of the inner city were demolished by bombing or slum clearance and the new estates were built.

It is easy to notice the benefits which the industrial towns possess in contrast to the big city, and to overlook the real poverty which also exists in them. The decline of a specialised industry on which a town had depended hits people very hard, who are often less amenable to change than city dwellers. Those who find themselves rehoused in areas where family ties are seen to be strong know they are outsiders; often they feel even more isolated. A social worker who had moved to work on an estate in St Helen's said that there was a terrible feeling of inferiority and depression; people felt they were stigmatised because they lived on that estate. Wigan faces the present recession with a strong sense of having been here before. When George Orwell wrote *The Road to Wigan Pier*, the town had the worst unemployment figures in the North West. The current recession has revived old feelings of frustration and resignation. Poverty hurts in an industrial town too, but in many ways it is different in kind from what is experienced in urban life.[2]

On the large Merseyside estate which I am describing, unemployment has been a major issue from the beginning. Merseyside has consistently had double the national unemployment figures; this area has consistently had double Merseyside's figures. It used to be said before the recent recession that industrial countries must learn to tolerate 5 per cent unemployment; that meant that large communities such as this were being asked to accept that as a normal state of affairs they should tolerate 20 per cent unemployment. At the time of writing the figure has stood for some time above 30 per cent and in parts at 50 per cent, so we are discussing not a temporary trough of bad unemployment but a chronic situation.

A large comprehensive school, which has regularly produced good achievements and has an excellent name, had 350 leavers in 1980. At the beginning of 1981 forty-nine had found jobs. Five years earlier only about half their school leavers had jobs by the beginning of the following year. Putting those figures together shows that many who are twenty-one and older have never had a regular job. Young people used normally to find work through their parents, aunts, uncles or friends who knew about an opening. When there is very high unemployment in a whole community, the ability of families and friends to help each other to stand up for themselves is seriously crippled.

Questions are sometimes raised about whether unemployed young people really want to work. It would take enormous self-confidence to bounce back after repeated disappointments; such self-confidence is in short supply in areas where opportunities to achieve in ways that are recognised are few. Not one, but a series of vicious circles follow. Fourteen and fifteen year olds in schools on this estate have for years been asking out loud what is the point of working in school, if you're going to find no work or only a dead-end job when you leave school.

Many young people get themselves into a second circle: it hurts too much to go on looking for work, so you cover up by having a laugh at anything and everything. Liverpool's humour has certainly helped people to survive very bitter experiences. It can be greatly enriching; it can also be a way of hiding your eyes from stretching demands to dismiss everything with a joke. A group came to the funeral of one of their number. They had drifted since they left school; they're above average intelligence, good-looking young men, about twenty-four years of age. They knew the vicar well; they had offered him pot the first night he arrived years before, for a laugh, to see how he'd react. They were full of caring for their friend's mother, yet had somehow brought down the shutters in their minds against the causes which over four or five years had led to his death. They could not free themselves from the group's own momentum and way of life. They had built up certain pressures on each other, and were trapped into a set of hedonistic values. The only way some have broken away from the group has been when a steady girl friend has put her foot down, and they've been married.

There is a third circle in the background; it is often said that it isn't worth providing a training scheme if there are no jobs to go on to. At the same time employers are saying that it isn't worth bringing jobs if there isn't a better trained work force.

Unemployment is a hard experience in a more obviously felt way for those who have known what it is to work most of their life. One such couple, both in their fifties, and their son in his twenties have all been out of work for some years. The son is 'skilled at recycling'; he found a cooker on a dump and has mended it, so that it is working in their kitchen. He would be willing to travel across the country for a training in electronics. The husband told me they moved to the estate with his firm. He was made redundant seven years ago. Everyone seems to have given up any expectation that he'll find a job again. He now is only expected to go down to the Unemployment Benefit office four times a year, and they post him his Giro cheque every week. What does he do? He walks a lot. That day he'd been for a fifteen-mile walk with the dog to a country village. Unemployment brings hidden poverty with it. There are two sides to this; first people feel that society doesn't value them. Secondly they do not have enough money to live more than a grey existence.

Increasing the sense of powerlessness which unemployment brings are people's feelings about the bureaucratic machine. You must be able to do two basic things to get the machine to work for you: fill in a form and use a telephone. Many residents are short of confidence about those skills too. Very few council officials live among their neighbours. It all seems very remote. Top of the list of needs for many people on the estate come housing repairs. It is normal, not exceptional that if, say, a glass panel on the door is broken, it will not be mended that winter. It is quite likely to take twelve months. When a young couple talked about mending it themselves, they were told sharply by their neighbours not to do it because it was the council's responsibility.

Housing transfers seem to be hedged around with mystery and helplessness. Once a bad name is attached to a district, it becomes a Hard to Let area. At least one family set fire to their own home on this estate in order to get out of it. Many single-parent families are inevitably dependent in large measure on the bureaucratic machine. Those who operate it can make them feel that they have no right to be full citizens.

As I walked recently beside a wire fence, the rubbish was piled quite thickly against it for perhaps fifty yards. I said it had been like that when I stayed a night there some years before. 'Oh, they're always clearing it—perhaps four times since you were here—at least once a year.'

Councillors and officials are caught between two fires. Many of the councillors live on the estates. The Local Government District of Knowsley is comprised largely of these large post-war estates. They have faced enormous problems with scarce resources, and there are few long-standing institutions to help. Government money through the Rate Support Grant has been considerably reduced over the last few years. Knowsley misses out on the Inner City Partnership money, though its population is made up substantially of inner city people who face the same pressures in the estates as are met in the inner city itself. Politics are raw; community groups spring into life when there are particular issues like a rent strike or rehousing those who were stranded in the blocks that other tenants had abandoned. It is difficult to raise sustained support for long-term goals.

There are distinct flickers of hope to be seen, if you have eyes to see. Many who live on the estate are happy to be there. They mean to hang in there and build a good community. Many strongly self-reliant families live there, determined to give their children a good start. There is great generosity among the poorer families in giving time to neighbours, especially in tragic moments or through community efforts. There are some fine schools; for example, I spent a day in a large comprehensive school. I was asked to give away the prizes, but only provided I came to see the regular life of the school—all day. It has always kept its head steadily above water; a wide variety of intelligences and abilities are being helped to develop. There are good achievements to be measured. I was surprised and delighted to see fifteen and sixteen year old boys, a normally self-conscious age, dancing their hearts out in scenes from their production of *Grease*. How had this happened? It was because of a young teacher who was an old boy of the school; he had qualified as a teacher elsewhere and had now come back to teach in his old school. He lived on the estate like other teachers and nurses, who had grown up there and are determined to stay. The boys would risk making fools of themselves for him.

There is some resilient Church life. We have accepted, for example, a number of men from this parish for the ordained ministry during the last few years. I said resilient. There is a determination not to give in to vandalism and despair; if there is a service or occasion to which people come by car, it will be normal to mount guard over the cars while the service is going on. The Church congregations might have taken on embattled attitudes and become very inward looking in such situations; but members are involved widely in the life of the community.

As Chairman of the Area Board of the Manpower Services Commission for Merseyside and Cheshire I see quite a lot of the Youth Training Scheme. To start with it seemed to be no more than a stopgap, a poor second best, because there are so few jobs for youngsters to go on to. It has its severe limits: after twelve months in districts like this probably half go back on the unemployed register. But many projects offer definite disciplines, the opportunity to try out a number of different kinds of work and to do something genuinely needed in the community. Some Community Service projects have been criticised for not offering training for 'real work'. The emphasis in plans for the Youth Training Scheme to replace the Youth Opportunities Programme is often placed on persuading major blue chip companies to offer training places. That is important and overdue. But substantial parts of Merseyside have been described as an industrial desert. Our problem is that the blue chip companies are not to be found there. In areas like these the most realistic training schemes in the medium term will be those which teach skills, self-discipline and a will to offer service in the community. Measuring the usefulness of a project in an industrial desert will need different yardsticks, because the future beyond the training year is not likely to include traditional employment.

The very substantial resources of the Manpower Services Commission have come at a timely moment after the years when community development philosophy had taught many to look for leadership from within their own community. For example, in one twenty-storey block of flats on another estate no community room had been provided, even though the flats were largely for old people. Sponsored by local community groups together with some local business, Church and social-work people, the Youth Opportunities Programme trans-formed a ground-floor flat into a large sitting room with a kitchen beside it. Various community groups meet there. There is also a cooperative food shop there once a week. Old people, who have often been afraid of young people and hostile to them, now greet youngsters in the street, whom they know because they clean and do their shopping for them. Some continue to visit the elderly people whom they have met through the project after they leave it.

Some speak only of problems when they mention these estates. There are many others who see great possibilities along with the problems. The problems have to be faced, if there is to be true hope. Hope is not inspired by shutting your eyes to harsh realities. The same people who tell me about the signs of hope also make it very clear that they know how deeply hurt many in the community are. A vicar on the estate I have been writing about told me, 'I'd hope more than anything, that people's confidence in themselves and in God should grow against all the odds. The odds include lack of confidence, anger, the risk of mental breakdown and the shortage of money.' Yes, in order to redress the balance there has to be a bias.

The Inner City—interlocking deprivation

My first look at losers in the urban race has deliberately been in a modern housing development, not an inner city slum.

Already the subject has been the experience of life of inner city people: David Eversley rightly says that the inner city is a concept about people and their environment, not a geographically confined place.[3]

There needs also to be a decisive bias in favour of the inner city itself to begin to redress the balance there. It has sometimes been questioned whether the inner city's needs have not been exaggerated out of proportion to those of other parts of the city. Certainly there are great needs elsewhere, but large parts of the inner city must always be in the first list of priorities.

The needs of inner and outer areas are interrelated. For example, I returned from a parish visit to another outer corporation estate, Norris Green. This was an inter-war public housing development. As its first settlers have grown old and died many good houses have become vacant. It would be a healthy policy for the estate if young couples who've grown up there could now move into those houses. But they're not allowed to. I tackled the City Council. Surely this was a foolish policy. There were two parts to the answer; first there was no proper mixture of size of dwelling when Norris Green was built. They should have built plenty of smaller properties for newly marrieds and for the elderly as well as the family houses. Arising out of the unbalanced stock of housing came the second part of the answer; the urgent need of families in substandard inner city housing had to come first. They agreed with the point about young people being able to find housing in their own area, but the other need was so great that it must take priority. This argues that, if only we can get housing in the inner city right, there will be a ripple effect of better housing, because housing stock on other estates would then be available for their own needs.

Parts of Liverpool's inner city have been described as a disaster area. Many of the better-paid workers have moved out. Those left behind are the least able to cope. Housing standards are bad. Side by side with that comes poor health, low educational achievement, low incomes, high crime rates, many problem families and unemployment from 30 per cent to 60 per cent. Youngsters from these areas enter the labour market with many handicaps. Examination results are so far

27

below the national average that the gap is almost as wide as between Britain and some Third World states. One survey in 1979 found that only 3.5 per cent had five or more 'O' Levels compared with 22 per cent in the North West of England as a whole. Another survey of the inner city area (described as Roundhouse) notes the way in which children of six and seven years are already socialised with a sub-culture which makes it psychologically difficult for them to take advantage of educational and other opportunities that occur thereafter.[4] It is often assumed that everyone has a car nowadays. The contrast between car ownership in areas where there are many professional and managerial families and the inner city in Liverpool is dramatic. It ranges from over 70 per cent in four suburban planning zones to less than 10 per cent of families owning a car in ten inner city planning zones.[5]

In 1972 Peter Walker, then Secretary of State for the Environment, set up an inner areas study of three major cities—Birmingham, Liverpool and London. The final report of the Liverpool Inner Area Study in 1977 described disadvantages experienced in housing, jobs and schools. It reported that social polarisation was increasing. Professional and managerial people moving into the high-status areas in the five years prior to the 1971 census were raising the status of these areas still higher, whereas the increasing proportion of unskilled workers moving into the other council estates had an equivalent lowering effect. A similar divergence was occurring in the rooming house area, intensifying the social differences between its more and less affluent parts.[6]

Job opportunities in Liverpool have been seriously reduced. It was always a commercial rather than an industrial city. The proportion of semi-skilled and unskilled workers has always been much higher than the national average. The port has declined dramatically; in 1939 there were 45,000 dockers. In 1981 there were fewer than 4,000. The demolition of the inner city, first by bombing and then by redevelopment, took away much of the untidy (to the planner's eye) jumble of small businesses. It is one of the flickers of hope to see the bustle of new life of small businesses near to the centre of the city; new advance factories have been built by the City, and have been well taken up. But it would take an awful lot of such businesses to replace the jobs lost through recent closures.

In Liverpool alone (not Merseyside) 39,000 jobs were lost in five years, 1977–81, in notified redundancies. The closure in 1981 of Tate and Lyle's sugar refinery accounted for 1,500. They had long been a large family employer in the inner city's North End. Nearly a quarter of Tate and Lyle's production workers came from the Vauxhall area, where the unemployment figure was already 46 per cent.[7]

There is not one issue which by itself blocks God-given gifts in the inner city. People have a total experience of life, made of a confusing set of interlocked factors; it is neither the housing problem nor the employment problem, but life in their district. But as soon as local ideas have to be fed to the top, they have to go into separate channels, marked 'employment', 'housing'.[8] Unemployment is only one of a vast range of issues which face young people in the North End of Liverpool's inner city. Many young people have very poor preparation for leaving school, for example in interview techniques. They've been conditioned that they're not going to get a job anyway. The allowance for those on the Youth Opportunities Programme (£23.50 in 1982, including an allowance for travelling to work) is very low. Their friends are drinking beer, buying records, getting married earlier. If they go back on the dole (as more than half do in such a high unemployment area after a YOP programme) they are more disillusioned than they were in the first place. 'This disillusionment really has to be felt.'[9]

The marks of being grown-up in that area were described by a Roman Catholic priest to me: 'You are in trouble with the police. You go for your Giro (for Unemployment Benefit). You smoke and you drink.' He went on, 'In order to be grown-up, you have to be stretched; young people expect to be stretched. Who's going to take responsibility for putting work in front of these young people and saying, "This is what you're expected to do"?'

There is a poverty in Liverpool which crushes the spirit. Compared with Calcutta or Bangladesh, there is not starvation poverty. But relative poverty truly hurts. Before the World Wars no one expected to have any control over his future.

During the wars and in the years after them that expectancy has been lifted. We are brought up to believe that all are to be citizens and all able to make choices which truly affect their destiny. The letdown, when that proves not to be possible, is so much greater. Advertising tantalises the poor. Endless choice seems to be only a stone's throw away in every advertisement of the consumer society. Yet it is not true for the poor. It is frustrating to the point of provoking both anger and despair.

A study was made of sixty-five families living on Supplementary Benefit on behalf of the Family Service Units and the Child Poverty Action Group in 1980.[10] It found that the families in the survey were not able to meet from their basic Supplementary Benefit all their normal day to day living requirements. It is difficult to live any enriching life in a city without spending money; a shed, a garden, countryside, all offer interest and possible resources to rural or suburban people. They are not available to the majority in the city.

The families who appear in the study, *Living from Hand to Mouth*, are experiencing a crushing kind of poverty in a nation as affluent as Britain. Parents talk of the misery of always worrying about money; 'Having to live from day to day, you can never plan anything.' 'I send the kids to the shops, because if I went, I would see something I wanted and couldn't afford it.' Mentally it is a constant strain. 'I worry from Friday to Tuesday (Family Allowance day) that I'll run out of money.' 'We receive £19.50 each week after all deductions, but this doesn't allow us to buy extras or treat the kids to any outings or day trips. Even ice cream is a treat. Birthday parties for the children would be great, but we just can't afford it.'

'If I had some money, I'd buy tools to make things for the house, shelves and so on. But I can't do anything.' 'Walking by shops with nice clothes in the window makes me sick.' 'We have to spend so much time going to see officials, DHSS, housing, asking for help, asking for advice. They ask you the same questions over and over again. We feel so ashamed, so low, as if we are beggars.' 'Rooms are too large to heat adequately with Supplementary Benefit.' 'Sometimes it gets the better of you and you overspend. That's even true for bills you can't see at the time—gas, electric.'

Merseyside's Child Poverty Action Group produced a study in 1977, 'Cut off and Cold'. They interviewed 130 families who had had gas or electricity cut off; fifty-three families were without both gas and electricity. The average length of disconnection was eleven months. The survey found little evidence to support the widely held view that those who are disconnected are feckless scroungers. 'The main point we want to make is that many poor families can't afford adequate fuel, and we need a fuel policy which takes this into account.'

Repeated surveys and studies can add to the problems they look at. When professional-looking people ask questions, at first it raises hopes that someone is going to do something to tackle the problems. Repeated enquiries, when nothing appears to have been done, lower the thresholds of bitterness and disillusionment. They may also measure what is going on by inappropriate yardsticks. For example, *The Sunday Times* published a series of articles on inner city areas in 1977. In the article about Liverpool a series of 'failures' of projects was listed. The only success that was marked up was of a 'nationally-known boxing club'. What yardstick was being used? Did the commentator acknowledge that it sometimes takes heroic resilience not to slip back any further against the odds? In *Alice Through the Looking Glass* the Red Queen said that it took all the running she could do to stay in the same place. The loaded odds from generations of being left behind are ignored when many attacks are made, for example, on teachers, because children have achieved less well in acquiring a number of skills. In a school serving an area where all who have achieved well move out of the district, you start again with the next generation, not at Square One, but at Square Minus One. To achieve the same results as in a previous generation possibly ought to be saluted as a remarkable success. The life experience of those who have had to survive in family or community life in the inner city is a great resource. We should treat it with very great respect. Teachers and other professionals need to acknowledge and welcome what parents' groups and community bodies can give.

31

The Liverpool black experience—generations of under-achievement

Liverpool's black community has the general deprivation of the inner city to face, compounded by the lack of opportunity which racial prejudice brings. It has to a large degree stayed within well-defined boundaries. One vicar moved to this area from a South London parish where there was a substantial black population, most of whom would have come to Britain in the last twenty years. The Liverpool situation initially shocked him. In South London most black people were employed, and young people at school looked forward to good employment. He found an area with massive unemployment, particularly among the black community, and where there was depression and a rather tired anger at being neglected or patronised.

We are often told that if only there was less talk about race relations and time was allowed for immigrant communities to find their way in Britain the problems would be surmounted. But the long experience of black people in Liverpool disproves this belief. There has been a black community in Liverpool for over a hundred years. But Liverpool-born black managers, foremen, lawyers, teachers and clergy are hardly to be seen. The blocks in the way of good employment are far worse than that; a black girl asked me when I met the fifth form at Paddington school in Liverpool, 'Why don't black people get jobs in Liverpool in the stores or on buses or trains? They do in London. I know, because I've lived there.'

Most Liverpool white people claim that we have no race relations problem. They believe there has been long-standing tolerance in a great multi-racial seaport. Tolerance can sometimes be the polite name for ignorance or indifference: in this case it often means no more than not hearing stories of violence until the explosion of 1981 and not seeing black people around.

Liverpool has been made aware of its neglected black population on more occasions than has been supposed. Between 31 May and 10 June 1919 there was a series of riots; at 11 p.m. on 10 June the situation became so serious that

32

the police made several baton charges on the crowd, assisted by the mounted police; subsequently 'arrangements were made for a number of the coloured men to return to their own country'. An enquiry in 1929 believed that there were then about 1,350 coloured children in Liverpool.[11] Another working party in 1939 visited 225 coloured families; of the 206 male heads of families four were old-age pensioners or invalids; of the remainder 149 were unemployed, (74 per cent while the corresponding figure in 1939 for white men was 34 per cent).[12]

In 1966 Lord Simey made a speech in the House of Lords; he said that he came from Liverpool, 'where our coloured fellow-citizens are nearly all locally born'. They had been educated in our schools, spoke the common language of Liverpool, but because of their colour, they were given un-skilled jobs. They were the first to become unemployed in a slump, they had the worst accommodation, the worst social services and the worst neighbourhood to live in. 'We are creating a Harlem . . . What now applies to Liverpool, and has obtained for sixty years in increasing degree, will shortly apply to all the big cities in England. And may God help us, if we lose equality of citizenship with people merely because they are coloured.'

Wally Brown, Liverpool born, then Chairman of the Community Relations Council, wrote in 1980, 'In Liverpool we are dealing with generations of under-achievement; those of school age see around them parents and grandparents who have not achieved, and thus feel there is no use trying.'[13] Some say, 'You don't only want me to be twice as good. You expect me to be a pioneer, going after jobs where no black people have gone before.' A director of a major store in Liverpool said, 'Yes, we only have two black employees. And we've had no black applicants for two years.'

A move in the right direction is that Liverpool City Council in 1980 voted to set up a liaison group with the Community Relations Council to monitor the number of black employees in all the different departments of the City Council. Six or seven years before, a senior officer was saying that it was a fact that black youths were no worse off in employment terms

than their white counterparts in Liverpool. He felt the City
Council had been very wise to decide not to separate the
unemployment statistics by ethnic origin, because, he said,
this would in itself be discriminatory. Now this was reversed.
Employers could only see what was happening if they kept
accurate statistics. At least one large firm has gone out of
its way to recruit from the black community for a short
induction course paid for by the Manpower Services Commission. They have found that youngsters who would not
have got through their normal recruiting procedures have
proved their ability to surmount them, when the course has
given them this opportunity.

As in other deprived parts of the city uncertainty has hung
over schools in Toxteth for some years. Many black families
felt happy with Paddington and Arundel schools. They had
developed teaching staffs who had taken real trouble to understand the black community. With the greatly reduced numbers
of children in the whole city it was proposed in 1978 to close
both these schools. On appeal, the Secretary of State for
Education and Science in the Labour Government, Shirley
Williams, refused to allow the closure of Paddington. Within
two years the City Council brought back that proposal. They
made much of the small number of parents who made
Paddington their first choice; in saying this they did not
comment on the effect of threatened closure hanging over a
school, nor the repeated leaflets issued by their own political
party, explicitly encouraging electors to vote for them in order
to protect other named schools and to prevent their children
being sent to Paddington, which was named in several leaflets.
This proposal was also rejected by the Secretary of State in the
Conservative Government, Mark Carlisle.

The City Council undoubtedly had a serious problem with
falling school rolls. But they refused to see that the building of
Paddington, a fine, large (too large) comprehensive school for
inner city children, had been a grave symbol of a bias in favour
of the most disadvantaged area. Symbols are very important
when it comes to matters like race relations. To close it and
propose that it should become a selective school was seen to
express a bias against those at a disadvantage.

Teachers and employers need to see the potential more than the problem in the lives of black young people. The appointment of black teachers and youth leaders lifts the confidence of children and parents both that they will be understood and that perhaps they too could 'make it'.

The black American in Ralph Ellison's book, *Invisible Man*, first published in 1952, says, 'I was pulled this way and that for longer than I can remember. And my problem was that I always tried to go everyone's way but my own. I have also been called one thing and then another, while no one really wished to hear what I called myself. So after years of trying to adopt the opinions of others, I finally rebelled. I am an *Invisible* Man.'[14] Liverpool black people have often acted as though they were invisible. The point of Ellison's book was not only that the black man was invisible to white people who ignored him, but that he was invisible to himself. He did not see black people in the front ranks of society, and did not think of significant jobs being possible for him. There is hope in the growing assertion that it is good to be black and that black self-help groups can breed self-confidence and build bridges with businesses, schools and city councils.

From that point of view the riots and the aggressive attitudes in the succeeding months of some black community groups may carry within them the seeds of new hope. There was an element in these events of saying, 'We're not going to be pushed around any more. We're going to stand up for ourselves.' This could be a significant first step towards greater self-confidence and responsibility in community groups and their leadership. At the same time there was great pain which nearly tore a community to pieces; there was pain too for emerging leaders to stay with the challenge of leadership which both expressed the feelings of their own community and at times had to stand up to those feelings. It would be wrong to hide that pain.

This chapter has shown how decisive a disadvantage has to be overcome to survive, let alone compete in the urban race, by those in corporation estates and in both the white and black communities in the inner city. Many have felt robbed of the power to make significant choices. This sense of powerlessness can lead on to the still more damaging feeling of worthlessness. The poor are then robbed of a central part of being human. If we ignore this kind of deprivation, we deserve the conse-quences which follow.

CHAPTER THREE

How Liverpool's Poor See the Church

Sectarian divisions and their legacy

The Churches have had a high profile in Liverpool life; more so than in most British cities. The first reason for that, sadly, is the Protestant/Catholic sectarian one. One ethnic group has sometimes felt severely threatened when another group has arrived in very large numbers. This has certainly been true in Liverpool. Over 300,000 people came through the port in the one year—1847—at the height of the Irish potato famine, and many stayed in the city. In turn the immigrant group felt great hostility from the others. That set a pattern which lasted a very long time. Housing was confined to Green or Orange in several areas. For example, St Alphonso's in Scotland Road became a great rallying point for the community in those streets. They were filled with families from Armagh and Newry; as immigrants do, they were often found somewhere to live nearby by cousins who were already there.[1] Jobs were reserved for those who professed the same religion as the boss, the foreman or those already employed there. The bitterness of Northern Ireland was found in Liverpool too. Sectarian religion intruded into everyday life, for example when dockers stood 'on the stones'; hoping to catch the foreman's eye.

In such a setting the Churches became rallying points for ethnic groups, as in the United States; they rehearsed the memories of the community, kept alive its particular culture, emphasised its beliefs and practices which were different from the others. Within its separate fortress each community of faith developed great warmth of belonging and of caring for those in need. They didn't necessarily feel any obligation to 'the others', who were often in effect invisible to them. This still happens when very different groups live in the same

37

parish. 'The others' feel that they are invisible to Church people.

I met members of an inner city parish together with representatives of the community there. The discussion began with one senior Church member saying how much the district had changed; 'It's like a transit camp now,' she said. Another Church member had lived in the parish all her life; she said, 'There are no children in the parish any more.' Next to me was sitting the head teacher of a nursery school in the parish. She told the group that she had eighty-nine children on her school roll. There was disbelief on the face of the Church member who had said there were no children in the parish any more. My interpretation of what was happening, as I listened to the discussion, was that she saw the life of the parish entirely through her Church experience. Children from the parish used to come to Sunday School; now they didn't. The children in the parish were of different social groupings; many were black. She did not see them as potential Sunday School children, so they became invisible to her.

In strongly sectarian Church life religion was fulfilling the functions which those who study the sociology of religion have always observed in it. Religion has strengthened the identity of clan, tribe or nation all down the centuries. Those who study Church growth have also noticed that numbers are more likely to grow in Churches which serve one cultural or ethnic group. But it has to be asked then if the Church is being true to God and His calling to be catholic, reaching across all human groupings. Those outside the circles of Church life have felt, whether because of sectarian Church life or preoccupation with Church matters, that members of such Churches were not interested in them.

It is a natural reaction of a group which feels shut out from the main stream of life in a country to strengthen its own community life; it is natural for Churches to be focus points of such a community, as black-led Churches are today. But such separate development can never be God's last word. A deprived group sometimes needs to find strength in belonging to a like-minded Church and community; but once that strength is there, the challenge of Christ's teaching about the Kingdom of

God calls them to come and make their special contribution to the whole of Church and society. For many years in Liverpool Catholics and Protestants not only lived in enclaves of separate development, but frequently in bitter hostility too.

Central to Jesus's teaching is the elusive, very non-Western, idea of the Kingdom of God. He was reaching out firmly beyond the idea that God was concerned only for the Jewish people or for the religious, the steady and respectable. Samaritans were in the Kingdom; deadly rivals of the Jews, they were playing a leading role in the Kingdom of God which Jesus talked about; so were tax-gatherers and prostitutes. It was to be a Kingdom, not a clan, which would have been made up only of those who were like-minded and had similar self-interest. When Church life develops separately, as it did in Liverpool for so many years, it serves clans, not a Kingdom. However strong it may be numerically, it misrepresents the Kingdom of God, if it ignores or hates other Christians or other groups outside the Church.

The Anglican tradition of F. D. Maurice, William Temple and Michael Ramsey has insisted that the teaching about the Kingdom of God must not be confined to spiritual ideas internal to the personal life of the Christian or to the Church. Justice and truth in society and the quality of life of all people are the concern of the Lord and of His Church.

The Kingdom of God would have been a concept Jesus's Jewish hearers would have understood. The Old Testament led the Jews to believe that a king would reign in righteousness, fulfilling all the hopes begun in King David. This king would judge the poor in justice. God's healing hand would reach to the whole of His creation; the wolf would live with the sheep, and the leopard lie down with the kid. The earth would be filled with the knowledge of the Lord.[2]

In the Gospels we are taught to pray that God's Kingdom will come, and that His will should be done on earth as in heaven. The Kingdom is to come in full power beyond this world, conquering sin, death and oppression; but the belief in that future hope is not to make us indifferent to suffering and injustice in this world. Jürgen Moltmann says that the more seriously we take the future promise of God's Kingdom, the more unbearable will be the contradictions of that promise which we meet in the present.[3] The Kingdom of God is about what we think of as 'spiritual'. It is also about breaking down barriers in the whole of society. These spiritual and social matters are all mixed up together. The Kingdom is about a God who forgives sin, yet who confronts evil. It is about a generous, giving, healing God. It is about prayer and the secrets God will show those who become His willing partners. It is about the possibility of being born over again. It's about how He will bring in His Kingdom by the way of the Cross. There are repeated surprises at the kind of people who are receiving special attention in the Kingdom—tax-gatherers, prostitutes, the poor, the lame, the sick and the blind.

When it comes to interpreting the Bible in our own situations, we need to notice the powerful influences which tint the reading glasses we wear or the assumptions we make as we read it. Our own particular religious experience, the social and economic realities of our life, colour what we read far more than we want to admit: the shape and character of the Kingdom of God which we assume bears an uncanny resemblance to the Church and the society we belong to, or long for.

I asked a minister in Northern Ireland to explain to me what he thought people understood they were responding to when Ian Paisley preaches the Gospel, using all the historic Christian words. By way of reply he described how a man had come to him in great distress. He had been recruited to join the Ulster Defence Association, a Loyalist para-military organisation. That had led to his murdering a number of people. He was now bitterly repentant. When invited to join, he had been asked if he would work 'For God and for Ulster'. It was a vivid way of answering my question. When Ian Paisley preaches the Gospel, it is as though he is a man speaking on television, while pictures and diagrams appear on a screen behind him, showing what he stands for—his 'image' we might say, if it did not annoy such a fierce Protestant too much to be told that he had an image. In his case it is 'For God and for Ulster', meaning an Ulster with particular political, social and economic arrangements.

I learned something more, when I thought about that. All

preachers who speak, all Churches which put out welcoming notices, have behind them a series of pictures or images which, fairly or unfairly, people see them to stand for. Jesus understood this very well; He never said, 'Follow Me' until He had repeatedly, by an action or a story, said 'The Kingdom of God is like . . .' Like Him we must think out how the reign of God should break into the whole situation, spiritual and secular, in which we find ourselves. Our dreams for the community in which we find ourselves should be shaped by our best understanding of the Kingdom of God. And, if we are to be seen to be servants of His Kingdom, we must commit ourselves to action on behalf of what we belive to be just and true.

The Greek word *oikoumene*, from which the word ecumenical comes, means 'one inhabited earth'. Just as Jesus's teaching about the Kingdom of God must not be restricted to Church matters, so the ecumenical movement should be about breaking down the walls which divide God's one inhabited earth. Indeed we should be found to be in opposition to the movement towards one inhabited earth, if we were to turn inwards and spend all our energies on negotiations between the Churches. Yet Christians are not likely to be given any credibility when we try to break down other human barriers, if we have not done all that is within our power to remove Church divisions. The connections were properly made when a black boy in Liverpool said, 'In the old-fashioned days the Catholics hated the Protestants. Now they don't do that any more. Perhaps one day black and white people won't hate each other any more either.' The change in attitudes between the Churches in Liverpool have provided a strong hope for many people who long for something better.

The Church leaders of all denominations in Liverpool have developed a high degree of trust; we meet regularly for prayer, for study (when twice a year we deliberately take on issues we know we do not agree about), for consultation and planning. We have issued several joint statements. The Roman Catholic Archbishop of Liverpool, Derek Worlock, and I have acted together on a number of matters, for example concerning unemployment and race relations and following the riots in Toxteth. The picture of local Church cooperation in the parishes is patchy; some continue to live in frosty separate development. Many Churches have entered into increasing partnership in community projects in tackling human needs, visiting the housebound, mission services and study groups. A request has come for what would be the first shared Church in the Liverpool Diocese between Catholics and Anglicans. The Diocesan Planning Adviser went to consult local people on this corporation housing estate; he wanted to be reassured that they fully supported their vicar in this request. They said, 'We grew up with a lot of division in Liverpool. We want something better for our children.' Active efforts were made at the time of the Pope's visit to Liverpool in 1982 by extreme Protestants to fan the flames of old fears and bitterness. But I have no doubt at all that the majority of Christians of all Churches here feel a deep sense of rightness and relief that partnership and brotherhood are the main features of our day.

Moral standards and social class

The poor have often seen the Church as being only for the respectable. That has been seen in a muddling mixture of moral standards and of social class.

A vicar, born and brought up in Liverpool, described his interpretation of the history of his inner city parish. The social composition of the parish, as with many others, changed when the merchants and shopkeepers moved house to the growing suburbs. In this parish the move took place largely in the nineteenth century. Some of the Church people who emigrated physically to the suburbs felt a strong calling to travel back to worship in their former parish. Churchwardens and Bible-class leaders were often drawn from such commuter worshippers. 'It might be too harsh to assert that the Churches were closed to the new working-class people coming to Liverpool, but I suspect it is more true than otherwise. Those who joined Church life and observed the "initiation demands" would soon learn how to aspire to a "better life" and within a generation leave for better pastures themselves.'

Working-class communities felt that 'their sort' were not accepted by Church groups. Stories went the rounds expressing a sense of resentment and communal apathy against the Church. One of the results has been that working-class groups have been prepared to relate to the Church on a dependent level—baptisms, weddings, funerals—but this is the relationship of dependants or casuals, not of peers.

That vicar, like many others, firmly believes that local leadership can and should emerge. Over a number of years local people have come to believe that they are wanted and that they can become the leaders and decision-makers in their Church.

A change in where the power of decision-making lies brings some confrontations where it is often not very obvious what is at stake. This vicar rang me up when he had been in the parish eight or nine years; was it possible to see me the same day? He's a very resourceful man, and I felt this must be urgent. At first I could not understand what was so important. An argument was going on in the parish about whether the keep-fit class in the Church hall should be required to have prayers at the end of each class. Gradually I realised that underneath the surface a great deal was at stake, which had been patiently worked for. The keep-fit class had grown over a number of years; its leaders were a group of local inner city women, growing in self-confidence, gradually coming into the life of the Church. They didn't want to force saying prayers on to a group which was a first stepping stone for those who were still outside the Church.

Older members of the PCC, most of whom grew up in the district, but have for years travelled back to it, saw it differently. They regarded having prayers as a way in which the Christian identity of activities in the hall was maintained and of making sure that they were not swallowed up in the secular neighbourhood's social programme. Perhaps underneath there was a certain struggle about who was going to make the decisions. Was every new group going to have to fit into the pattern the older members insisted on? Were they in fact feeling the strength of a rival group which might want to take over the running of the Church next? The upshot was that the keep-fit class has been left to work out its programme. A growing number of its members have taken part in five house groups; this has led on to Confirmation for several of those women.

In another inner city parish I was repeatedly told during a parish visit that those outside the Church, whom we were meeting, felt that they were too bad to belong to it. That is a legacy of how Church people were seen and saw themselves. The membership of a relatively strong inner city congregation was described to me as 'good working-class', with the emphasis on *good*. The great majority would be in employment. There would be strong, unspoken assumptions about activities which are right and wrong for Christians. There is a vigorous emphasis on standards of behaviour. That leads some, who don't feel they measure up to those standards, to feel they would not be wanted in such a fellowship.

Before we call their attitudes harsh and judgmental, we need to remember how frightening the wolves at the door sometimes seem. 'I won't let Kevin and Johnny play in the yard with the other children,' said a mother to a Church visitor. She was afraid they would pick up bad habits. 'Why do you always believe the others are stronger?' asked the visitor. Yet that fear is a natural one.

There is a tightrope for the Church to walk. We are called to witness on one side to lasting values, on the other to the grace of God, which meets people where they are. A new chain reaction of making the first move is set in motion by the grace of our Lord Jesus Christ reaching out to us. That is the basis from which Christian morality starts, rather than a brittle insistence on clinging to outward standards of behaviour. Grace leads us on from meeting people where they are to a deep commitment to lasting values as well. Christians have to walk this tightrope repeatedly; one example is how the Church deals with those whose marriage has broken down. One single-parent family found their way back into a Church fellowship after a strong sense of being rejected by one congregation. The mother said, 'I've appreciated the way I've been welcomed, not gushingly, but people clearly wanted us to be there. Now there are five or six single-parent families in that Church. In the Church that I left, I know it would have been very different.'

Patterns of Church presence

The Church of England has inherited the parochial system from previous generations. Many inner city churches have been closed; that has been because the population there has dropped dramatically, overall by a half. Whole areas of housing were demolished, leaving churches standing isolated from any parishioners. Redeploying clergy to serve those who were moving into the corporation estates on the perimeter of Liverpool meant that fewer parishes could be staffed in the inner city. The policy was necessary, but some inner city people felt that the Church had withdrawn from needy areas. However, the structure and staffing of the parochial system has been maintained.

The Church of England has stretched its resources to the limit to maintain a presence in every parish. On average there would be a parish for a population of 8,000, including people of all denominations and none. The commitment to the parochial presence has meant that by comparison, say, with the Episcopal Church in the USA, much smaller resources are given to special programmes and projects.

The mainstream Free Churches and the Independent Churches have not been able to provide ministry or church buildings in many of the newer estates. Wherever possible the mainstream Free Churches want to share in ministry in such estates together with the Church of England.

A Methodist minister underlined the problems of the Church in Liverpool's inner city; he said that we needed to know what urban man is saying. In some senses we knew what urban articulate man was saying in suburbia. He said that the strong Churches of Methodism were in suburbia and its laymen were the good middle-class people in middle-executive range and in responsible posts in the professions and local government. We listened to them.

There was an urgent need for the Church to listen to what urban man in the inner city is saying. 'He is not less articulate, but he is not heard in many Churches because (a) he is not present and (b) where he is present, he is overwhelmed by his more powerful suburban colleague.' He did not decry the

45

place of preaching, but said that the evidence was that special events like the ten-day mission were less and less effective. 'The type of work is now the ongoing mission that holds a balance between service in social and community terms and the presentation of the Gospel truths, demanding a response.'[4]

Other Churches do maintain the old style with the emphasis strongly on preaching. A study was made in 1974 by Jim Hart of the Protestant Churches of Toxteth, in the South End of Liverpool's inner city. He concluded that local people do not see the Church struggling and working locally. 'Their only exposure to the Word is the annual knock-on-door.' Jim Hart's enquiry looked at ten Churches, of which three are Church of England. It happened that all were Evangelical in tradition and belief. Of the worshippers 331 lived in the area of the ten Churches; 1,099 came from outside. Two of the Baptist Churches had very substantial commuting congregations. The majority of lay people holding office in the Churches came from outside. The three Church of England Churches had more members living in the area than outside it, but perhaps 40 per cent came in from outside. They also have considerable involvement in serving the community, running open youth clubs, a drop-in centre and a Youth Opportunities Programme project. Since the survey was made there has been further growth in local membership.

In the poorest part of the area studied, Brunswick, there were thirty-nine Protestant Church members in a population of 12,630. More than half of those were elderly, single or widowed women. Perhaps a thousand children were involved with the Churches, about seven hundred and fifty living in the study area. 'Very few indeed will attend beyond their thirteenth and fourteenth birthdays.' 'I have discussed social problems with many Church groups in Toxteth. The majority voices held strongly judgmental views about young people and minority groups.'[5]

It is difficult to do justice to the faithful ministry which clergy and lay workers have maintained to many individuals, whether they belonged to the Church or not. The city has had many projects which have come and gone after three years or so. There has been a continuity of the Church presence through the parishes. This ministry has been unsung; it has been to children, to the elderly, to all sorts of people at times of suffering.

Such slender beginnings may lead to people trusting the Church at important moments in their lives. One couple came to have their second child baptised. They said, 'We'll be in Church next week.' They've come regularly ever since. A remark the vicar made in the Baptism Service had touched a chord. Ten years before they had been thrown out by their parents. The vicar in their parish had let them sleep in the hall for a week; he had pestered the Housing Department until they were offered a home. The couple had told each other they wanted to respond to this help they had received from the Church; the baptism of the second child had reminded them. They have stayed in the Church fellowship. The husband has been out of work seven years; the curate taught him to read. They feel that Christ is for them in the reality of their situation.

In many areas people have to learn to survive in the face of failure. The vicar, who has seen a small but lively congregation come into being on that large new estate, told me, 'I want to say something about new vicars; they've got to be able to live with failure.' He said, 'People are pleased when I fail. I wouldn't say pleased exactly. But they experience failure so much. If I say that I've failed again, that reassures them. Sharing it reassures me too. We clergy don't have to be too anxious about people seeing our humanness.'

In the face of poverty on the estate members of the Church community help one another practically, for example, with something as mundane as mending electric cooker rings. People support each other a lot on a more consistent level than people do in the wider community. There's a very warm Church fellowship. There's a danger in having a very strong in-group. Subconsciously it can lead to the rejection of new people. That vicar spoke of the importance of a continuing Christian presence; 'The Church has just got to survive. It must maintain the worship of God—and yet in such a way that it is open to the community. As long as the congregation is indigenous, there is very little danger of not being open.'

Seeking such limited targets as surviving and living with

47

failure can sound very unbelieving. I was taken to task by a student in the chaplaincy group at Liverpool University. He had been to hear my lectures on 'The Divine Bias for the Losers'. He thought I had described the realities of life in the city quite truthfully. But all I had to offer, he said, was flickers of hope. 'If the bishop really believed in the power of God, he ought to be talking about great streams of light.' I understood his challenge. But on Good Friday there were no obvious streams of light. Many parts of Liverpool are facing Good Friday situations. Then it may be a great testimony to Christ's power when people don't give up.

The Church has consistently been present; it has not always been present in a listening kind of way—listening to what people in the neighbourhood feel and have to offer. Nor has it always been seen to stand for justice. Many of those who are at a disadvantage would instinctively believe in God's bias to the poor, but would not believe that the Church reflects that bias.

A spirited defence of the Church of England's record was put up by E. R. Norman in 1976 in his book *Church and Society in England 1770–1970*. In 1979 he was to deliver the BBC's Reith Lectures, in which he attacked what he called 'politicised' Christianity. The thesis of his 1976 book is that in fact the Church was heavily involved in the nineteenth century in caring for the poor. He defends political economy, *laissez-faire* and the encouragement of individuals to improve themselves. He attacks those, particularly William Temple, who speak of the guilt of the Church on the ground of its lack of will to change a society in which so many suffered. Church leaders, Norman says, reflected the views of the intelligentsia; rather, they caught up with the fashions of the day just in time for them to become out of date. He says that the working classes themselves, 'progressively soaked in practical *laissez-faire* ideas did not look to the Church for interference in earthly conditions and would have resented the clergy if they had attempted it. English popular spirituality actually expected the Church to cultivate an 'other-wordly' concern to elevate and direct them to another realm of values altogether.'[6]

It is right to say that the Church was heavily concerned in charitable works and was committed to providing educational opportunities; but as far as the poor are concerned, these opportunities were for the individuals who would improve themselves—and move away. Those who were left behind in the race saw the Church as kindly, but not prepared to stand for justice, if the going became tough or if it was to their disadvantage.

My experience has been that working-class people in East and South East London and in Liverpool are not helped by clergy and congregations to believe that Christ could be for them. It is certainly true that they want to know that Church people have deep spiritual roots; but their interest disappears if they discover that there is no willingness to be involved in issues which affect the quality of life of the whole community. It is their complaint that they have not seen a bias for the poor reflected consistently in the Churches.

'The Church always rode with power,' said a Kirkdale, Liverpool man. There are folk memories which are very influential. During a visit with an industrial chaplain to a factory in Kirkby, I had an hour's discussion with the shop stewards. Some of them attacked the Church; 'We don't think your track record is too bad, but the Church is hopelessly compromised; bishops sit in the House of Lords. All twenty-one bishops voted against the Government in the Dock and Harbour Bill.' I said I would be very surprised if so many were present (that would be nearly a full bench of bishops in the House of Lords), but I would find out and write to them. I found from the voting record that, out of many amendments to the Bill, there was one amendment on which one bishop, then chairman of our Industrial Committee, and therefore likely to be well informed, had voted against the Government. Folk memories die hard, and the likeliest explanation of 'All twenty-one bishops voted against the Government' is that memories were going back to the Great Reform Bill, when all the bishops voted against the Bill. But that was in 1832.

It is true that William Temple and other Church leaders have argued for a more just society. But working-class people have seen powerful laymen defending the status quo. They know that they, and not just the Church leaders, are the Church. And it is not only powerful laymen. There has always been a connection between belonging to the Church and the self-improvement which goes up in the world. This often proves to be at odds with a bias to the poor. Its effect on inner city Church life has already been observed.

I asked a group of young men in a Liverpool housing estate parish if they were in employment. All of them had jobs, an engineer in the bus depot, a laboratory technician . . . I asked if they had friends or neighbours who were out of work. None of them did. Everyone who came to Church had a job, they said. They thought the fact that they belonged to the Boys' Brigade had helped them to obtain the jobs they had gone after. I said I was surprised they knew no one who was out of work. The curate then said that there were parts of the parish where many were out of work. He said to one of the group, 'You'll get out of the area as fast as you can.' 'It stands to reason,' came the reply, 'that if you can send your children to a school in a nice middle-class district, they'd have a better opportunity.' Another said, 'If I could afford it, I would send my children to a public school, because that would give them a much better start.'

That whole process is natural enough. But if we want the Church to be able to root itself firmly in urban working-class life, we must give up regarding that sort of social mobility as inevitable and right for all who are able to 'make it'. One of the flickers of hope is that a good number of Christians are determined to stay and work out their faith within their own community. Such personal motives need to be supported by more mixed-housing policies. It is another flicker of hope to have seen such policies producing modest-price private housing estates in inner city Liverpool. It must be to the advantage of the whole community if those who've grown up there and want to buy their own home are able to do so without moving away.

The sale of council houses to their present tenants is a more complex matter; it depends on the housing stock which a council holds. In principle it ought to make for a more mixed community. The difficulty is that tenants will only want to buy on the better estates. That could make the keeping of a balance on other estates very difficult. Once an estate has a name for tenants with rent arrears, noisy tenants, 'problem families', its houses or flats become hard to let. We've then created major problems for those who feel trapped in it. The possibility of easy transfers, which help people to move within reach of family support systems, depends on having a balanced housing stock.

I'm not sure whether politicians want to break down these divisions which segregate people into vast one-class quarters: some have a vested interest in keeping cities polarised, so that their electoral base is safeguarded. We lived for nearly twenty years in the inner city in London. No major political figure visited any of the three safe Labour constituencies in which we lived at election time. They all went off to the marginal seats. This has led me to argue for proportional representation, perhaps in larger, multi-member constituencies, which will give minority groups a better chance of being represented. It is not only Socialists who have resisted the development of more mixed housing. In London the building of council estates in outer areas has always been fought by Conservatives in the outer boroughs. A Christian living in an executive suburb of South London realised how much his own sectional interest affected his judgment. He said of proposals to build a council housing estate in a comparable area, 'If I'd lived in that place, I think I would have voted against the housing estate. And I'd have known it was a sin.'

The one striking exception to the patterns of Church life in England in relation to urban working-class and poor people is the Roman Catholic Church. In the eyes of the poor there was the advantage that the Roman Catholic Church was not the Established Church. Nor did they see powerful Roman Catholic laymen in comparable positions of power from which they could have been expected to change injustices. Archbishop Worlock and I were asked about this; he said that poor people would probably have blamed my predecessor for not bringing about change, but that they would not have expected his Roman Catholic predecessor to have the power to do so. By contrast in Paris, Brussels, Madrid, Milan or Turin the Roman Catholic Church found itself in a position much more akin to the Church of England position which has been described. In each of those cities there are huge areas where scarcely any working-class men go to Church. In Liverpool and other British cities the experience is different; the largest numbers in inner city parishes came from Ireland. The Church became a rallying point for an ethnic group which was facing the bad experiences of immigrants in the worst housing and with the least security of jobs.

The relationship of Liverpool working-class people to the Roman Catholic Church is not quite as predictable as might be expected. Before 1844 the priests worked under lay committees. The first four Roman Catholic Churches in Liverpool were built by the better off laity, with many Church of England members subscribing. There were long-established Lancashire Roman Catholic families; they saw to it that the presbyteries were built solidly with fine brass fittings, to let it be seen that the parish priest was an important person. On the whole the leadership in the Church was felt to be identified with the status quo; this was the appearance given, even though parish priests were closely identified with the people in the very harsh conditions they experienced.

A sense that those in power were against them was felt quite early by Roman Catholics in Liverpool. Until 1841 Roman Catholic children went to the free schools and were allowed to use the Douai Bible there. Then the new Tory administration came into power in Liverpool; their first act was to forbid the use of the Douai Bible. The Roman Catholics then withdrew their children into denominational schools. There were at that time 9,000 Roman Catholic children of school age in Liverpool. Only 800 were in Roman Catholic schools. For many years hostility to 'Rome on the rates' was a vote-catching political argument. All this helped to drive many Roman Catholics, particularly in inner city parishes, into the beleaguered fortress mentality. Many devout Roman Catholics felt it would be better to keep your nose clean and stay out of community and political involvement.

The many who did involve themselves in the Labour Party felt some tensions about continuing their involvement with the Church. Hardcore Labour groups often included more lapsed or fringe Roman Catholics than those who practised their faith regularly. The great slogan of the French Revolution rang very different chords for different members of the Church. For a dock labourer Liberty, Equality and Fraternity sounded like his natural music. For Pope and bishops they were the words of those who had thrown out the established Church in France. In 1864 Pope Pius appended the Syllabus of Errors to an Encyclical. Its last section condemned 'errors which tend to present-day liberalism.' Historians have been inclined to play down its significance; they said it sprang out of a political situation of the moment, when the Pope lost his lands after a thousand years of ownership; that the fight over it concerned the doctrine of authority in a particular Church, and that it was a matter only of theology and not of European politics. But impressions which are widely held are more significant than the precise details of what is said and in what circumstances.

Owen Chadwick in his book *The Secularization of the European Mind in the Nineteenth Century* says that the assessment that it was only a matter of theology and of a situation of the moment gravely misunderstood the European importance of what happened. The Syllabus was a symbol of something bigger, namely, the stance of the Pope in the age of Garibaldi and the Risorgimento . . . Europe saw the Pope condemn liberalism—whatever that was the Pope condemned it . . . Ethical ideals were associated with the slogans of liberalism, words like liberty and fraternity, freedom of conscience, tolerance, justice in the way of equality before the law. 'Many Western Europeans had the sensation, not just that the Pope was wrong, but that he was morally wrong.'[7]

Many who grew up in the different Churches have given up practising their faith because they have had that sensation; their Church has seemed to them to be morally wrong in failing to support attempts to deliver the poor. It has indeed been one of the great forces in the secularisation of minds.

At that sort of time in Liverpool the Roman Catholic Bishop Goss preached against the beginnings of the trade unions and against Liberalism, which he connected with free thinking. The Methodists had felt the same connections when they framed their No Politics rule in the 1790s; many working-class Methodists followed Tom Paine on *The Rights of Man*. One of the fears was that they would follow his arguments against revealed religion in *The Age of Reason* as well.[8] In the 1930s Pope Pius XI denounced Socialism, meaning Communism. This caused great heart-searchings in some devout Roman Catholics, who were deeply committed to the Labour Party. Great pleasure and relief was felt when it was spread about in 1945 that the Pope thought that the British Labour Party was all right. But the suspicion of Socialism was part of the background to the existence for many years of a Catholic Party. It was also because there was a Protestant Party. Within months of coming to Liverpool in 1928 Archbishop Downey dissolved the Catholic Party. He held that every Catholic had an inalienable right to belong to any political party, provided he waived nothing of sound Catholic principles. No priest was to stand as a candidate. A lady in her seventies told Father Alger about the song they sang in her Church school, when their parish priest, Father Rigby, stood for Parliament against the Labour Party:

> Vote, vote for Ben Tillett
> Throw old Rigby in the dock

Until Bessie Braddock was elected for the Scotland Exchange Constituency, it was usual for a Roman Catholic Conservative to be elected there. One of the reasons for that was that until 1945 businessmen had a second vote in the constituency where their business was located.

Slum clearance and redevelopment have broken up some of the very strong Roman Catholic communities. 'The Church really depends for its practice on a strong community,' Bishop Augustine Harris told me. 'The reasons for a strong community may be external pressures, such as bad times or sense of other people's hostility, or internal pressures, such as strong faith and fellowship. As the external pressures ease off, because Catholics feel themselves fully accepted in the wider community, the practice drops off.' Habits built in during childhood still have a momentum. Very large numbers of Roman Catholics will still practise their religion in working-class areas of Liverpool. But there has been a substantial weakening of faith in many people; 'The teaching element about the faith has not only changed; it is very often absent . . . A survey of one street in a strongly Roman Catholic parish found that there was only one family presenting their children for Confirmation.' Proportionately far fewer will attend Mass. The breakup of communities has much to do with that. Archbishop Derek Worlock says that the emphasis now has to be on deepening the faith rather than on the externals which bound a community together. Lay people increasingly see that they have an apostolate; the factory where they work is their parish. An increasing number of lay people accept responsibility and leadership in the life of their parish and community.

As in other Churches, Roman Catholic clergy with whom I talk feel that the poor still often see the Church as superior and standing over against life. A sister who lives in the area was walking by when a youngster swore, using foul language. He saw her and covered his face. It did not occur to him that she had heard it all before. A parish priest said, 'We've blinded people to the God who's really in the middle of their life.'

A woman of thirty approached a priest about an abortion. She was thinking about her life and also genuinely about her husband. She was not too worried about the teaching of the Church. She had been on the pill. She felt she'd made great efforts in trying to find ways out of her tangles. The priest said, 'You must be angry with God.' 'I don't think anyone's told Him about me.' 'You don't really believe in God, do you?' She stayed silent for a long time. She'd never thought that He could come into her situation. 'God's not out there. If He is only out there, then I don't believe in that One either.' She hadn't connected her worship with her life, certainly not the parts that were tangled, messy and frustrating.

'As long as He's walking on the water, people can say, "We couldn't be like that".' People often want to keep nuns, clergy and bishops on pedestals too. But the Incarnation meant truly entering into a world where there was indignation, corrupt authority, sickness, adultery, betraying, agony and bloody sweat. If we can believe God is really incarnate, He is frighteningly close; then He meets us where we are, calls us to take the steps from there which can actually be achieved. The followers of Jesus have to live in that world too; like Him we are called to meet people where they are.

Roman Catholic priests who come out from the walls of the fortress and enter into secular community life receive the same criticism as clergy and ministers in other Churches. It is supposed by the critics that the involvement is for the sake of being trendy or in order to prove that they are not too pious. For many the motive is to do with what they believe about Incarnation, Creation and Redemption.

Father Austin Smith wrote about the area in which he lives. It has been described as a social malaise area; he said a Creation thing was happening, if he saw or enabled someone to take control over some aspect of their own destiny. God's creation was becoming fruitful, even if it was a tiny acre. At the same time there was pain and suffering. 'The pain comes from the efforts being made by a friend or friends, those I love, to walk but one yard in asserting human dignity. Why should this child have to suffer so much to gain one small iota of respect? Why should this family suffer so much stress from causes beyond their control? Why should my black brother or sister fight for equal acceptance in a world boasting equality for all?' He believed his calling was to exist with his neighbours, whether they were in the Church or not.[9]

The Church which is learning painfully to exist with people has also a Word which God has entrusted to it. When we have earned the right, by listening, by receiving, by giving, we also have to speak that Word, which will sometimes be over against the community with whom we exist.

Church people of all denominations find the going hard enough to survive in disadvantaged areas of the city. It is very understandable that many are influenced by the fear that 'the others' are stronger, and that they will drag us down from hard-won standards. The Church will not feel like home to the poor, if our welcome is only on our terms—'provided they fit in with our ways.' The thrust of this book is that we must listen to the poor, exist with them, try to stand in their shoes; and then be willing for them to take a full share in leadership and decision-making. That would mean uncomfortable changes for each of our Churches. The Church must risk losing its image of respectability. A study of how it can reflect a bias for the poor must not stop short at advice for inner city parishes. Many of the disadvantages of the inner city are maintained by policies which defend the self-interest of the suburbs, where Churches are often stronger. The vision of the Kingdom of God—or of the City of God—takes in how all of us live, and how our lives affect those in other parts of the city. More affluent Christians must be seen to stand for justice on behalf of the poor, even when that may be to the disadvantage of themselves and their families. Only then will many of the poor believe that the Christ whom the Churches preach could be for them.

CHAPTER FOUR

Black is Vulnerable

South London generations

The winter after I moved to Liverpool (1975) I was asked to go back to South London to take part in the annual conference of the Evangelical Race Relations Group: it was held in Brixton. By comparison with Liverpool the black community was extremely visible, vocal about their situation and determined to change it. The conference was about the black experience; the speakers were all members of the black community and professing Christians.

They spoke of the generation gap between older West Indians and their children who think of themselves as British blacks. Many parents 'are still living in the West Indies', as far as their outlook and attitudes are concerned. Their England-born children could not enter into their dreams of the Caribbean. Nor could the parents enter into the actual experience of British schools, which their children lived in. Parents used corporal punishment as a means of discipline without loss of affection; many children were at schools where it was not used. English school methods were not understood by parents and were interpreted as weakness by children. Parents had been lectured by the courts for disciplining their children in ways they believed were right.[1]

They said that young people found confidence when they saw black people in positions of authority. There would be a breakthrough when they saw black policemen and teachers. When Church leaders were always white, respect for the Church was diminished. 'There are no leaders who can calm the people as the economic squeeze proceeds. White people will look after themselves and unemployment will fall upon the minorities.'[2] Black Church leadership had largely missed out on this generation and fourteen-year-olds did not want to know about Jesus Christ. Many black Church leaders offered leadership only within the Church. 'Some of our Church leaders should set an example not inside the Church only, but outside the Church, where young people can identify with them.'[3]

The black experience, they said, included inequality in education and menial tasks in employment. More than that a black person 'lives in an atmosphere of tension between his own self-concept and that imposed from outside, from the white culture. In this society a black man's manhood is tested daily.'[4]

The problem was not a black problem, but a white problem. When people said that they didn't have a race problem in Bournemouth, they meant that no black people lived there; but 'There's a bigger race problem in Bournemouth than in Brixton.'[5]

'The black Church in every aspect should be independent of Europeans. The land of my forefathers has been so exploited by Europeans that I cannot feel justified in allowing them to take control of something so sacred as religion. What do we mean when we say that Jesus saves? We must mean not only from sin but also from all the backlashes of society, from oppression . . . but I reject the concept that God will do for us what we can do for ourselves . . . the things we would do for ourselves invariably have political overtones . . . I believe that when we move, we shall move not only for the black race; we shall be moving for the whole community. Therefore I believe that there is a necessity for us to be working apart.'[6]

In discussion this need to work in separate Churches was challenged; 'The Lord Jesus went to the Cross in order that He might break down the barriers, so forming a single new humanity in Himself. I want to be a member of that new humanity in Christ.' Others said that was a fine ultimate goal; more immediately young black people should be prepared through education and opportunities given them within the black Churches to take up responsibilities, for example in the social services: then from a position of equality and not from a client position, they could cooperate in forming the single new humanity.

That conference of Christians who held conservative views of the Bible raised a series of questions which need to be examined; the identity of young British black people; their relationship with the police; inequality in education; menial tasks; heavy unemployment; white attitudes; the issue of control and leadership; the question of separate homogeneous Churches; cooperation which follows on respect for equals rather than clients. That is a formidable agenda for action. I shall attempt to consider each of these issues.

There is no doubt of the tone of the black voice, especially of the younger generation; it is a very bitter one. The report, *The New Black Presence in Britain*, acknowledged how much bitterness was felt; newcomers to Britain had found a kind of barrier-system which was perhaps more frustrating than straight poverty. Young black people felt there was subtlety and deviousness which kept them at the bottom of the heap. They seemed to have discovered very little solidarity with white working-class people. The Labour movement might be democratic in the sense of standing for the right of the majority, but the majority were not the most disadvantaged.[7]

A sympathetic criticism of the New Black Presence made the point that it is not simply a question of listening, but knowing to whom to listen. There are different voices speaking from within the black community; the report was a shade patronising towards those who had made what it called 'a prosperous adjustment'. They deserved as much attention as those who were severely alienated. 'I recently went to a party of black young people who I hadn't seen for four years and was impressed not by the extent of unemployment, homelessness, crime and illegitimacy, but rather by the sense of an emerging way of life which was distinctly black, but with little sign of social dislocation. Several young people, for whom one had predicted a bleak future, were in fact making "prosperous adjustments", and to underrate that world over against the more dramatic world of rude boys and rasta-bandwaggon riders, is an irresponsible distortion of the future of the black community.'[8]

Police/Community relations

In 1969 I became Bishop of Woolwich and moved from the
East End of London to South London, where there was a
comparatively large black community. It seemed an important
priority to meet and listen to members of that community. At
the end of one day of listening I joined a group of black
community leaders. For the first hour they insisted that I
listened to what they had to tell me about the police. I heard
what has become over the subsequent twelve years a familiar
tale: allegations of harassment of young people, planting
evidence and lack of respect for senior members in the black
community.

In 1981 Brixton and later Toxteth erupted into violent
riots. The patient, loving work of many black and white
people had not succeeded in shifting the situation sufficiently.
The Brixton Council of Churches said that the riot arose out
of frustration, unemployment, homelessness, alienation and
confrontation with the police. The same causes were listed by
a senior judge, Lord Scarman, who was appointed by the
Government to enquire into the Brixton riot. The flashpoint in
Brixton was an incident with the police. The black community
saw police/community relations filling the foreground, though
they knew very well that other long-term issues lay underneath.
To them the heavy-handed deployment of the police was an
arrogant assertion by society that there was no need to take any
notice of their pleadings or complaints. The Toxteth riots
were also triggered off by an incident with the police; black
and white people were involved together, though a specifically
black sense of injustice and deprivation was an important
factor.

Police bear the brunt of frustrations which are felt against
society. At the meeting with black community leaders twelve
years ago a sort of parable was told; the experience of black
people was as though they were going up to a big house. They
wanted to see the man in charge of the house. But he sent his
butler to get rid of them. They were angry with the butler,
though their real frustration was that they could not get a
hearing from the man who lived in the house. The police are

like the butler in the story; they become the objects of the frustration and anger of alienated young people.

Among Lord Scarman's recommendations were an independent procedure for complaints against the police, longer recruit training, in-service training, the establishment of liaison committees and a re-examination of policing methods.[9] The Chief Constable of Merseyside introduced a policy of community policing which accorded with this recommendation. Foot patrols were to be reintroduced in coordination with mobile patrols. Home beat officers were to be given greater status. More experienced police officers were drafted to the area designated for the experiment. A local police station for the area was established, and determined attempts were made to meet with community groups.

It has not been easy. A great deal of bitterness was felt by parts of the community; this was expressed in a campaign for the dismissal of the Chief Constable, which was not acceded to by the Government. Several black community groups boycotted public police/community meetings, though privately they continued to have some discussions with the police.

Getting local policemen back on the beat has underlined the dangers which police face. Police officers walking in pairs have been ambushed and violently attacked by gangs of young people. Yet it is an essential part of policing, which needs the consent and support of the community. I experienced a taste of the alternative in New York. I was walking on the sidewalk in Harlem with some black clergy. We passed a large group of black young people on the corner. As we walked on, I suddenly heard a loud voice over my shoulder: 'Keep walking!' A police car was moving slowly along and moving on the crowd with the loud hailer on its roof.

When that is the nearest the police come to parts of the community, we have lost any notion of intermediate policing. In the same way, if a police officer calls too quickly on his radio for help, and if there is an over-reaction so that vans arrive with large numbers of police and dogs, a minor incident rapidly escalates into a major confrontation. Whether there have been such confrontations or not, it is very helpful if local police follow the matter through with community leaders.

The police commander in Tower Hamlets in East London recently made a promise that the home beat officer would follow every incident involving an attack on an Asian with a home visit. The sense of the police being 'our police force' will be greatly strengthened, when it is seen that they are determined to offer protection to ethnic groups when they are in a vulnerable position.

Much good work has been done in community relations by police liaison officers. They have the most difficult task of all bridge people. Sometimes they are regarded as having the soft option, while others claim to be doing the real policing. There is no value in appointing home beat officers, if, when decisions are made about policing that community, their advice is not sought. Former Chief Constable John Alderson stresses the value of interchange between home beat officers, community relations experts and other operational branches by promotion and other means.[10] It is very unhelpful when views of policing are debated in a polarised way between hard and soft approaches. For example, a hard view may regard consultation with community groups about ways of dealing with street crime as undermining the independent judgment of the senior police officer. That does not follow. 'Consultation informs judgment: it does not pre-empt it.'[11]

Assumptions are made about hard and soft approaches in police attitudes to other professions. It is often assumed that youth workers, social workers and clergy will always have a soft approach. But there are bridge people there too; they will encourage those who have witnessed a crime to put away their fears of reprisals and come forward to give evidence. They will risk hard-won confidence of young people by encouraging them to come with them to meet police officers. In Peckham, South London, a black detached youth leader and a police liaison officer patiently worked at bringing together over a whole winter a group of black youths and police officers.

It is worth such costly investment in time for the police to try to stand in the shoes of parents, community leaders and young people in the black community. Spending time in community activities and getting to know those who are respected in the community can build up vital links. Police complain at times that black community leaders do not denounce lawlessness. Two answers may be given to that complaint. First, they probably denounce lawlessness privately as frequently as senior police officers rebuke policemen who abuse black people. Secondly, we need to understand that the forces of law and order are believed by many black people to be against them; if we expect leaders in the black community to line themselves up publicly with those forces of law and order, we need to give them the respect which is given to other leaders in the community. This has not always been done; sometimes community leaders have themselves been aggressively moved on by the police; sometimes they have been ignored or turned away, when they have tried to intervene at a flashpoint between black youth and the police. Police officers have not always taken the trouble to recognise community leaders; it is an important shift of consciousness to stop saying that all black people look alike to a white person. It is a further shift to acknowledge that in a multi-racial society leaders in each community need to be known by name and treated with respect.

If such relationships are to develop mutual respect, we need to understand better the pressures on each. Police officers face many situations when it would be superhuman not to feel afraid. Put yourself in the shoes of two young police officers in Liverpool:

> Allan: It's frightening when you go towards a crowd that's fighting outside a pub, because you look young, and they're going to treat you as young. It puts you below them, you know—people are going to treat you as a kid.
> Helen: You also never know which way a crowd is going to turn. That can be terrifying.[12]

High morale and strong bonds of support are needed within the police force if they are to go out and face such situations. Fear leads sometimes to over reaction, as does natural anger. If a woman police officer is attacked and severely injured by two men whom she is trying to arrest, it is understandable when her colleagues separate them and beat them up. Understandable but wrong. It represents a breakdown of self-discipline, which teaches a police officer not to over-react. That discipline is very severely tested; a Chief Constable told me that his police officers had to learn to stand in a line at a demonstration with spittle running down their faces, abuse hurled at them, and not to hit back. That asks for a very high order of discipline.

As the task of policing has become more dangerous, so the temptation has grown for police officers not to discuss their work outside their own profession. Sometimes clergy may have shared the blame for preventing a good interchange from taking place. If we have led police officers to understand that we believe law enforcement can always be achieved without any use of force, we should not be surprised if they refuse to discuss policing matters with us. We must acknowledge that sometimes their choice is between the lesser of two evils, and that evil is a reality in human beings.

It is understandable that police react sharply to criticism. They have an increasingly tough task; they do a great deal of it very well. They deserve a lot of praise, and often don't receive it. But it doesn't help if senior officers deny, for example, after the 1981 riots in Brixton, that anything has gone wrong in police relations with the black community; nor does it help for them to say that the trouble has all been stirred up by political agitators from outside. Those who hold such theories of conspiracy need to ask what outsiders could achieve if there was not the seedbed of resentment already there.

In its worship the Church should notice and pray for those who play significant parts in community life. Few play a more important part for good or ill than the police. They should be frequently in the prayers of Christians. As we show that we believe that this is a very important calling, we will encourage people, black and white, to offer themselves for service in the police force. To be bridge people for black people will be a very tough calling.

In Liverpool police officers felt very hurt by the grant of £500 made to the Liverpool 8 Defence Committee by the Community and Race Relations Unit of the British Council of Churches. The Defence Committee organised transport for relatives to visit those who had been arrested and were being held at Risley Remand Centre; they offered advice and support in obtaining defence lawyers. As well as these straightforward activities they organised a march through Liverpool, calling for the dismissal of the Chief Constable, whom they held to be responsible for the police tactics in which a young man was killed by a police vehicle.

The Church leaders issued a statement dissociating ourselves from the campaign against the Chief Constable, but asking understanding for the need to offer support on occasions to groups in a massively deprived community. The Community and Race Relations Unit did not have to ask our consent. Over several years it had made a number of modest grants to self-help groups in the Liverpool black community.

We Christians found ourselves deeply divided about this grant, feeling the pain, as people who were very close to us expressed opposite points of view. My wife and I spent an evening a month after the riots with a group of friends. One clergy couple lived close to the scene of the riots. They saw matters very much through the eyes of inner city people, whom they felt the police had picked on unfairly over the years. Another clergy couple then told us that their son in the police force had his face permanently scarred by a brick on the first night of the riots. We were rightly and uncomfortably feeling torn in half between two groups of people, knowing that we belonged to them both.

I spent a morning with the clergy in Toxteth, a little fearful that we might tear ourselves apart. For there are very different communities and attitudes in Toxteth. Church people and clergy are likely to reflect these different views. Though different opinions were strongly expressed in the Toxteth clergy meeting, there was a consistent readiness to listen to one another.

There are those in Toxteth who say, 'We are good working-class people in our street. What we need is a strong dose of law and order'. That is one authentic Toxteth voice. There are others who say, 'We're all deprived on our estate. It's nothing to do with being black or white'. That is a genuine Toxteth voice too. There are others again who say, 'There is deprivation for everyone here. But if you're black, the difficulties of finding a job, and of receiving even-handed treatment from the police are much greater'. That is also a true Toxteth voice. Those different attitudes emerged when Liverpool City Council made a door to door survey of Toxteth designed to find which matters caused greatest concern to residents. The response rate was 50 per cent. One question was, '*Are there things to do with policing and the prevention of crime that you would like to see something done about in your area?*' Two of the answers people could give were 'Bobbies on the beat' and 'Poor police attitudes'. Two areas make up one parish, which elsewhere in the book I described as made up of good working-class people. Their response was:

Bobbies on the beat	31.7% and 36%
Poor police attitudes	9.5% and 7.9%

Two other areas had the following response:

Bobbies on the beat	17.9% and 14.7%
Poor police attitudes	15.3% and 16.9% [13]

The division of attitudes was also expressed in angry letters received from several suburban Parochial Church Councils; they demanded that, if any further grants were made, they should be given through local Churches. Part of the pain of a debate about a bias to the poor is to question what such letters expressed; was it proper Christian indignation against law-breaking? Was it the fear and anger of the suburbs, refusing to listen to the bitter cry of alienated people? Or was it an unwillingness to help, unless people belonged to the Church?

The leaders of the Churches in Liverpool were approached by local black community leaders, who asked us if we would help to sponsor a law centre. This would offer services to all people in the area; its management committee would include three Church nominations, and would otherwise be elected at a public meeting. It seemed to us right to offer what support we could, to help a community to stand up and take its own responsibilities. That cooperation has made me aware of some of the conflicting pressures which fall on those who begin to take a lead in a community which has for generations accepted the bottom line.

Following the riots the Prime Minister sent a Cabinet Minister to Merseyside. Michael Heseltine, the Secretary of State for the Environment, spent three weeks in the area with a strong Civil Service support team. Then a task force was set up for twelve months to try to attract new businesses and offer new training resources to Merseyside. It was a redirection of resources already allocated, rather than any substantial fresh aid. There was a particular attempt to bring fresh opportunities to Toxteth. Advance factories, a small firms workshop, an information technology centre, a sports hall and a community refurbishment scheme were among their plans for the area. Black young people were making use of some of these; but the developments which would win the confidence of many more had still to come. That would involve black adults in management positions.

At the time of writing there remains a great deal of distrust of the City Council; it has threatened, as part of economies caused by Government cutbacks, to remove the grant from one of the few black-run organisations, the Charles Wootton Adult Education Centre. It has been said that grants were not being used in the most cost-effective way, and that the same courses could be run on Education Authority premises. There seemed to be little understanding of how important it was to black organisations to have the security of controlling their own premises. Then a visitor can be a welcome guest and not a threatening agent of the controlling institution. There is a parallel in the black-led Churches which flourish in London and other cities where more recent immigration has taken place. To established Church leaders they seem to be marvellously free of the heavy costs of maintaining large buildings. But, if they are asked what they most want, the most frequent answer will be to have a building of their own, which will help give them independence and identity, and where they can worship with the dignity which is due to God. They find it galling to worship on a Sunday morning in a hall still heavy with the stale smell of beer and tobacco, or to have to hurry their prayers and praises, because the caretaker is impatient to lock up.

Unemployment and underemployment

When unemployment is mentioned as a particular issue for black people, the reply is often given that in a time of depression unemployment hits every group in a country alike. That is not true. Unemployment falls unequally on regions such as Merseyside and on groups such as black people. Rates of unemployment for black people are generally more than double those for all workers of the same age group. For example, a 1978 survey showed that unemployment was three times as high among black as among white school leavers in Lewisham.[14] The Political and Economic Planning(PEP) survey in 1974 showed that there had been a drop in racial discrimination since their survey in 1967. Yet more than half the plants investigated in 1974 practised some form of discrimination against black people in their hiring practices.[15]

There is not only an issue of unemployment; for a long time there has been an issue of underemployment for black and Asian people. Many have to take jobs far below what they are qualified for. Selecting one example from many, one man was a personnel manager for a very large international company in his own country. He is a member of the Institute of Personnel Management. When he came to England, his company told him there would be a job in the English company. He did get a job with them, as an office messenger. He was told that everybody starts at the bottom in an English company. After a year he was still an office messenger, and left.

In 1980 a study was made in Nottingham. Identical written applications were made for white-collar jobs by three test candidates. One was a native white person, one was of West Indian origin, and the third was an Asian. Standard letters of application were used and handwriting was equally matched. In 48 per cent of the tests either the West Indian or the Asian candidate, or both, was refused an interview, or not replied to, whilst the native white candidate was offered an interview. The separate figures for the West Indian and Asian were almost identical—evidence that employers who discriminated did so mainly on the basis of colour rather than ethnic grounds.[16]

A black woman told me she had visited a large works in the London area and met the managing director. He said that there was no prejudice and that many black people were working on the factory floor. She asked, 'How do you get to do your job?' He answered, 'Probably you would join as an apprentice.' 'All right. Tell me about the apprentices you took on this year.' 'There were eighty apprentices.' 'How many were girls?' 'Four.' 'How many were black?' 'Zero.'

If we want to get rid of racial discrimination, there are two policies which employers and trade unions should follow. First we need to keep accurate statistics; secondly accept the principle of affirmative action. Without accurate statistics no firm can know whether it is discriminating or not. As far as white-collar jobs are concerned, discrimination often results from the fear of those responsible for recruiting for junior posts that they will displease their senior management if they take on more than a handful of black people. Sometimes the fear is the other way round; management fear that office and shop-floor staff will resent the promotion of black or Asian people. These assumptions are rarely tested and are not spoken about. Firms, local authorities, nationalised industries, the Civil Service will not know whether there is prejudice or not, unless they monitor the numbers of applications and appointments at every level of seniority of both black people and Asians. Sometimes the prejudice is more explicit. British Leyland recently pleaded in court that they had not refused the application of a worker because he was black; the reason was that white workers said they would not work with him because he was black.

Affirmative action does not mean giving someone a job just because he is black, even though you know he is not competent to do it. It means that special and appropriate training should be offered to those who are at a particular disadvantage, to help them reach the starting gate. In one firm it is settled practice that the managing director is shown the application forms of all black people applying for jobs, whether they have been taken on or not. The personnel officers soon realised that the firm meant business when it said that it practised no colour prejudice.

It's easy to laugh at the presence of 'statutory blacks', and 'It's better still, if she's a woman.' Some may, because of past loss of self-confidence, struggle to keep up. But such positive compensation for deprivation is a necessary step along the way.[17] A younger black generation will see that it is possible to use their gifts in a responsible post. Their expectations will be greater, and in due course they will enter those jobs with a different level of confidence.

The General Council of the Trades Union Congress has commended to unions a model clause on equal opportunities for inclusion in all collective agreements. It concerns recruitment, training, promotion and redundancy. If trade unionists acknowledge that black people are at a disadvantage, they too must argue for affirmative action and keep accurate statistics, within their own organisations as well as in their places of work.

I have chosen to use the term favoured in the United States, *affirmative action*, rather than *positive discrimination*. I am talking about action, which affirms the abilities people have, and determines to intervene in order to offer them equal opportunities. In this sense positive discrimination reflects a proper bias to those who have been robbed of equal opportunities. It is not the same as reverse discrimination, with which it is sometimes confused. This would offer black people both more than their share of jobs and also posts for which they were not qualified at all. This confusion leads some to grumble at affirmative action. It is said to add fuel to the fire of the white backlash. If there has sometimes been affirmative action, we should not apologise for it, but explain why it is necessary and right. Without such open debate prejudice can never be brought into the open and examined for what it is.

Underlying the debate about positive discrimination or bias to the poor is a debate about justice. The great prophets of the Old Testament, like Isaiah, Amos, Micah and Jeremiah, spoke about God's concern for righteousness or justice (*tsedeq* in Hebrew). *Tsedeq* topples over on behalf of those in direst need.[18] This justice is not the same as fairness, as though everyone started from the same line. It is not portrayed by the blind-eyed Goddess of Justice. We owe that picture of justice to the Greeks. The blind Goddess properly stands over the Law Courts. She does not look to see if the plaintiff or the defendant has the greater needs: she is blind. She dispenses even-handed justice. She assumes that she is settling a dispute between equals.

In the Bible the righteous God is not blind; His eyes are wide open. Because He is against sin, which distorts relationships between His children, He pushes away the oppressor and is active on behalf of those in special need. He sees the need of widows, orphans, foreigners, the oppressed and He acts for them. At times this is in contrast to strict justice. C. H. Dodd commented on the famous phrase in St Paul about Christ justifying the ungodly. Had St Paul written in classical Greek rather than the more colloquial Greek of his day, the words could only have meant that Christ condemned the ungodly. But he understood deeply the thought of the Old Testament; God's righteousness topples over in favour of those in dire need; so the righteousness of God, as shown in the work of Jesus Christ, is not the righteousness of the law, which gives each man his just desserts. It is the righteousness of divine grace.[19]

When we argue for affirmative action in favour of groups in the greatest need, other groups will complain that it's not fair. They want the even-handed justice of the blind Goddess which leaves the advantage with those already in possession. If we are to reflect the character of the living, eyes-wide-open, God of grace, we should argue unashamedly for policies which will intervene on behalf of those in special need.

Progress for black people in the United States

It was a revelation for me as an Englishman to go to the United States in 1977 and 1979. I saw black people taking with confidence their proper place in society. They were to be seen in the front rank of education, business, the arts, public administration and the Church. These advances were not brought about by playing down the issues of race relations, nor by black people staying quiet. The Civil Rights Movement of the 1960s brought about massive changes because black people would no longer tolerate their suppression, and took the initiative. And many white people with enormous courage stood up to be counted in the Civil Rights years.

By comparison with Britain theirs was a different earlier history. There was a long period of conscious segregation with the slogan 'Separate but equal', when black schools, universities and Churches helped black people to qualify for the professions and for leadership roles. Where black people have risen to prominence, for example, as mayors of their cities, there is generally a majority of black people in those cities. In other words the black people made their advance through the electoral support of their own people, rather than through the enlightenment of the whites.

Black people won some great victories in the 1960s. They won the right to vote in the South and the right to representation in the North. Segregation was broken down in housing, jobs and schools in many areas. President Johnson proclaimed the War on Poverty; he wanted in particular to see that black people got something fast. Sargent Shriver, the Director of the Office of Economic Opportunity, set no less an objective than the abolition of poverty within a decade.

After those heady years, the stubborn persistence of poverty for urban black people has led to a lot of bitterness and despair. In June 1980 6.8 per cent of white Americans were unemployed; 14.7 per cent of black Americans were jobless. In several cities, where the inner ring of the city is largely black, unemployment figures are very comparable with what I have described in Liverpool. For example, in Detroit it was estimated that in the summer of 1980 65 per cent of black youths and 40 per cent of the total black work force in Detroit were unemployed.[20]

Frances Fox Piven told the Urban Bishops' Coalition of the Episcopal Church of the USA that the bottom line of US urban economic policies was to be found in the actual, tangible experiences of the inner city poor. The toll had been most catastrophic for the black urban poor. 'The bottom line has to do with the persistence of unemployment . . . with the utter collapse of the low-rental housing market . . . under these circumstances the communities of the poor collapse, so that whatever they have in a capacity for self-help is gone.' Because of reductions in public spending (long before President Reagan came into office) 'whatever neighbourhood services the older cities once provided for the casualties of our economic policies have been cut back.[21] Now even more drastic cuts have been made.

Later in this book I shall examine some of the Poverty programmes and their effects. The impression grows that it is not more surveys or speeches about concern that are wanted. The needs of the urban poor are well known. What is wanted is the political will to act. In a similar way the countries of the Northern hemisphere hide their unwillingness to act behind a wall of concerned rhetoric about the Brandt Report on the Third World.

In a survey of chronic truants in an East Harlem junior high school the question was asked, 'What do you most want to be when you grow up?' The response uniformly was to draw a blank. They had 'no hopes, no dreams, no visions for the future.' At the age of twelve or thirteen life simply had closed in.[22] Sometimes this blank leads to apathy, sometimes to violence which makes some US cities very dangerous places. The slum clearance and public housing programmes of the New and Fair Deals had perpetuated segregation. Massive housing projects, undertaken with the most benign intent, had become 'jungles—places of despair and danger for their residents and for the cities they were designed to save' wrote Bobby Kennedy in 1966. 'The violent youth of the ghetto is not simply protesting his condition, but making a destructive and self defeating attempt to assert his worth and dignity as a human being, to tell us that, though we may scorn his contribution, we must still respect his power.'[23]

Urban poverty is vividly described in an oral history of a Puerto Rican in 1976. 'When you're poor in Puerto Rico, you're not really poor. It's a different thing. Everybody around you is in the same category. You don't feel poor. No one makes you feel poor. When I came to Eighth Street in New

York City, it was like falling from a high place. The whole neighbourhood was black and Puerto Rican, and at that time at each other's throat. I have never seen a bum in Puerto Rico. I mean I had seen poor people, and I had seen drunks, but they belonged to a family somewhere. Here there were people sprawled over the stairs, completely gone. They were junkies. I mean, nobody was doing anything about it. Nobody knew. Nobody cared.'[24]

Programmes of affirmative action on behalf of the black people have been very important in developing opportunities. But how seriously priority programmes are taken is to be seen most clearly, not in times of expansion, but in times of cutback. Cuts across the board appear to be fair. In fact they are a rejection of any sense of priorities. Last in, first out appears to be the fairest way. The effect of such a policy has been to make black people suffer most, for example in New York City in the police force and among teachers. That has destroyed the hard won gains of patient affirmative action. Promises and programmes raised poor people's hopes; when the programmes were ended and the promises broken, the disillusionment was even greater.

The lessons from the 1960s, which black people in the United States would say they have learned, are that they themselves must take the lead in bringing about change; and, although they must have clear long-term objectives, they must work for short-term goals, which are consistent and achievable. In Philadelphia a largely black Episcopalian congregation had been very much involved in trying to bring about a change of mayor in November 1978. The election brought about the change; on the following Sunday the sermon at the Eucharist was preached by a woman who had been for many years a leader in the community; 'The hands that once picked cotton are now picking the elected officials in our cities,' she said.[25] An inner city group which I met in Pittsburgh said, 'We must become sophisticated, competent and skilled, and not forget the whole black community.'

Whether in Pittsburgh or in London there is a temptation for more successful black people to distance themselves from what may seem the less respectable black community. In

Shepherd's Bush, London, a residents' meeting was objecting to plans to start a hostel for black youths. The chief spokesman for the residents was a black man. The scale of the barriers which block the way for the black community cause some intelligent young black people to forget their whole community; instead they settle, as many white people have done, for personal advance. The philosophy of the day for so many self-confident young people is to seek status and security for themselves and their family. Some young black people are no exception. If they can get through the turnstile themselves, they are tempted to forget those who are still outside, and to take advantage of the individualist opportunity which is now theirs.

That's not the whole story: if black youths are to see the value of education they need to see black people in the front rank of society. The achievement of Asian children in school is dramatically better than that of black children. This reflects the different nature of the communities; Asians who have come to Britain include many who have the background of having run their own businesses. Many have been used to living as a minority and automatically made arrangements for extra-curricular coaching. Young Asians can see the achievements which educational success brings to other Asians. It is not that West Indian parents value education less; but many of them lack the self-confidence which comes from having done well in school themselves. Children of West Indian origin have often suffered in Britain from very damaging labelling, which has placed many children in low streams and in educationally sub-normal schools, who should never have been there. In its interim report the committee of enquiry into the education of children of ethnic minorities spelled out a cycle of under-achievement of children of West Indian origin. Its roots are established in pre-school years. A disproportionate number of married West Indian women (68 per cent compared with a national average of 42 per cent in the 1971 census) were forced to go out to work because of their economic circumstances. Their children were often left with unregistered child-minders. The proportion of West Indian males employed on night shifts was almost double that of white males. Therefore many children did not receive the vital time with their parents, when home conversation and story times develop language and ability.

The disadvantages in the way of black children achieving well in an inner city situation in Britain add up to a formidable list. A Department of Education and Science survey of school leavers' qualifications in 1979 in six urban education authorities showed a remarkable difference of achievement between children of West Indian and Asian origins. The number of those who obtained five or more 'O' level exams (not lower than Grade C, or CSE Grade One) was:

West Indians 3 per cent, Asians 18 per cent, all others 16 per cent. The figure for the whole of England was 21 per cent. Those who obtained at least one 'A' level were:

West Indians 2 per cent, Asians 13 per cent, all others 12 per cent. The figure for the whole of England was 13 per cent.[26]

I will take up the question of educational opportunities for those at a disadvantage in a later chapter. Here I make the point of how much expectation influences children's achievements. That includes what parents, teachers, friends and the children themselves expect. The committee did not believe that more than a tiny proportion of teachers held openly racist views; yet unintentional attitudes patronised and stereotyped black children. I recall visiting an infants' school in South London where the majority of children were black. The head teacher in a kindly manner said to me, as we entered the school assembly, 'Of course, they won't achieve much, but we try to make them happy.'

The achievements of black individuals will lift what black young people expect of themselves. But if the whole community is to be enriched, ambition to change things needs to be corporate and not simply for the individual and his family. 'It's easier to say, "Here I stand. I can do no other," as an individual, than to say "Stand with me." '[27] Black Christians in the United States said to me, 'The recent poor have taken the values of the white middle class in working for material goods and status. Then a bit later they come and say to us "What have we done to our teenagers?" '

77

There can be no serious doubting the massive disadvantages which black people face in Britain and still in many cities in the USA. Sadly there is resentment among those who see themselves as poor whites, if programmes are established to help disadvantaged black people. The fact that black achievement or non-achievement is literally visible in a mainly white society reveals what happens to other disadvantaged groups. If we could learn how to deal with the disadvantage of black people, we should at the same time learn how to help other poor groups. A further look will be needed at enriching whole communities, at the experience of white pain and at the effectiveness or otherwise of poverty programmes.

CHAPTER FIVE

Solidarity

Those who have been shut out

The need for pride in the black community raises major human and Christian questions. Separate development is an evil contradiction of God's purpose for 'a single new humanity';[1] when it breaks into Church life, it ignores our belief in one holy, catholic Church. It was a shock when we started to hear black people talking about black consciousness, development of black community life and black churches.

It is a central thrust of this book that God calls us to break down the barriers between races, classes and Churches. That does not suggest that one class or nationality should dominate others; minority groups should not be absorbed into one dominant culture. If immigrant groups were to allow themselves to be absorbed, and to learn to fit in with the way of life of the host country, they would have to let go the distinctive features of their own culture. They would then lose the distinctive flavour which they can bring to the great enrichment of the whole community. Those who have been shut out from the main stream of national life have to make an assertion of the solidarity of the group they belong to. For many people that is a necessary step to self-respect before they have enough confidence to bring their distinctive gifts to the whole human community.

That group solidarity may properly express itself in black consciousness or a black Church. It is never the last word about solidarity; the last word is the solidarity of the whole human race. Learning respect for their own clan or group is the first step many need to take. It is at the same time a basic canon in education never to teach anything which it will be necessary

79

to unteach, so there needs to be an awareness of a wider world from the beginning. There needs to be some understanding of how difficult it is for those at a disadvantage to see beyond their own needs. 'When your group is fighting from a position of powerlessness, you cannot engage in self criticism. There is bound to be a period when you are pressing to prove that you can be top.'[2] What is true of black solidarity is also true of solidarity expressed in class terms, for example in belonging to a trade union. When such a group has enriched its own community, there is a call to bring its resources fully into the whole community and to have particular concern for other groups which may then be in the weaker positions.

A black evangelist wrote that Black Power was the most encouraging thing in race relations in recent years. He rejected black racism and emphasis on violence. 'However as a Christian I welcome a philosophy that encourages men to accept their innate sense of human responsibility. I want people to control their political, economic and educational destinies. Black Power encourages blacks' awareness of their humanity, and for that reason should be welcomed as an ally and not an adversary.'[3] The report 'The New Black Presence in Britain' saw great hope in the black community going through 'a phase of sharpening its identity and discovering its points of leverage in relationship to the rest of society'.[4] There would then be opportunities for a great new wealth of variety and vigorous diversity.

The American dream of the melting pot, from which one American way of life emerges, has been rightly questioned. America is more of a stew than a soup, and it is in the strength of its various ingredients that the flavour of its life can be enhanced.[5] It was when black Americans realised the strength of the Irish-Americans, the Jewish-Americans, the Italian-Americans that they began to see the connection between a sense of identity and political and economic power. So Afro-Americans started to talk about 'putting the hyphen back'. Churches in Britain have taken an important step in affirming that Britain is now a multi-racial, multi-cultural and multi-religious society.

We live in a pluralist society; some regret it, but faith in the living God, who is active in the continuing creation of the world, should help us to see such changes more positively. 'Yes, our society is pluralist in that it is overwhelmingly urban, full of jostling philosophies,' wrote Don Cupitt. Our contemporaries and we ourselves often dream of an older and simpler order of things, a small-scale society in which religion and morality are built in, taken for granted and not worried about; a social order which will give us our beliefs, and tell us our rights and duties. 'We dream in a word of retiring to the country. But it is only a dream, and even if we could realize it, we should lose a great deal more than we should gain.'[6]

It needs to be recognised that race relations are between communities. It is only individuals with exceptionally strong self-confidence, who can cross these gaps by themselves. A member of the black community who read these words of mine commented, 'No individual can cross these gaps by himself.' He had underlined no twice. And it is well-nigh impossible for these relationships to be good when one community is plainly much stronger than the other and with no prospect of change. If the weaker is to repudiate the dangerous self-contempt which such an unchanging situation engenders, then there must be some assertion of its distinctive life.

There are often two voices heard from groups which are at a disadvantage; one says, 'Leave us alone; our culture is as good as yours.' The other says, 'Give us a share of the common future.' The voices are in conflict. The conflict reveals something of the hurt which groups feel, when they know they are shut out from the opportunities a society claims to offer to all. The sense of national harmony and unity, for which we long, lies on the far side of tackling this issue. There is a sequence in relations between communities; first identity, then self-confidence, then an acknowledged interdependence.

Asians in Britain

I have written very little about Asians in Britain, though there are more Asians in this country than those of West Indian origin. This is because in the areas where I have lived and worked comparatively few Asians have settled. It is also true

81

that many Asians are from business communities; they have a long history of landing on their feet in many parts of the world. This, together with a strongly distinctive and unbroken culture and different languages has meant that it has been possible not to see Asians as being particularly among the vulnerable in the community. But it is becoming clear that this is not the whole truth. Many have come from very poor communities in the Indian sub-continent; they find themselves living in some of the worst inner city housing and doing the most unpleasant jobs. And the brown generation born and brought up in the inner areas of British cities shares in many of the confusing and alienating experiences, which the same generation of black youth faces.

Some Asians came to Britain with their families. Many more came alone, in the hope that they could save enough to call their families over later. Nearly all originally came determined to spend no more than seven years. Everything took longer than they expected; they had to take low-paid jobs. They had to send money home to maintain wives and children as well as their parents and relatives. Then there was often a waiting period of two or three years before their families were allowed to enter Britain. So seven years stretched out to a fifteen-year period. Now they were middle aged; to return to their country would be very difficult economically. People retire in India much earlier than in Britain, and middle-aged men have little chance of finding jobs. The longer they stay in Britain, the more their children become Anglicised. So the parents decide to stay on until their children complete their education. Now they must stay twenty-five years at least; that means they have grown old. Their children have grown up in Britain and have no wish to go to the Indian sub-continent.

There is much sadness in the life of the Asian immigrant in Britain. Dr Bhikhu Parekh writes that several Indians in their early sixties have put it to him that they cannot bear the thought of getting old and dying in this cold and alien land, and yet they cannot see how they can avoid this. There are many who do not speak English after years of living in England. They have not grown accustomed to the culture of an industrialised society. They have suffered racialist insults and indignities. In many cases they have not been able to obtain decent houses or jobs which match their abilities.

Attitudes towards the British from old colonial days, anxiety because of repeated harping by British politicians on floods of immigrants and of police searches for illegal immigrants, together with explicitly racist attacks by the National Front on Asian shops and homes—all these make the Asian immigrant, as distinct from his children born in this country, nervous and timid in his relations with white Britons. 'He walks in the shadow and close to the wall. He avoids confrontation, "plays dumb" and swallows his pride.'[7]

The second generation Asian's attitude is different. He thinks of himself as a brown Briton. He competes with his white contemporaries, often excels them in education and employment. He is therefore free from his parents' deep-seated feeling of inferiority and insecurity in his dealings with white people; he feels much less inhibited in standing up for his rights.

Family ties remain very strong among Asians. To a remarkable degree they have contained the tensions between the generations, though hardly any Asian family is entirely free from them. Some Asians, born in this country, are critical of their parents for maintaining traditional Asian customs, especially those relating to sex. They think their parents are too submissive, that they lack political self-reliance. They look for their own leaders among those whose attitudes are those of the working class or lower middle class instead of being drawn from business or the professions.

In spite of the different experiences of young Asians the structure of the Asian family has continued to give its children strong emotional interdependence. Their rebellions are more symbolic than actual. 'In a population of a million Asians there are not even a hundred cases of children leaving their parental homes.'[8] The majority of young Asians believe that they should marry within their own communities and approve of arranged marriages. The relationship between father and children has a mixture of authority and vulnerability. At one level the father is remote and is expected to be obeyed without question. At another level he is dependent on his children, freely acknowledges his failings and deficiencies, and expects to be protected. His children therefore feel both deferential and protective toward him.

In a novel by Mulk Raj Anand, a Sikh adolescent is described; 'Lalu was taken aback by the onslaught, even though he had expected it. One part of him longed to struggle. But the feeling of docility and respect that had been inculcated in him since birth made him dumb and unresisting, though he smouldered with rage and self pity.'

In a report—'The Half-way Generation'—a young Asian says, 'Our religion has everything to do with family. I mean religion says that we should live together. This is one of the biggest things, respect for your elders. My brothers, they can come in the house, say something—I've got to do it, whether I like it or not. Say, for example, I refused him once, which I did. This was when I was working at the market, and he just turned round and slapped me in the face. I was 19 then. See, if I'd been an English lad myself, I know this, I would have turned round and hit him one. But not me . . . I just turned, started working.'[9]

Attacks on Pakistanis and Bengalis in the East End of London have roused young Asians to a much more belligerent spirit. Vigilante groups have been formed. Some young Asians join the Anti-Nazi League. Many vote for extreme left-wing candidates who campaign on a strongly anti-racialist platform. Asian businessmen are in a sense natural Conservatives, but their strong feelings about how the Asian community is treated have turned some to other parties, while others begin to speak up within the Conservative Party. The Asian and the black vote may increasingly need to be sought by British political parties. Nevertheless fears about the prejudice of white voters seem to prevent parties from putting up candidates in electoral seats which they have the possibility of winning. So there are still no black or brown Members of Parliament.

Christians and other Religions

The migration of Asians means that there are today in Britain substantial communities of Muslims, Sikhs and Hindus. The religions are sometimes brought face to face; on occasions religious groups who have moved into an area ask to buy a church building no longer needed by Christians who have moved out of the area. The thought of removing Christian symbols from redundant Church buildings, releasing them to become places of worship for other religions, has naturally raised deep anxieties in the minds of Christians. But, if the Christian Church has no further need for a particular building, it is a proper response to the needs of a minority community, to make it available to them. To offer such practical help as we are able, to treat other religions with respect and to enter into friendly dialogue is not to abandon the belief of Christians in the uniqueness of Jesus Christ. It reflects our common humanity and our common experience of the love of God.

I believe that Jesus Christ is in a wholly unique way the Son of God. That can be said in two quite different ways; it may be said in an *exclusive* way, which claims that no other religion has anything of any lasting value to say. Or it may be said in an *inclusive* way; then God's revelation of Himself in Christ is seen to be of relevance to everyone and everything in the universe.[10]

If Christians obey Christ's call to go into all the world, they will meet people of other cultures and other faiths. The manner of the meeting should include respect for the convictions of the others. Christians will not believe that we can give to others, but never receive. So dialogue is a more appropriate way of meeting than monologue. Dialogue will include being true to the experience of those who live by the Word and Sacrament of the Gospel. We continue to believe that Jesus Christ, in whom all the fulness of the godhead dwells, makes Himself known in the life and worship of the Church. So at the right moment, with courtesy and respect, we shall bear our witness to Christ. Dialogue will also include being 'open to receive the riches of God, which belong properly to Christ, but have to be brought to Him'.[11] We may receive those riches through men and women of other faiths. The atmosphere of mutual respect and caring will mean that it is no proper concern of the Church to defend its own present position in society; we should be glad if we are able to help other religious groups to have the facilities to enrich their community life.[12]

Ethnic Churches

Within the Christian household of faith there is a good deal of evidence that Church growth, understood in numbers attending services, is likely to be more successful if worshippers are encouraged to stay with those who are like-minded. That would be one thing, if it was possible to operate on the separate but equal principle. It would still mean disobedience to the calling to be a Catholic Church, in which Christians learn to live in a body enriched by a variety of cultures and backgrounds. In practice, separate but equal is not possible in Church or State. Perhaps the most crucial questions which prevents it is, 'who makes the decisions?'

Those who have been left behind in the urban race often feel that the Church of the settled and successful is not for them. They say they are tolerated up to a certain level and up to certain numbers. But other people make the decisions about what kind of Church programme there is going to be. The movement of ethnic groups makes newcomers feel the same. For example, a large Puerto Rican population moved into the South Bronx in New York. The Roman Catholic parish of St Angela Merici had been established late in the nineteenth century to serve mainly the Irish and German population of the Bronx. From the mid 1960s the population changed until the majority became Puerto Rican. The other parishioners tried either to ignore or resist their presence, even when the majority of Sunday worshippers were Puerto Rican. The newcomers wanted a parish which would offer a sense of ethnic identity.[13]

In the United States black-led Churches were a natural part of life which was segregated in all respects. They came into being both in the 'main line' Churches and in the many 'store front' Churches of US cities. In Britain black-led Churches came about as a direct result of a sense that black people were not wanted in white-dominated Churches. At best they found that they were tolerated; but there was no share in the decision-making. 'Some were politely told not to come back, or to go and form their own organisation: some were shunned or not given any opportunity to express themselves within the organisation.'[14] It seemed that they were expected to take a subservient place in *white-run* Churches. So many withdrew into black-led Churches, where black people are able to decide the style of life and the programme. They have always emphasised that white people are welcome. In Birmingham alone there are more than forty different denominations which are black-led. It should be said that there are a number of mainstream Churches where black membership and share in leadership have been growing strongly. But it is the exception rather than the rule.

Black Churches offer cultural identity, practical mutual support, leadership opportunity and personal faith.[15] Many youngsters belong, though some black young people challenge the black-led Churches for being so concerned with the spiritual life and the fellowship of Christians that they do not ask questions about the whole community and the secular life which their members have to face. Many pick up families in a minibus and take them across the city to a day of worship and fellowship. The Rev. Jeremiah McIntyre wrote in 1974, 'We are at present moving away from the internal work of the Church. The first ten years were spent gathering the people together, but being increasingly confronted with outside problems, we have been forced to become more involved with matters not directly concerned with the Church.[16] Leadership is sometimes autocratic with demands of tithing and strict discipline from members. Certainly many young people have turned away. This is partly because they feel the church avoids the issues they have to face every day; it is also because black-led Churches are not immune from the processes which make many urban white-led Churches seem to be places for the respectable and the successful. Five children were sent home from Church in a black Episcopal parish in Detroit, because they were not clean enough.

A visiting speaker at a club service, in the Methodist Youth Club in Liverpool 8, challenged members to decide for Christ. Three girls tackled the youth leader afterwards. At school they were in a small minority; in the club, which was entirely black, they felt safe and at home. 'Don't ask us to make a decision,' they said. 'We feel all nice here. Now you're asking us to be different again.' When I visited the club a few years later, the three girls were asked if they would like to talk to me; they declined. They were Bible-carrying Rastafarians. They were still searching for God, but they felt that the finding could only take place in a black milieu. The first time they had seen a religious group run by black people had been when they met Rastafarians.

As with Christians Rastafarians have widely different levels of seriousness with which they take their faith. For some there is honest commitment, which has thought out a philosophy, touching the whole of the natural world. 'There is a rich and eccentric pattern of Biblical imagery and contemporary expression. Since they rely on inspiration not information without any historical anchor, the movement could well end up as a curiosity, or a fad, or a form of self indulgence.'[17] Yet a book entitled *Bias to the Poor* cannot avoid looking wistfully at such a movement. It has given slum-dwellers in Jamaica a sense of identity. They see the West as Babylon. A Rastafarian in Jamaica expressed God's commitment to the poor, 'God say, he shall take the base things of the earth to confound the wise and prudent. You couldn't look for a man in St Andrew who is in a big house and live into a big category. You'd have to come to a place like where you is now, in the slum, to look for one of the base things that shall rise to confound.'[18]

A bias to the poor leads us to understand why black churches have come into being and to offer support to them. It is a step along the way for those who have reason to feel shut out from the main-stream opportunities of secular and Church life. It is not God's last word to them. Nor should it be used as an argument to support the idea that God is content for like-minded people to keep themselves to themselves in worshipping congregations. This idea has been elevated to a principle by some of the writing of the Church Growth school of Fuller Seminary, Pasadena, California.

Peter Wagner acknowledges that the 'homogenous unit' theory of the Church Growth school has caused controversy. He has written *Our Kind of People* to defend the idea that 'congregations develop into healthy communities, when they concentrate on only one kind of people'. The dust jacket of the book proclaims, 'Wagner transforms the statement that 11 a.m. on Sunday is the most segregated hour in America from a millstone around Christian necks into a dynamic tool for assuring Christian growth.' Wagner admits that this position raises some ethical problems. 'Ethical issues, such as learning to live in peace and harmony with those of other homogenous units' should not confront people at the point of conversion or 'discipling'. They come later. 'Men like to become Christians without crossing racial, linguistic or class barriers.' Turning away from racism would be part of the 'perfecting' process of Christian living. Since evangelism occurs best in Churches that are made up of one kind of people, the Church should no longer feel guilty about segregation or try to change what must be considered a natural inclination of the human species to withdraw from those who are different.[19]

As long as the Church makes growth in terms of numbers its yardstick, so long will it blind itself to the plain meaning of the New Testament. Conversion is no more than a trip to personal reassurance, if we are encouraged to think it asks no questions about the company we keep. The call to follow Christ must always be in obedience to a vision of the Kingdom of God.[20] As we have seen, that vision will lead us to be indignant at those features of life which contradict God's promise of the Kingdom. Nothing contradicts that promise more consistently than the barriers which have been allowed to stand between classes and races.

The remarkable number of churchgoers in the United States has a lot to do with the ethnic nature of the United States and the ethnic nature of the Churches there. Bishop Paul Moore writes of parishes in New York often being captive to their members' sub-culture, which differs from that of the people who live in the neighbourhood: white instead of black, American black instead of Hispanic, West Indian instead of American black, Hispanic instead of Chinese, Puerto Rican instead of Cuban. In addition there are more subtle cultural problems: middle class instead of poor, middle age instead of avant garde youth, married instead of single. Few are able to have more than a friendly relationship with other denominations. So a difficult question faces Christian leaders; 'Should a bishop put the unity and well-being of the institutional Church ahead of the reconciliation through the achievement of justice of suffering neighbours? . . . Is our ministry to the desperate outsider or to the Church members who wish to be comforted?'[21]

The Ecumenical movement is about one inhabited earth. It calls us to work at breaking down the barriers between races and classes. We must reject the route by which one dominant group—even the Christian Church—expects to absorb others into its culture. That is not Christ's way. Nor is the way labelled 'separate but equal'. We must allow distinct cultures to be strong; that is especially important, if they are an expression of the life of a group, which has been shut out from the opportunities of the main stream of society. The Church has a calling to be a meeting place, where different groups, especially those commonly regarded as on the margins of society, can meet each other with equal respect.

CHAPTER SIX

Jews and Gentiles

Ideas have been put forward in the previous chapter about solidarity, which need testing against Christian roots. I have welcomed the fact of a multi-racial pluralist society. I have tried to look at the issues which the indefinite existence of ethnic Churches, or Churches for 'our kind of people', raise; this has acknowledged the need for those at a disadvantage to experience the sequence which moves through identity and self-confidence to acknowledged interdependence. The New Testament Church faced many of these issues head on in the controversy about Jews and Gentiles.

To try to interpret what the New Testament has to say to our present approach to race relations I shall use a 'hermeneutical circle'. This is described as a circle because its different parts should keep on relating to each other. Here are four parts of a circle of interpretation:

1. Pay attention to the world of ideas and experience of the Biblical writer and his readers. What glasses did they wear?
2. Notice the ways in which people today, including ourselves, are conditioned by our experience of life and of the particular Church tradition to which we belong. What glasses do we wear?
3. Commit ourselves to action in obedience to what we believe God is saying in our particular situation; and reflect critically on our action and the theory from which it stems. This is what Liberation Theology writers call *praxis*.
4. Let the Biblical text speak back to the questions we bring to it.

BIAS TO THE POOR

The Early Church and its divisions

First the New Testament Church knew the experience of division. It was almost torn in half by the issues of whether Gentiles should be welcomed on equal terms with Jews. Three parts of Scripture allow us to see the first generation of Christians wrestling with questions about 'the others'.

Acts Chapter 10 describes what moved Peter to open the door of the Church to Gentiles, who had previously been excluded. In a trance he saw a great sheet of sailcloth. In it were creatures of every kind, whatever walks or crawls or flies. Then there was a voice, which said to him, 'Up, Peter, kill and eat.' But Peter said, 'No, Lord, no: I have never eaten anything profane or unclean.' The voice came again, 'It is not for you to call profane what God calls clean.'

While Peter was still puzzling over the meaning of the vision messengers arrived. They came from Cornelius, who was a Roman centurion, a religious man, who had also had a vision, telling him to send and find Simon Peter, and to listen to what he had to say. At Cornelius's house there was a large gathering. Peter said to them, 'I need not tell you that a Jew is forbidden by his religion to visit or associate with a man of another race; yet God has shown me clearly that I must not call any man profane or unclean.' As he preached about Jesus, 'The Holy Spirit came upon all who were listening to the message.' Peter said, 'Is anyone prepared to withhold the water for baptism from these persons, who have received the Holy Spirit, just as we did ourselves?' Then he ordered them to be baptised. They asked him to stay with them. He found that he had to live with his theory and actions; he couldn't hurry away back to his Jewish Christian friends. [1]

Some years later in an atmosphere of heated controversy the first Council of the Church was held in Jerusalem, to discuss the matter of the Gentiles' coming into the Church. Some of the Jewish Christians said, 'They must be circumcised and told to keep the Law of Moses.' Peter appealed to the experience he had had in Cornelius's house; 'God made no difference between them and us; for He purified their hearts by faith . . . We believe it is by the grace of the Lord Jesus that we are saved, and so are they.'[2]

Luke, who was the author of the Acts of the Apostles, had been Paul's companion in his years of mission to the Gentiles; this had repeatedly stirred up controversy and brought bitter hatred upon them. He tells the story at length, because he means his readers to understand that this is a turning point in the life of the Church.

Mark had also been personally involved in the mission to the Gentiles. He includes in his Gospel a short 'Gentile section'. The second part of Scripture I have chosen is part of it; Jesus's ministry was to the lost sheep of the house of Israel. Under the never-ending demands that ministry laid upon Him, He went into Gentile territory, looking for privacy. A Syro-Phoenician woman broke in on Him with her urgent demand. She begged Him to heal her child. She would do anything to get help for her—even perhaps suffer degradation, going along with a Jew's contemptuous view of her race. Jesus's reply was no more than she had feared; 'It is not fair to take the children's bread, and throw it to the dogs.' But she would not be put off; perhaps her reply was witty. More likely it was bitter; 'Sir, even the dogs under the table eat the children's scraps.' Jesus listened to her bitter cry; 'For saying that, you may go home content; the unclean spirit has gone out of your daughter.'[3]

The main interest of Mark in the story is the attitude of Jesus to the Gentiles.[4] Stuart Blanch sees this moment as a turning point in Jesus's awareness of His own calling. 'Hitherto He had conceived of His mission as to the lost sheep of the House of Israel. Now the staggering truth is borne in upon Him that He is the Saviour of the World. In the woman's plea He hears His Father's voice.'[5]

In the Nicene Creed Christians say, 'We believe in one Holy, Catholic and Apostolic Church.' The fullest New Testament outworking of the idea of the Catholic or universal Church is in Ephesians, which is the third part of Scripture I have chosen. Paul had been given the particular task of proclaiming the good news of Christ to the Gentiles. He writes of the secret of Christ, which had not in former times been disclosed to the human race, but has now been revealed;

'Through the Gospel the Gentiles are joint heirs with the Jews, part of the same body, sharing together in the promise made in Christ Jesus.' The secret was 'hidden for long ages in God the Creator of the universe, in order that now through the Church, the wisdom of God in all its varied forms might be made known to the rulers and authorities in the realms of heaven'.[6]

Paul takes the belief that the Gospel was not a religion for one people alone but for all people, and raises it to the highest possible standing. This is the secret of Christ. Only because the Church contains people of all races and classes can the wisdom of God in all its varied forms be made known; through this Church, with its tiny membership by comparison with the present day, the many-sided wisdom of God was 'made known to the rulers and authorities in the realm of heaven'. They are pictured perhaps like Satan in the Book of Job taunting God that His followers only served Him for what they and their own kind could get out of Him.

Paul had the scars to prove his commitment on behalf of the Gentiles. He risked splitting the Church, so that the secret of Christ, that there was One Body, should be faithfully made known. The minds of Mark's Jewish readers would have been arrested by the story of Jesus helping a Gentile woman. They would have felt total sympathy with the idea that a Gentile dog had no right to grasp at what belonged to the children of the Jewish Kingdom. They would have been aware of the drastic turnaround from that attitude, when Jesus responded to the woman's cry. Like many of Jesus's words and actions it changed their perception of what kind of Kingdom God was bringing in. His Gentile readers would have very quickly seen in this story the message that the Gospel was for them too.

Luke's readers would have shuddered with fellow feeling when Peter was told to eat whatever walks, crawls or flies. It went against every food law, every scruple which their parents had so jealously guarded. Their generation was already very afraid that the distinctive identity of Judaism and its standards might be diluted or lost for ever. There were so many contacts with the wider world and the Hellenistic culture which dominated it. No wonder some of the Jewish Christians feared that they would be swamped by a flood of Gentiles, if they were allowed to come into the Church on equal terms. But Luke records Peter standing firm; no one is to be called profane or unclean. God makes no difference between Gentiles and Jews. They are rescued by His grace, His undeserved love. They matter to God simply because they are human.

Stuart Blanch at the Lambeth Conference of all the Anglican bishops in 1978 pointed up the influence of our own culture upon our understanding of issues. He commented that many parents in Britain have been worried in recent years because their sons wear their hair long and take no sporting exercise. In the first century the Jewish rabbis were afraid of the influence of Greek culture on the purity of Judaism; they were disturbed that their young men wore their hair short and were always going to the gymnasium. The assumptions they inherited from their parents and their fear that another culture would take them over decisively influenced the way in which they looked at life.

Our own experience of racial prejudice

The second part of the hermeneutical circle asks us to notice the ways in which people today, including ourselves, are conditioned by our experience of life and of the particular Church tradition to which we belong. What glasses do we wear? I write as a white Christian, part of the dominant majority in Britain. I must engage with my fellow white Christians and look at what effect our own religious, cultural and economic experience has on the way we look at issues of race and human solidarity. Part of the hermeneutic circle is to try to understand the experience of other contemporaries. These chapters have included an attempt to stand in the shoes of black and Asian people in Britain and the United States and to listen to what they say out of their experience.

Our religious experience provides something like stained-glass reading glasses when we open the Bible. When we read the story of the Gentile woman in Mark, Anglicans might recall the Prayer of Humble Access; 'We do not presume to come to this your table, merciful Lord, trusting in our own righteousness but in your manifold and great mercies. We are not worthy so much as to gather up the crumbs under your table . . .' This familiar and lovely prayer can make us see the woman kneeling alongside us in worship. We instinctively feel that her cry for help is a humble one, emphasising her own unworthiness. But if we ask, not what we understand as we read, but what Mark understood, her words seem much more likely to be the pressing cry from someone who feels shut out. The words are very likely to have been bitter. We are not used to such voices being raised in Church. A bias to the poor calls us to listen to many who may not be so helpless or so grateful as we expected. They may address us with very bitter voices.

If belonging to the Church is an important part of our experience, we shall feel strong pressures which have to do with the maintenance of the Church fellowship. In a time of inflation Christian giving has to be placed frequently in front of Church people; actions and words which challenge white people about injustice done to those who are black or brown may upset those whose financial support is important. Numbers may be smaller when the Church takes a strong line about a matter like race.

Our experience has for so long been in a Church which is divided denominationally and ethnically that we can scarcely think in terms of one Church. We take for normal what should be a scandal. The fact that we have for so long tolerated denominational differences and lived in separate Churches has a major influence on our inability to allow people of another culture and colour to share in the decision-making and shaping of 'our' Churches.

The main Churches in the United States and Britain have for some years committed themselves publicly to saying that a multi-racial society is what God intends for our countries. For example, there was strong opposition from the leadership of the Churches to the British Nationality Law. That should not lead us to assume that the majority of their members welcome a multi-racial society.

The action of Churches has been generally of a limited and sporadic nature. Race relations have been seen (if at all) as one among a number of ethical problems with which the Churches must deal rather than as a personal and theological issue. It is for this reason that the Churches could plan three year crash programmes and delegate large budgets to these and then turn their attention elsewhere. In a study of American Protestantism and race relations Jean Russell argues that it is because this has been considered as an ethical problem 'out there' in secular society that the white Churches and white Christians are so easily discouraged by their inability to solve the problem, and are so easily led into indifference or cynicism.

The Church and the world stand *together* in the face of sin and death, which manifests itself in racial hatred. The Church does not stand by the world, as though impervious to this power of death; it knows that it too has 'fallen victim to hatred, that it has allowed itself to be torn, shattered, rendered impotent and controlled by racism'.[7] Racism is *our* problem, within our own hearts and minds and within the Church.

Many of the assumptions we make about 'the others' are conditioned by our own cultural experience. Many Christians will make strong statements about all peoples' being one in Christ. Then what they think of as the British way of life seems to be threatened by the arrival of other groups and the cultural influence becomes very powerful. One black observation about Britain needs to be heard; 'Religion has never been a controlling thing in this country. It has always been subservient to the nation thing.' Many British people who live in what inner city people call the White Highlands feel that in some dark, unspecified way the coming of black and brown people is all part of the undermining of values and standards that they value. They see race relations in terms of problems, not of opportunities.

Others, including many Church people, simply say, 'It's not our problem.' They argue that the agenda of a parish Church should concern parish issues. They can't see the point of giving time to educational programmes concerning race relations. Bernard Nicholls, Church Missionary Society Secretary for Community Relations, published a letter, 'Dear Mary . . .' to a friend who had said to him, 'It's not our problem'. He reminded her of the remarkable sense of connection with far-away people that her Church felt through overseas missionary giving and prayer. Yet her letter assumed that, while concern for far-away people was a 'must', Britain as a multi-racial, multi-cultural, multi-faith scene did not need to be a matter of serious concern.[8]

The majority of black and brown people live in inner city areas; most of those who exercise influence and control in regard to these areas in political, administrative, social, educational and ecclesiastical matters do not themselves live in those areas.

Our own social and economic experience of life will also colour how we understand God's concern for those in particular need. If the cry for justice from the inner city calls for more Government spending—more taxation—many Christians who are comparatively settled and successful may feel that what is being said about the needs of the poor is a lovely ideal, but impractical in our time. If property loses value, because black or brown people have moved into a suburban street, white house owners may start to feel less clear about equal opportunities.

Organisations like the National Front do their recruiting among those who feel they themselves are deprived. Britain has become less wealthy. Unemployment is high for all groups in inner city areas. Many feel that they are injured parties. To recognise people by their colour as an alien wedge, whose coming coincided with Britain's decline, is to seize on an easy scapegoat to blame.

It has all happened before. Caroline Adams has shown the very similar propaganda which greeted the arrival of two groups of immigrants.[9] The foreign Jewish community arrived in the East End of London at the turn of the century and the Bengalis during the last twenty-five years have settled in almost exactly the same areas. The *East London Advertizer*'s headlines in 1904 included, 'The Flowing Tide, London's Foreign Flood, The Invading Army of Aliens, Swamped by Aliens, Europe's Paupers swarming to London, Russian Deserters Invade Whitechapel'. Headlines in the 1960s and 1970s have included, 'Powell Warning of Erosion of Britain by Alien Wedges, Asian Floods, Asian Invasions'. The Dean of Norwich in 1901 'urged the working men of England to rise in all the majesty of their manhood, and all the strength and purity of their glorious cause to reject the dumping of alien paupers in their midst'.

For many centuries the Jews were 'the others'. Everyone else could be expected to fit into the dominant culture of countries like Britain. Alan Ecclestone shows how significant our attitude to the Jews has been and is. 'With his fatal inability to be "like all the nations", the Jew offered a target for all injured parties.'[10]

We would fail to understand the difficulties of race relations if we did not admit that there is white pain. People fear the breakdown of law and order; mugging is frequently ascribed to black youths alone, though it is widespread, for example, in several white parts of Liverpool. Bernard Nicholls says that his wife has been attacked twice on the streets. Her assailants included both black and white youngsters. She did not seek to condone or excuse the wickedness represented in such incidents: but felt that, often for less reason than some of the disadvantaged city youngsters had, violent industrial action, violent student demos, violent police overreaction had marred our national life. She saw the danger of making scapegoats of a minority group which was marked out by colour. Friends of mine in the East End of London told me how they had always wanted to stay in their own district. Their housing is not very adequate. For years they have been on a housing list. They ask me why families, whose roots are not in this country, should go in front of them on the housing list. I wince as I hear them talk about 'these people'. It hurts particularly because I have just given them the bread and wine of the Holy Communion: the giving of Christ's body and blood broke down the dividing walls between peoples. God's love calls those who have been faithless to Him 'my people', not 'these people'.[11] Another East End comment, when we were discussing hostile statements about immigrants crowding into sub-standard housing, was quite different. It reflected strong fellow feeling. 'That's how we had to live when times were bad.' Part of the Gospel to the working classes should always be that, when they fight for their needs, they should remember other groups whose needs may be even greater than theirs.

The National Front plays on the fears of 'poor whites', those who feel themselves deprived of the opportunities that the affluent society promises. Their complaints are given much too much weight in the setting of the agenda for race relations. In Britain as in the United States politicians have argued that we must beware of inducing a white backlash, perhaps by moving too fast in removing disadvantages which are in the way of black people. A white backlash can only mean that those members of the majority group still deny the rights and humanity of minority groups. Talking about the fears of the white community (96 per cent in Britain) ignores the effect on the black and brown communities (4 per cent). They feel very hurt at the constant harping on the issue of immigration numbers. For children growing up in Britain it is a profoundly hurtful experience to hear and read public statements which make them feel that neither their parents nor themselves are wanted here. The young daughter of a black clergyman turned to her father when the racist statements of some politicians were being reported; 'Dad, why do they talk about us like that?' she asked. The pain on her face was unmistakable.

John Hick points out correctly that there has been no disagreement between the main parties in Britain for ten years about restricting any further immigration to very small numbers. 'It is therefore a thousand pities that Mrs. Margaret Thatcher's much discussed speech on immigration in January 1978 made the subject a centre of party controversy.' That election speech, which talked about the danger of being swamped by immigrants, drew a letter to *The Times* from Reginald Maudling, a former Conservative Home Secretary, 'Any British Government which has regard for justice and the rights of individuals has very little room for manoeuvre. Suppose that the new Conservative proposals reduce the flow of coloured immigrants, which is what the argument is all about, by 5000 a year. This would amount to one less immigrant for every 11,000 people already living here. That is the measure of what is involved. It hardly represents the difference between being swamped and remaining on dry land.'[12]

A comparatively small island has every right to limit the number of those who can come into it. That is proper and just. It is not proper or just to do so on the basis of colour. That demonstrates that a country does not accept that it is a multi-racial society. The 1968 Immigration Act, brought in by a Labour Government, was effectively racist; MPs of all parties were very uneasy at what they were doing. When the Bill was passed, the number of those who did not vote was extremely high. The final vote was only 145 to 31.

In 1981 a Conservative Government introduced a British Nationality Bill. Despite repeated pressure from the Churches and others it refused to include in the Bill a direct affirmation that our nation is multi-racial. They also refused to alter provisions of the Bill, which took away the fundamental principle of *jus soli*, that anyone born on British soil should be British. There was Government talk about children of tourists and students in justifying this, but much less about children born to work-permit holders, who are also affected by the limitation of *jus soli*. An amendment was passed to allow children born in Britain who live here for ten years to have a right to citizenship. That still left a child of ten and upwards, who has for whatever reasons been outside the country for more than ninety days in any of the first ten years of its life, with no entitlement to citizenship. The need to prove continuous residence and the subsequent dependence on documentary evidence, with no system of appeal to courts of law, leaves such children very vulnerable.[13] The introduction of this Bill showed a great lack of awareness of the hurt caused to black and brown minorities by its assumption that they were not wanted, and by weakening their sense of security. It has often been argued that strict immigration control is necessary for good race relations inside Britain. That claim puts all its emphasis on the need to soften the white backlash, rather than on the importance of making minority groups feel accepted and secure.

The only way forward for a people like the British is of repentance and heartfelt commitment to a multi-racial society as God's best plan for us. We need to repent, because attitudes of superiority have been with us for centuries. Whenever we have encountered others, on their territory or ours, we have expected others to fit in to our ways. Heartfelt commitment to a multi-racial society will include standing up to the white backlash whether it is inside our own minds or in other people, and giving priority time to an educational programme which will help different communities to understand and respect each other.

Action and critical reflection

The third part of the hermeneutical circle is *praxis*—action and critical reflection. It is properly part of the circle of interpretation, because, once you have acted on your belief, you do not see things as you did before. Our actions will then need to be subject to critical reflection, to discover what we have learned from our experience.

The danger in suggesting action in response to such a pervasive subject as race relations is that we try to take on everything. We then become 'promiscuous do-gooders', in the telling phrase of a retired professor to the clergy of the East Harlem Protestant Parish.[14] Different members of the body of Christ must take on different priorities.

A number of possible examples of *praxis* are described elsewhere in the book; for example, those who have influence as employers or trade unionists should consider what practical steps they could take to keep accurate statistics and to employ effective policies of affirmative action. Police officers and community leaders or clergy should look at possible ways of initiating and sustaining dialogue between police and community leaders and with black and brown youth. Those who have grown weary and discouraged after the Civil Rights years in the United States, or who have seen disappointing results from three-year programmes, should not give up trying to build these priorities into the regular life of Church and society. Attitudes are shaped everywhere where human meeting takes place; a lady in retirement told me, 'Three of us have promised each other that we shall never let a racist remark go unchallenged.'

The *praxis* for some is to offer resources to help disadvantaged communities to stand up and help themselves. How help is given, and what strings are attached to it, is a vital question, whether the aid is financial or personal, and whether it is from statutory, voluntary or Church bodies. The philosophy of offering aid is a good example of how *praxis* is part of the circle of interpretation.

In 1977 the General Synod of the Church of England passed some strong resolutions affirming that Britain is a multi-racial society. It called for an educational programme. Some of us believed that the educational programme would be given a sharper edge if the whole Church of England was challenged to raise at least £100,000 a year for self-help projects in the black and Asian community. The money that is given is channelled through the Community and Race Relations Unit of the British Council of Churches. The controversial grant of £500 to the Liverpool 8 Defence Committee certainly sharpened the debate about the need of the inner city and ways of helping.

When we were discussing how the Church of England might best offer resources to self-help groups, members of a small working party undertook to sound out the views of different groups in the black and Asian communities. I went to Manchester to meet a number of community leaders. Though there was a warm personal welcome, it was a painful evening; I was pressed to say why the Church of England was wanting to help at this stage. The voices of all those who spoke rejected the idea of help from this source. Next morning I rang one person who had been rather quiet, and asked what he thought I was meant to hear. He told me that a number of younger leaders, who had remained silent, were rather upset that another point of view was not expressed. He said that several would welcome help; the crucial point I was meant to hear was to do with control. Making grants, while keeping control of how they are spent, is felt by many community groups, not only black, to be a kind of colonialism, which keeps people as clients. It is an extremely sensitive issue for those who are trustees of public and charitable funds. They have to find ways of keeping a proper check that funds are spent honestly and of allowing community groups to run their own life, which may include actions and statements which would embarrass the funding body.

The concept of charity is a stumbling block to groups who

are developing their own self-confidence. Wilfred Wood wrote to me. 'The outstanding need in the black community is a self-image of which we can be proud. The outstanding need in the white community is to adjust to a proud black man.'

The issue of control has a great deal to do with help which white-run Churches may offer in the important matter of buildings. A great deal has been done very helpfully, leading to happy links, in the renting of Churches and Church halls to black-led Churches. They very naturally want some security; part of the eagerness to buy their own premises stems from the wish not to be dependent. An example of a way forward, which could be a model for similar or smaller schemes, is St Matthew's Church, Brixton.

For many years the parish had been deeply involved with community groups. The Parochial Church Council had been concerned about the dominant position in which they found themselves in relation to other groups. They could allow community groups and black Churches to use their premises; but the control remained with the PCC. In 1979 they eventually found their way through the legal thicket; the parish Church itself, a large and fine building in the middle of Brixton's traffic, now belongs no longer to the Church of England. It belongs to a community trust.

The vicar has to be chairman of the trustees, who meet only occasionally, to see that the trust deed is adhered to. The chairman of the Management Committee is currently the black pastor of a Pentecostal Church. That is one of twelve community or Church groups, including St Matthew's, who use the premises regularly and are represented on the Management Committee. St Matthew's people no longer have control over other bodies. Their need to worship and to use the building is safeguarded. They share its use on equal terms with other bodies. Each body also shares in the responsibility for maintaining the buildings. Because of their wide community use public funds are available, which would not come to a Church of England parish. If that shedding of security and power and that wide community use are possible with a historic Church building, comparable schemes must be possible with other Churches and Church halls.

The matter of who makes decisions reveals whether we truly want to relate to strong black people. The Church, no less than trade unions, management and political parties needs a determination to see black leadership at every level within not too many years. A Baptist minister in Handsworth, Birmingham, said in 1973 that black membership of Churches was not dependent upon particular forms of worship. 'White churches in theory may desire all people to be won for Jesus, but in practice it is only within certain ratios.' Black people wanted to participate in the running of the community. That would mean in some areas that they would hold the dominant position; white Christians would need to accept this.[15]

In Churches of all denominations, wherever black people become churchwardens or deacons, the possibility grows that other black people will feel that this church regards them as equals. When a black priest or minister is appointed to the charge of a parish, black people take notice. It is important that such appointments should not only be made in areas where there is a very large black population. They should take their place naturally among the Church's leadership. In the United States John Walker was made Bishop of Washington in 1977, the first black Diocesan Bishop in the Episcopal Church of the USA. It is noteworthy that only ten years earlier he was the first black rector to be appointed in the Episcopal Church except to a wholly black parish.

Clearly we live in a phase when some black Christians will continue to worship in black Churches. The main denominations in Britain should treat them in every way as sister Churches. Local congregations should find every possible occasion when they could meet together with black Churches for worship, for music, for celebration, for meals, for discussions or weekends away together. Pastors and ministers of the black Churches should be encouraged to play a full part in Councils of Churches. The British Council of Churches has mounted a series of conversations between Church leaders over some years. New York Theological Seminary, as well as offering full-time ministerial training, has Saturday courses for the part-time ministers of black Holiness and Independent Churches and Hispanic Pentecostal Churches, one of whose ministers is on the staff of the seminary. Ray Selby, former Principal of the Northern Ordination Course in England, visited the seminary. He saw these courses as a daring and enthusiastic attempt to deal with a real problem; they were setting out to offer those who had widely different educational experience an adequate ministerial training for widely different settings. He recognised the need for respect for different Christian understandings of the faith, at the same time hoping there might be a more rigorous and critical approach to study.[16]

The Principal of the New York Theological Seminary puts the other side of that coin. The Pentecostal clergy and black pastors have brought new insights to the life of the seminary. Most of them come from a conservative position on Biblical authority. They have been eager to understand what the arguments of Biblical criticism are all about. The important matter, as far as they are concerned, is that their members really know the Bible story. The staff of the seminary, trained to break down Scripture by scholarly tools into small segments, have learned a fresh discipline from these students, to memorise a whole story and to give weight to the whole. They found themselves taken back to the Bible by people who were trying to work out their faith amidst the realities of urban deprivation.

There has been also a meeting of minds on the issue of the Church as spiritual community versus the Church as a base for social action. This is a debate I shall return to in a later chapter. Black and Hispanic storefront ministers came to the seminary with great distrust for the phrase 'Social Gospel'. They did some reading of the history of the black community in the United States and Liberation Theology from the Third World. They discovered, for example, the importance given in Paul to 'principalities and powers'. When they consider the possibility that the board of education, the criminal justice system, the medical delivery system in New York City are principalities and powers, their Biblical understanding and their daily experience of the poor deal given to black and Hispanic people come together. 'Suddenly there is a Biblical mandate for action and responsibility. It brings a new unity between the necessity to picket and to pray.'[17]

The *praxis* of many inner city Christians does not bring

much visible success. That would not be a very appropriate
yardstick for the ministry and mission of an inner city Church.
A faithful ministry for twenty-five years may be marked by
increasing problems and even greater deterioration. Bob Nind
in Brixton said, 'Surely our role is to sit in the middle of the
storm and suffer it with everybody else.'

The Biblical texts and our questions

The fourth part of the hermeneutical circle is to let the Biblical
text speak back to the questions we bring to it.[18] This seems
to me a necessary discipline, not always followed in the
hermeneutical circle of some Liberation Theology writers.
They properly emphasise the importance of our action on
behalf of the poor and our own experience as sources of
learning. These parts of the circle need to be held side by side
with the words and experience of the New Testament writers.
The texts I have been examining are not marginal to the main
truths of the New Testament. The chapters in Mark and Acts
describe turning points in Jesus's understanding of His ministry
and in the Church's decision about the divisive question about
the Gentiles. That in Ephesians is the most carefully worked
out statement of God's purpose that the Church should be
universal.

Three questions have been surfacing during this discussion.
First 'Is it right to encourage like-minded groups to stay with
like?' There is no doubt that many members of the New
Testament Church expected to go on belonging to a company
who shared the background and culture of being Jews. It made
it more difficult for many to belong to a Church in which
Gentiles were equal members. The leaders of the New
Testament Church risked splitting it, because they believed
God had made it plain that the Church was for all people. Too
much was at stake to give in to the natural wishes of settled
Church members for an undisturbed sense of belonging.

As far as the group which had been excluded was concerned,
Paul resisted every effort to absorb them into the pattern of
Church life which was already established. Gentile Christians
had particular insights, gifts and leadership to bring to the

whole. No doubt separate congregations continued to exist for some time. But from the beginning they were reminded that they belonged to a world-wide Church. For example, Paul called on them to give generously for the poor Christians in Jerusalem.[19] This meant that they were being asked to support the very people who had wanted to exclude the Gentiles, unless they came in on the terms laid down. Their response was overwhelmingly generous, because they recognised that they were part of the same body.

The Biblical texts examined would not encourage settled groups of Christians to encourage Church fellowships only made up of 'our kind of people'. They would make at least two points plain to those who have felt excluded; first they were not called to abandon their own distinctive culture. Secondly, if it was necessary for a time for them to worship separately, they must acknowledge by deeds as well as words that they belong to the one holy catholic Church.

The second question is, 'Will we not lose distinctively Christian identity and standards, if we allow other social and racial groups to come into our congregations on equal terms?' The Jewish Christians had the deepest fears that this was going to happen. But Peter would not give in to them. No one is to be called common or unclean. We should give this same answer when a middle-class, white congregation fears that their children will be influenced harmfully if working-class or black youth come in to the life of the Church. We have much less ground for assuming that the culture and values of suburbia are better than those of inner city people, than Jewish Christians had for believing their culture to be superior. And, like Jesus Himself, we might hear God's voice speaking to us in vital ways, if we will listen to some of the bitter voices of 'the others'.

What people's opponents say about them can often be revealing in ways the opponents didn't intend. Christians have long gloried in the charge Jesus's enemies made that He was a friend of tax-gatherers and sinners.[20] Another charge was, 'Are we not right in saying that you are a Samaritan?'[21] The stories He told and the people He went to meet sometimes made them feel He was more interested in the outsider than in the faithful

people of God. He was the Man for others, and they hated him
for it. The distinctive identity of the Christian Church springs
from worshipping and believing in the God of all grace. He is
constantly reaching out to those who are in greatest need; His
followers are true to Him when that reaching out beyond our
own ranks is central to our life as the people of God.

The third question is, 'Are we right to welcome a multi-
racial society and Church?' Each of the Biblical texts examined
strongly suggests that we should welcome a multi-racial
Church. It is impossible to believe that God's purpose for the
Church is somehow at odds with His purpose for the world.
According to the text in Ephesians the secret of Christ was that
through the Gospel the Gentiles were joint heirs with the Jews,
'that through the Church the wisdom of God in all its varied
forms might be made known'. The wisdom of God can only
be known through the Church in all its varied forms, if the
Church is made up of people of all races and classes; the world
can then see how these different groups can learn to bring their
different gifts to the whole body.

The Greek word translated 'in all its varied forms' is
polupoikilos. Its literal meaning is many-coloured. Would it be
too far-fetched in our situation to say that the many-coloured
wisdom of God can only be fully seen through a Church which
is multi-racial? A Church properly called Catholic must reach
across the barriers of race—and of class. We can never be
ultimately content if Churches live a separate life in homogeneous groups, however much their numbers may grow. 'In
spite of our talk of a Catholic Church,' writes Alan Ecclestone,
'we are all very much inclined to live in pockets of our own
choosing, and these to a large extent shaped by our social
standing.'[22]

It is perhaps easier for professional people to meet other
groups in their working life or in conferences, perhaps without
committing themselves very deeply to the common life of a
parish. Many feelings of intense parish or denominational
loyalty have developed in the hard struggles for survival which
less mobile people have faced. Then rising above group fears
and prejudices is massively difficult. They are much more
difficult to overcome than many personal fears.

We should not expect to see a complete social and racial mix in every congregation. But it is not good enough for world-wide Churches to content ourselves that somewhere else across the city there is a congregation, where other ethnic and class groups feel at home. God's calling to every local Church is to reach across human barriers, as far as lies within their power. That should increasingly mean planning and working out projects together with other Christian denominations; it should also mean giving a welcome to twinning arrangements between congregations in inner city and suburb. The dangers of condescension and dependence can be avoided; each can find ways of giving and receiving.

We live in a world which desperately needs to see that it is possible for people from different interest groups to hold and argue for their views with deep conviction, and at the same time to stay committed to a common future. The Church will indeed show the many-coloured wisdom of God if our shared commitment to Christ is tough enough to hold together groups whose ideas and interests are at times in conflict. Such a holding together of different groups will mean that many Christians, black and white, must be willing to be bridge people, with all the pain which that frequently brings.

A black Anglican priest working in a multi-racial area of Birmingham was asked by his bishop, Hugh Montefiore, if he could see examples of the glory of God in the inner city. He wrote, 'I find myself accepted without constraint for the first time in my life. It feels like coming in out of heavy seas on to dry land. Being black is a positive advantage here . . . I have discovered what it means to be a representative person, someone in whom deep aspirations are focussed, around whom hope flickers . . . It is as though for me for the first time incarnation makes sense. For the first time the word has become flesh, and dwells with me as an abiding glory. God has made Himself accessible. He has made it possible for us to identify with Him.'

Hugh Montefiore wrote in a paper to a small group of bishops that the priest had written this to him one morning. But that very afternoon something dreadful had taken place. He found himself abused, slapped about the face, chanted

110

down, abused by black young people. It came about because he asked for contributions for a sponsored walk. It ended because he would not say that he believed in Haile Selassie, King of Kings and Lord of Lords, but could only confess that Jesus Christ is Lord.

The priest wanted to say that the inner city is unredeemed. He found the glory there not in the sense of fulfilment, but in his rejection by Black Consciousness, the very people for whom his heart yearned. He writes, 'Perhaps there was a kind of glory in being there today. They saw me hurt, minding.'[23]

CHAPTER SEVEN

The Future of Work

In a city like Liverpool unemployment fills the foreground of the picture. A succession of closures of firms raises the question of what industrial and commercial base there will be, if and when the national economy starts to expand again. Other questions arise too; will there be full employment again? Should we regret it, if dull and repetitive jobs are taken over by new technology? What is work?

It's worth pausing to ask why we are so worried about unemployment. In our industrial society we have expected people to be able to make a useful contribution to society through their work; and through payment for their work that contribution has been recognised by society. Unemployment seems to take away the opportunity to make a useful contribution and that recognition by society. Perhaps paid work is not the only way. Thinking of those who have least opportunities for being recognised, it will not do to say, 'We'll pay you to stay alive. But we don't really need you or your skills at all.' The burden of unemployment, which follows shifts in the market or changes in technology, does not fall equally. The heaviest burden falls on the semi-skilled and the unskilled, those who have in the past been able to hold their heads high, because they could sell their strength or their willingness to work in a gang.

In Liverpool's employment situation it almost seems like a luxury to ask questions about the quality of a job. Any job seems like a blessing. Yet, if God has given all people skills and brains to use, we cannot be happy if people at work are simply asked to be less efficient robots. So there are also questions to be asked about the type of work and the way in which it is organised.

112

Alienation over many years

The explosion of Toxteth in 1981 revealed an alarming degree of alienation; black and white young people alike felt they had no stake in this society. It was the tip of an iceberg; many more are characterised by apathy, which will not take any part in the life of the community; that is a kind of frozen violence. Suspicion of all those who work for the institutions of society, from the 'Corpy' to the Social Security, has been bred over many years. This has been generated both by the kind of work which has been traditional and the cutting away of those traditional jobs.

Bob Houlton, who teaches trade unionists and comes from a trade union background, says that you will not understand the Merseyside worker unless you acknowledge the dominant influence of the culture of the Dock Road. Once a huge proportion of Liverpool's labour force worked there. For generations dockers stood 'on the stones' (in East London 'on the bricks') in order to be visible to the foreman, in the hope that he would choose them. In the cut-throat competition of casual labour, man was against man. That culture of the Dock Road bred a deep suspicion of all who held formal, institutional positions. If your mate became a trade union official, you stopped drinking with him. You suspected that he'd sold out to the big institutions. When young hopefuls in the trade union movement went off to university, they were removed from the background of those they were to represent.

In the Royal Docks in East London a similar suspicion passed into folk memories. In a discussion in our flat in Canning Town a woman said, 'Bevin sold out to the bosses. All our fathers believed that.' She was speaking forty years after the event, which was Ernest Bevin's building up the huge 'white' Transport and General Workers Union, and being resisted by the much smaller 'blue' Stevedores' Union, which continued for many years to exist in Liverpool and in London's Royal Docks.

Hostility and suspicion of institutions is still strong in Merseyside. It has a long history. For example, Anarcho-Syndicalism was strong in Liverpool in 1910–14. Syndicalism stressed direct action to bring about change rather than legislation through Parliament. They scornfully argued that, when representatives of the working classes were elected to Parliament, they were seduced by its club atmosphere into becoming slaves of the institution.[1]

The main strands of British trade unionism did not follow such a militant line. The majority of unions in Merseyside adopted a markedly pragmatic rather than ideological attitude. But the suspicions of Merseyside remained. There is a straight line from the attitudes of Syndicalism in 1910 to the power of the unofficial strike committee of recent years. Hostility and suspicion have been fed by insecurity and fear. As commerce ebbed and flowed, workers often felt that they had no secure stake in the future. Since 1945 the shift of trade and the arrival of the new technology of containers has drastically reduced the number of jobs in the Docks.

It is true that some loss of trade is because shipowners feared strikes in Liverpool. Bernard Levin wrote that the Transport and General Workers Union has become all-powerful, and that its elite members are the dockers. It seems a surprising history of an all-powerful elite that their work-force in Liverpool has dropped from 45,000 in 1939 to less than 4,000 in 1981. The power (often of an unofficial strike committee rather than the union) was the power to say No. The diminishing market and the way work was organised gave little opportunity for dockers to have any power for positive action.

Sometimes disputes have produced self-inflicted wounds. Sometimes they have been inspired by wreckers who want to destroy the system. The managing director of a large firm which was closing on Merseyside spoke of the work force as a whole as cooperative, led by the nose by six wreckers. But we ignore dangerous realities if we do not try to enter into the feelings of fear and alienation which influence a work force to follow such a lead. Strikes have often seemed the only bargaining counter, which must be played with a feeling of inevitability. I heard a speaker at the Pier Head in Liverpool refer to a closure; 'What will you say to your son in twenty years' time, when he asks you what you were doing when they closed the firm?' This is an emotional appeal; it is also deeply

114

felt, and was foolishly ignored when dockers were blamed for opposing the drastic reduction of the labour force. In Liverpool and East London large communities were based on the dock industry. It was a father and son business. Many sons of dockers were brought up to believe that they had a right to a job in the docks. It was a great club with a great deal of pride in the physical strength that was needed, in the loyalty of a gang and in the strategic importance of the trade.

Twenty years ago in working-class London the goal many parents put before their sons was to get a job in the printing trade. They believed that would give him a skilled job for life. Highly-paid printing workers seem to have behaved altogether irresponsibly in resisting the reduction of manning levels as new technology has been introduced. Such condemnation has again ignored the deep fears about their own jobs and equally about their children's jobs.

It has not been realistic to ask dockers, printing workers or others to acquiesce tamely in the rundown of their numbers, in order to bring about an upturn in trade. Vague assurances are given about the future of work; the assumption is made that new technology and greater competitiveness will produce more jobs. But no one spells out the alternatives which will offer real work to those made redundant—or to everyone's children. There are long-term promises of wealth through new technology; these could all be destroyed in the medium term by blocking actions inspired by fear, unless these human issues are attended to.

Preoccupation with unemployment should not prevent us from asking questions about the type of work offered; if the fears about unemployment were not so weighty, the promise that new technology could take away dull and repetitive jobs would be welcomed with open arms. An account of Ford's coming to Halewood was written by Huw Beynon from the shop floor point of view.[2] Ford's began operating in Liverpool towards the end of 1962. Something over 60 per cent of the first recruits were new to factory work. Liverpool began as a commercial rather than industrial city. Many who came from other experiences of work did not stay long. For example at the Paint Trim and Assembly Plant 1,140 manual employees left in 1966 out of a total labour force of 3,200. In 1967 the number leaving went down to 800, but in 1968 it was 1,160 and in 1969 it was 1,800.

I visited Ford's together with the Roman Catholic Archbishop in 1978. This past was not denied. There was now a much smaller turnover of staff; this is likely to be due at least in part to very high unemployment and to the fact that Ford's pay higher wages than most of their competitors in Merseyside. At Ford's, Dagenham, where they are competing with other industries which pay better, there was then a shortage of labour rather than a waiting list. Management had made great efforts to communicate better with the whole work force—though the number of Merseyside people in senior positions remained very small. In parts of the factory there seemed to be developing something of the pride which is to be seen in some heavy industries at doing a primary, strategic job which needs strength and skill. Yet this assembly line or track often produces glazed eyes. You are advised to buy a Wednesday car rather than a Friday one. The track never stops. They tell the story of the country lad, who couldn't believe he had to work on every car: 'Oh no. I've done my car. That one down there. A green one it was.' Or the man who went from the car production line to work in a sweet factory; he had to divide up the reds from the yellows. He left because he couldn't bear the decision-making.

On the assembly line you become an operative. Many are like the man who said, 'When I'm here my mind is a blank.' A group of unemployed youngsters in Liverpool were discussing jobs in 1975[3]; great emphasis was placed on job satisfaction—hours, conditions, interest, prospects. Some had had jobs which they hated; others resented the type of work done by their mates or families. 'It's worth travelling to Ford's for the money, isn't it? But you get like a robot.' 'My dad was at Ford's, and all he did was stick two bits of metal together all day long.' 'When my dad worked there, he just put one bolt in a gear box all day.'

When we visited Ford's, Halewood, the firm hoped they had moved into better times in industrial relations. Since then there have been a number of disputes. A shop steward in

Dagenham told me that he believed disputes were the result of a volcano erupting. Men hated the job, but couldn't leave because they couldn't find such good pay elsewhere. They were trapped into staying because of hire purchase and mortgage commitments, even though they felt alienated from their jobs. When an annoying incident happened, the volcano erupted.

A share in decision-making

There has been a long and frustrating pursuit of the dream that every worker should have a stake in how decisions are made. We should not give up the chase. It is disappointing that the Bullock proposals about industrial democracy are dismissed by many on both sides of industry. Many trade unionists have said they would rather not participate in the making of decisions; they would rather stay on the other side of the table and reserve their bargaining position. That sounds like settling for having no stake in positive decisions about a firm's future. From the management side it has been said that the most you can do is to civilise the fighting.

There is no magic wand that can be waved to make all workers feel they can share in the future of their enterprise. Putting workers on the board would not provide a short cut. Mutual trust is built by long, patient years of treating a work force and its representatives as intelligent and responsible partners and by trade union leaders responding in that way. Conflict and cooperation can go together in a vigorous partnership. Such a partnership exists in many firms. In many more there is a long way to go.

The offer of more participation must be matched by action; otherwise it can lead to an even greater sense of being let down. When they consult, it is important for leaders in management (or local authorities or Church leaders) to make it clear what is on offer. Some distinctions need to be made between offering information, consultation, participation and shared decision-making. One way of distinguishing between these would be like this; information makes it clear that management will make the decisions, but wants the work force to

117

know what they are doing and why they are doing it. Consultation would mean management putting plans in front of representatives of the work force; they would give them time and opportunity to make their suggestions, listen to them, but reserve management's right to make the decisions. Participation would mean inviting representatives of the work force to share in the whole process of making a decision. Shared decision-making would mean that clearly defined matters were the responsibility of the work force or its representatives. In each case it is important to make it absolutely clear what is, or is not, being offered.

Many believe that the dream of every worker feeling that he has a stake in the business can only be achieved by workers or the State owning the means of production. Marx never explained how this control, on which he set so much store, was to be organised. Some of the evils which he attributed to capitalism have persisted in Socialist countries. Enterprises have problems associated with scale, whether they are owned by a family, a multi-national corporation, a public company or by the State.

When Marx and those who have followed him have spoken of workers controlling production, they have thought of the economy as a whole or certainly 'the commanding heights of the economy'. In a mixed economy there is need to control the economy. This need is not diminished by workers taking control of particular enterprises. Either the economy is effectively controlled, in which case the managers, whether they are capitalists or workers, receive directives from the controllers of the economy; or the economy is not effectively controlled and the sense that the workers have of being at the mercy of events beyond their control is as great as ever. John Plamenatz believed that most workers in the industrial countries, whether capitalist or not, are more concerned that the economy and the organisations they work in 'should be efficiently run, so that they can benefit from this efficiency, than that they should take part in running them'. Yet experience has taught them that they must be strongly organised industrially and politically, to make sure they receive a larger share of the wealth created by greater efficiency.[4]

The scale of changes which industry and commerce face because of new technology brings with it many threats to trust. Len Murray, Secretary of the Trade Union Congress, says that it is precisely because trade unionists are involved in and affected by the results of change that there are 'pressures for us to be directly involved in the process of change at every level'.[5]

After the Winter of Discontent in 1978–9 I invited a group of Christian trade unionists of all denominations to come to our home. We discussed wage restraint, work sharing, the likelihood that there would never be full employment again in the old terms. Repeatedly the issue of control, or having a real share in decisions which affected their future, came up. This is highlighted when policies are put forward connected with new technology and fewer workers.

It is frequently said that trade unions have too much power. Norman Tebbit's Bill in 1982 set out to establish checks on them. As has been seen, their power has often been only the power to say No. If unions are not given a stake in planning positive steps forward, they are very likely to use the negative power they have. Working out ways of consultation or participation may seem to be going a long way round, but the cooperation they produce does mean that in the longer run they provide a more efficient way.

Many Christians are among those who resent the collective action of trade unions. Any cause which is represented as defending the rights of the individual against collective power can generally be expected to have Christian support. But standing up for the rights of an individual may deny the rights of a group of people who are less articulate, less influential, unless they act as a group.

The insistence in a closed shop agreement that every worker must belong to a particular union has outraged many of those brought up with an individualistic approach to life. For those who have grown up with a strong sense of solidarity in the community and at work, it seems obvious that you should belong; they would feel it natural that a worker should express solidarity with fellow workers and that it would be unfair to allow 'free riders' to have the benefits of union negotiations without belonging.

I make two comments; a Christian understanding of the way God has made the world should lead a worker to feel that he belongs to the company of his fellow workers. Many benefits he experiences would never have come about without the trade union movement. If he believes that some union actions are wrong, he should try to work from within to bring about change. A Christian worker who is critical of his union should be willing to expend a great deal of energy in trying to influence its policies. That may be very costly in time and on occasions might lead to standing up against hostility and threats. For there are situations where a trade union has blinded itself to anything except its own self-interest.

The second comment is that trade unions should feel confident enough about their own position to respect the conscience of an individual who feels that he ought not to join. It should be possible for such an individual—and not only on religious grounds—if he can show his conscientious objection, to opt out, and to pay his union dues to a charity.

Truth about the future of work

Underlying the anxieties, which cause many to resist change, lies a major question about the future of work. Christian thinking was very influential in giving great importance to the place of paid employment in people's lives; we still talk about the Protestant work ethic. At a time when there is a major question about the possibility of full employment, it is right that Christians should again join in the debate.

A Christian critique should start by insisting that we look hard at the truth as we best understand it. Slogans and dogmas must be challenged, if they prevent us from examining the truth. One slogan is 'We must oppose the deindustrialisation of Britain'. The assumption has often been made that fresh investment will bring more jobs. This has been challenged from within the Labour movement by Ivor Clemitson and George Rodgers in their book *A Life to Live–Beyond Full Employment*; 'If we look at what has happened in particular industries, the assumption that investment equals jobs tends to come apart in our hands . . . More "horsepower" has invariably meant fewer workers using the horsepower in the industries concerned.'[6]

Another slogan claims 'New technology always creates new jobs.' For a country's economy to be competitive, new technology is essential. But that doesn't mean that it must always be introduced without question. As some Third World countries have discovered, there will be occasions when intermediate technology is more appropriate to a particular situation.

Fears that jobs are disappearing are not going to be laid to rest by repeating over and over again, 'New technology always creates new jobs.' For example, Archbishop Derek Worlock gave evidence to the Parliamentary Select Committee on Employment, when it visited Liverpool. He had chaired a working party which had examined with care the likely effect of the introduction of micro-electronic techniques into the main manufacturing and service industries of Merseyside. He mentioned the figures which those industries had predicted for themselves; between 1980 and 1985–7 they expected a decrease in employment as a result of introduction of micro-processors of 7,500 jobs in manufacturing industry (out of approximately 150,000) and 19,800 jobs in service industry (out of approximately 375,000).[7] These figures have never been challenged by local industry, but one member of the Select Committee immediately dismissed any significance of the figures by saying, 'New technology always produces new jobs'.

We cannot be sure about the future. In the past there has been plenty of evidence to suggest that the new technology creates unpredictable new jobs even as it develops other ones. But today it is increasingly recognised that a delicate balance now exists between job creation and job removal. David Bleakley draws attention to the danger that the qualitative change brought about by the latest computer revolution based on micro-electronics will tip the scale towards a drastic and irreversible job loss.[8] Many large firms do not intend to employ more people, whatever the growth rate of the country. They regard the differences between a successful and unsuccessful business strategy in the modern world to be the rate at which numbers of the work force slim down.[9] Professor Tom Stonier pointed out that at the beginning of the eighteenth century 92 per cent of the labour force worked as farmers to feed Britain; today it needs less than 3 per cent; he suggests that it is probable that by early in the next century it will require no more than 10 per cent of the labour force to provide us with our material needs; 'that is all the food we eat, all the clothes we wear, all the textiles and furnishings in our houses, the houses themselves, the appliances, the automobiles'.[10]

We must face the truth that there is not going to be full employment again in the old patterns. Those with dogmatic beliefs in systems refuse to admit this. Some of them believe that a fully Socialist system would produce jobs for all; others believe that the free market is self-correcting and will in due course produce full employment again. Both assume that there are no limits to growth. Both seem to avoid the realities an area like Merseyside has known for years, and which much of the industrial world now faces. If we would only acknowledge that the old patterns of full employment will not return, the vitally important debate could begin about how all people can find a useful and valued place in society.

There is an urgent need for countries like Britain to find an ethic for today, not just for work on its own, but for work in the context of life as a whole. There are those who fear that this would cut a vital nerve and destroy the sense that people *ought* to work hard. But we should delight in the fact that new technology can make it unnecessary for human beings to do many dirty and dangerous jobs. Bishop E. R. Wickham has repeatedly encouraged Christians to glory in the possibilities of new technology. Taking the long term view, it holds out the promise of new jobs and of increased wealth. At the same time it allows us to realise greater potentials of human creativity and an increase in leisure.

An ethic for work in the context of life as a whole should have something to say to those who, unlike previous generations, face thirty or forty years of retirement. An ethic for today must help them to see that they can make a positive contribution during those years. Work is also about what housewives do, even though people say they are not 'working wives'. Work is about joining in the development of God's creation; it is about sustaining the good fabric of society. Real work calls for some real input; it is disciplined and purposeful. Bishop Wickham says, 'It is about the service we are called to render to one another. It is about the making of wealth—what is good for man—which properly understood and properly used, is honourable and vitally necessary.'[11]

Our concept of work is narrowed needlessly if we see it simply as what an erratic market requires people for. In Britain in 1976 Prime Minister James Callaghan called for a great debate on education. There was much emphasis on the feeling that schools and colleges were out of touch with 'the fundamental need of Britain to survive economically in a highly competitive world through the efficiency of its industry and commerce'.[12] Science and technology must claim an important part of education; but they must take their place alongside the need to learn about other ways in which we render service to one another.

Where the burden will fall

The emphasis on the need for a life ethic in place of the work ethic can lead to some bland and unrealistic talk about the value of more leisure. Let us assume that the present debate leads us to pay a reasonable social wage to all, whether they can find employment or not; such a social wage would need in all justice to be significantly more than the bread line of Supplementary Benefit. We may need to do this, to make it possible for those who do not have a job, or who may lose their job, to face future changes without fear. But many of those are the less skilled, and those who have not found a valued place in other areas of life. It might be one thing to encourage those who have experienced higher education to feel fulfilled by a life of leisure, but that is not where the burden will fall. Those who feel that their contribution in life is valued very little can less easily believe they are useful, unless this is expressed by a wage.

When jobs are scarce, those who are more skilled go down market and the less skilled are squeezed out. Between 1961 and 1971 there was a net improvement in jobs in Kirkby. But during the same period the takeup of jobs among those who live in Kirkby went down.[13] Firms found more suitable workers from elsewhere. Attempts to bring employment to areas of very high unemployment, inner city or outer area estates, will always run the risk that people from elsewhere will take the new jobs.

For centuries society has shown people that they are valued by paying them a wage; we must shape jobs in our community which are seen to be needed and valued. A job is the way young people register their entry to the fully adult, fully independent world. A job is the way many fit and alert old people keep themselves so. A job is often the one thing that single parents, the disabled, ex-prisoners, the recently re-covered sick need to lead an acceptable, self-respecting life.[14] There is a connection between being paid for what we do and a sense of self-worth. We need to strengthen the sense that all have the ability to render a service to one another.

The older industrialised countries are at present caught in a vicious circle. There are three parts to the circle; first, industry cannot be profitable if it is overmanned; secondly, de-manning will not be accepted by a work force, unless there are real alternatives; thirdly, we cannot afford real alternatives, unless industry is more profitable. The circle could be reversed and become a creative one. The provision of alternatives has been seen as something which can only be considered after the other two stages have been overcome. But it might prove to be the key which unlocks the door. If such alternative work was available, it could take away the fears of a work force which will so often resist change.

Once the point is acknowledged that market forces are not going to require all the available work force, it should not be difficult to recognise real work that needs to be done. Nor should it be seen as impossible to increase public spending. Large sums are already spent on providing the necessary cushion against the harshest effects of unemployment. Finding the cost to allow those not needed in the market to make their contribution should not be resented by those lucky enough to have better-paid jobs. It would be an investment worth every penny, if it removed fears and allowed changes to be faced.

A brief summary of some of the possible directions would include: environmental improvement, particularly in old dock and industrial sites or beside railways; draining and fencing allotments or fencing in defensible space and offering a choice of hard or soft surfaces, so that flat-dwellers and others in cities can have their own gardens; this would strengthen the development of what James Robertson describes as a gift and barter economy.[15] Community theatre projects, craft centres, working museums would offer much to leisure time, which can either hang as a dead weight, or be seen as a great opportunity. Then there are what might be called policing jobs; janitors for blocks of flats; nothing would improve the quality of life more for those who live in blocks of flats than to have their fears about intruders removed; patrols to protect public property, such as Sefton District in Merseyside runs in cooperation with the Manpower Services Commission; this has saved substantial sums of money in protecting schools; Sweat Equity housing projects, like U-Hab in New York, in which unemployed people have been able to improve derelict property, and own an apartment within it at the end of the project.

If community need rather than available cash was the decisive factor, there would be many jobs in schools, in adult education, in community groups, in home nursing and help, or as what have been described as barefoot social workers. From one point of view a natural growth was happening in education and social work, before it was cut back by public spending cuts.

Programmes like the Youth Opportunities Programme and the Youth Training Scheme which will succeed it have serious limitations because they are only allowed to offer a youngster a place for twelve months. That limitation damages what these programmes can offer in areas of very high unemployment. Young people, who have entered whole-heartedly into projects, lose that enthusiasm when the prospect of going back on the unemployed register looms up. They start to keep time badly, discipline suffers and they may steal from a project to which they have previously been happily committed.

One of the factors which damages the effect of the special

programmes is that young people are looking over their shoulders at friends who have obtained a real job. It might be a positive way forward to take all young people out of the employment market until they are nineteen. From sixteen onwards they would either be at school, in further education, in apprenticeships or in the Youth Training Scheme.

The special programmes should not be damned with faint praise: I became Chairman of the Area Board responsible for the special programmes in Merseyside and Cheshire in 1978. At first I only dared claim that it was better than doing nothing. Having seen a good number of projects on employers' premises and those which are sponsored by local authorities and voluntary organisations, sometimes in partnership with local firms, I claim rather more. For many young people such a project offers a better introduction to working disciplines than they would have received in many businesses. Everything depends on the quality of the supervisors; a grandfatherly figure, who may have been made redundant at fifty-five, may introduce young people to his enthusiasm for his trade. In addition he may give a more sympathetic understanding than some younger foremen would, and they may be given a whole new attitude to the community in which they live, for example, in the community service elements of a project. Some employers have used the Short Induction courses of the Manpower Services Commission to give youngsters from very disadvantaged areas the opportunity to prove themselves. Their experience has been that a number who would not have been chosen by their normal selection processes, have proved their willingness and ability. They have then taken them on permanently. In such cases the temporary programmes have altered the pecking order, and have given those at a particular disadvantage the opportunity to win their own way.

If we dare to look at the Third World, we see unemployment and underemployment which has been estimated at 30 per cent as an average overall. Charles Elliott made the point to the Lambeth Conference of Bishops in 1978 that the poverty of nations is the 'result of a series of relationships which enrich the rich and impoverish the poor'. The hope that, if the rich continued to grow, there would be a trickle down of wealth and benefit to the poor had not happened either internationally or nationally. Indeed the Green Revolution, giving more resources to the more efficient farmers, had sharpened inequalities and increased the actual numbers of those in acute poverty.[16]

Britain is most unlikely ever willingly to choose drastic alterations in trading relations to her disadvantage. We would be too determined to defend our high cash standard of living. What is much more likely is that Third World countries will increasingly develop their own industries and then protect their share of the market. An Old Testament prophet would say that God was taking away the high standard of living from Britain. The crisis for a country like Britain would not then be that we had a lower standard of living; it would be how we reacted to that lower standard. Those who lost cash, status or jobs could react with anger and fear. They could easily pick on scapegoats in those who had come most recently into the country. At that point those who are committed to the reconciliation of the whole world would have a vital role to play. All the work of World Development Education would not have been wasted.

There would be another implication; if our trading position became weaker, the burden would not fall on those who are strongest, but on those groups and areas which are already most vulnerable. Inequalities within a nation can be smoothed over if everyone can be promised more every year. If we once have to say that there is no more, or that we must all take less, those inequalities become much more inflammable. A commitment to justice and reconciliation in the Third World carries with it a commitment to justice and reconciliation of all parts of our own society, especially those which are most vulnerable.

Reflecting a bias in favour of those at a disadvantage is hard enough when the disadvantage can be spotted geographically. It is harder still when there is a depressed group within a depressed group.[17] In Northern Ireland Roman Catholics resent the fact that their community experiences two and a half times the rate of unemployment that the Protestant community faces. In English cities that is the experience of the black community with the same resulting resentment.

Unemployment has certainly been a major factor in causing the alienation, which has on occasions exploded into violence. If we care about removing the alienation, we must see to it that such depressed groups increasingly have opportunities to develop their abilities and to know they have a stake in our society.

CHAPTER EIGHT

A Crisis for Capitalism

Development, achieved by the skills of management and technology, is good news for the poor in the Third World; this is the claim of Liberal Capitalism. The existence of depressed areas, once needed by the market but now in the wrong place for market forces, presents a crisis for capitalism.

When there are changes brought about by technology or when unemployment hits a country, the burdens do not fall equally. They fall on the areas and on the groups which are already most vulnerable economically. A Christian critique of capitalism must examine the claims made on its behalf in the light of the effect of capitalist policies on the poor.

Liberal Capitalism insists that the way to give the poor a better deal, both in our own country and in the Third World, is by way of development. Unless the size of the cake is increased, it is argued, there cannot be the resources for programmes for the poor. The Christian case for Liberal Capitalism includes three major points; first, man is called to share with God the Creator in the development of the world. This must include wealth creation for the good of all. Secondly, efficiency is claimed. Liberal Capitalism harnesses enlightened self-interest. It is therefore realistic because it uses the natural drives of human beings and the natural laws of the market. Thirdly it is argued that it best protects freedom against totalitarian solutions.

Creation of wealth is good

Wealth creation is good. The hesitations which many have about such a statement are related to the unprincipled and uneven way in which wealth is distributed. That does not alter

God's calling to many to throw themselves wholeheartedly into the business of wealth creation. Capitalism claims that for the good of the whole it is right to appeal to enlightened self-interest in working for personal wealth. It is natural to want to provide adequately for the happiness and well-being of one's own family. To this is often added the wish to support good causes—philanthropic, aesthetic, moral or religious. Finally one of the strongest economic incentives claimed for the amassing of fortunes in a capitalist society is sheer exhilaration in the production of wealth—the wish to expand an enterprise to the limits of its potential.[1] It is acknowledged that each of these motives is capable of corruption; but law and the checks and balances of market forces and moral teaching will restrain these sufficiently for a good society. Zest for work combined with generosity in giving is a feature of parts of American life; Daniel Jenkins praises it by comparison with the grumbling shabby gentility of so much modern British life.[2]

The Protestant work ethic has come in for some criticism in recent years. Societies which have come under its influence may have narrowed the idea of work too much to what we currently think of as earning your living. But the Protestant work ethic contains truths which ought not to be shed. Central to it is the belief in 'the calling'. In the Middle Ages a calling from God was generally seen in terms of some sort of religious vocation. The Puritans in particular saw that there are callings to serve God equally by using their abilities in the secular world. Out of 'the calling' came drive and energy to develop the world in every possible way. Christians need to re-affirm the goodness and importance of productive work. It has been observed that today the children of industrialists and businessmen often do social studies at college, and go into one of the caring professions. At first sight Christians would be expected to be delighted at this, because they are caring about people. A second thought makes us realise what we have then said about industry and commerce; that is where so many people are damaged, because there is no fulfilment.

Many young people who might have been expected to go into industry or commerce have turned away. A major reason has been that they have seen it as a rat race, where ideals have no place and where profit is put before people. The question about how profits are distributed has much to do with it: but God does call His people to create wealth. Obeying that calling need not involve us in an inhuman rat race. The Church needs to be more visibly present in the world of commerce and industry, for the belief that God calls people to be involved in wealth creation is doubted on all sides.

Businessmen say to me, 'Bishop, you won't agree with this . . .' and proceed to describe their everyday business practice. They assume that the ideals a bishop might believe in would not work in their secular world. So they do not even attempt to apply them. They tell me they wish it were possible to practise the faith and the ideals they half believe in; but the pressures of reality, of market forces and industrial relations, seem to make it impossible.

In the Wisdom literature of the Old Testament the Preacher of Ecclesiastes breathes a similar pessimism. He says that life is meaningless; all is vanity. God is somehow in control, unchanging. But He and His doings are altogether beyond any understanding. There is nothing we can do about it. He finds his way through to a rather fatalistic philosophy by an appeal to patience; there is a time for loving, for laughter, for dancing, for peace, as well as a time for work and for mourning.[3]

The Preacher in Ecclesiastes has lost the vigorous urge to master life, which was a main strand in the older Wisdom book of Proverbs.[4] Proverbs breathes confidence about the man who trusts in God and in the good orders and institutions on which people can rely. He can expect to overcome life's difficulties, to shape it. Life is not kept in compartments. Wisdom calls to man, speaking about prudence and discernment in personal life.[5] Her call is also about public life:

> Wisdom calls aloud in the streets,
> She raises her voice in the public squares . . .
> On the hilltop, on the road,
> At the crossways, she takes her stand;
> Beside the gates of the city . . .[6]

Wisdom does not speak in the sanctuary, but in the most profane public place;[7] she will tell us how to master life. There

131

is almost a bourgeois feel to the Book of Proverbs. Prosperity and possession of goods are connected with being godly and good. That optimism has to be heard beside the pessimism of Ecclesiastes and the deep questioning of the third of the Wisdom books, Job. This is the story of the godly man who lost all his possessions, his family and his health, yet clung on to faith and integrity. Christians are called to reflect the character of the God whom we worship. Jesus showed us that He enters into the suffering and frustrations of the world, where Job asks his questions. Jesus lived out God's determination not to abandon His world.

God remains the Creator, the Sustainer and the Reconciler. Taking up the idea of the call for human beings to be creative, Christians have sometimes led people up a bypath, by encouraging them to believe that all work should be creative. However, God is not only the Creator; He is the sustainer of the universe. It is comparatively easy to see that some callings are fulfilling because they are creative; being a mother, a craftsman, an artist, an entrepreneur. Callings which reflect the character of God as sustainer should also be affirmed; being a supportive friend or partner in a marriage, a reliable accounts clerk, a maintenance engineer, in local authority work dealing with housing repairs or transfers; it is a necessary part of making the Creator's world the reliable place it should be that these services are faithfully and efficiently sustained.

In many firms it seems that the pursuit of self-interest by the individual and by the particular firm is all-dominant. The reassertion of the goodness of wealth creation brings with it the call to a re-entry of morality. Adam Smith's economic analysis was closely related to his social analysis; he believed men could safely be trusted to pursue their own self-interest without undue harm to the community, not only because of the restrictions imposed by the law, but also because they were subject to built-in restraint derived from morals, religion, custom and education.[8]

It is not possible today to assume such built-in restraints. Some firms and some economists resent any attempt at a moral re-entry. Our main institutions can carry on without our commitment. All they require is our acquiescence. A deep commitment to the goodness of productive work will involve at times a tough criticism of what the work process itself is doing to the people involved in it. The toughest and best criticism of an institution comes from those who care deeply for it.[9]

We are bound to use secular language in talking about daily work, because we need to engage with all who are involved in the world of work. But at times it is necessary to talk in religious terms, if we are to reach down to the deepest springs which motivate people. In a conversation sponsored by the Rockefeller Foundation it was noted that all would agree that the United States was experiencing a crisis in values. The point was made that a hundred years ago it would not have been called that: it would have been called a spiritual crisis. 'A crisis in values was something that happened *out there*. It was something which could be coped with through rational manipulation of institutions, of beliefs, of ideas. A spiritual crisis was something that happens deep inside a person and that had to be coped with in some inward way.'[10]

A Christian critique of the appeal to enlightened self-interest will say that the pursuit of economic self-interest does not need to be checked either by law and institutions or by inward and spiritual means: both are needed. Corporate policies and attitudes affect individual motivation. E. F. Schumacher observed that industrial society had produced among us 'a folklore of incentives which magnifies individual egotism in direct opposition to the Gospel'.[11] If we are to find our way through this sensitive time of widespread change in employment patterns, individualistic incentives must give way to much stronger concern for the community as a whole.

The assumption must be challenged that the one incentive which leads people to work hard is making more personal wealth for self and family. The heart and soul can find fulfilment in doing worthwhile work, in making a modest personal income and in contributing to the wealth of the whole community through taxation. Christians should take a lead in a public campaign to change the assumption that everyone pays their taxes grudgingly and unwillingly. Taxation is a proper way by which wealth is distributed more fairly and by which the poor and the whole of society are given better opportunities. A scheme of international taxation is needed, if the enormous gap between rich and poor nations is to be lessened.

The assumption that the larger the cake, the more the poor will receive, ignores the relative nature of wealth and poverty. Advertising suggests that the opportunities which are being enjoyed at the privileged end of the city are within the grasp of all citizens, whereas they are not. The assumption also ignores what Fred Hirsch calls positional goods. Superior housing, elite education with other children from the professional classes, a country home within easy reach of the city, a private garden, an apartment in Manhattan or central London—all these positional goods have an absolute scarcity. Because of their scarcity their cost becomes higher and higher, and must continue to do so.[12]

It is claimed that although the poor cannot have equal opportunities now, they will receive more soon, just because the successful have been allowed to press ahead. One illustration is that of scouts going in front of the main body. It is because scouts have found the goal that the road can be built for the less lucky or less energetic. This is used to argue that even the poorest today owe their relative material well-being to the results of past inequality.[13] Another way of illustrating the growth process is to picture society as a marching column. Wealthiest in the front, poorest at the back, the whole column makes progress. The last rank keeps its distance from the first, and the distance between them does not lessen. But as the column advances, the last rank does eventually reach and pass the point which the first rank had passed some time before.[14]

This illustration ignores the relative nature of poverty. It is just because some have opportunities wholly denied to large groups who live in the same small country that it hurts so much. And in absolute terms the picture of the road-building and the marching column are evidently untrue in the experience of inner city people in Liverpool and black people in Britain. They never reach the point which the affluent classes reached a century ago. There are social limits to growth. The United States is wealthy as very few countries in the world could ever be wealthy. Yet its cities contain massive deprivation. In New

York I visited Holy Trinity Church, Wall Street one day and St Ann's, Morrisania, South Bronx the next. The parishes are in the same city. Their members have massively unequal opportunities in housing, jobs, schooling, health, safety, transport and leisure facilities.

In the statement issued at the end of a consultation on urban theology in New York in 1979, Episcopalians declared that the American search for a higher standard of living was the most pervasive of all seductions. The pursuit of happiness, so defined, thrived on unquestioned assumptions about style of life, habits of consumption and control of the chance to participate in the economy. 'It directly affects our faithfulness to the Biblical direction to align ourselves as Church with the poor.'[15]

Efficiency matters to the poor

The second argument for Liberal Capitalism claims that it is realistic and therefore the most efficient way. It is argued that capitalism has led to the wealth of nations; it draws the greatest skill and enterprise out of the gifted. It reflects man's fallen nature—whether we like it or not, human beings are acquisitive—and provides the necessary checks and balances to protect the weaker.[16] As little government interference as possible allows the free market to work most efficiently. Capitalism relies largely for its defence on one of the oldest maxims of statecraft—that the way to social peace and prosperity is by harnessing the natural instincts and affections of men to useful objects.[17]

No doubt capitalism is efficient for the strong, though even that can be questioned. For, if the gap between governors and governed or between management and the work force widens, efficiency suffers. Where people have a stake in society or in a business, they are more likely to work hard for the good order of society or of the business.

A Christian critique asks if capitalism is efficient for the poor. J. K. Galbraith vividly described the imbalance between private affluence and public squalor in *The Affluent Society* in 1958.[18] Steps were taken in the following years to correct that imbalance by greater public spending. But the gap remains enormous between affluent, consumer, free-to-choose Britain and the other Britain described in this book. The first budget of the Conservative Government in 1979 responded to election promises to reduce taxation and increase incentives. The budget cut taxation by £4.5 billion; the richest 7 per cent of the community obtained 34 per cent of the tax cuts, In the following budget in 1980 smaller cuts were made; the richest 2 per cent still obtained 14 per cent of the net tax reductions. One of the results of these tax reductions was to reduce the living standards of the poorest.[19]

The emphasis on efficiency in the free market means that the inefficient goes out of business. As has been seen above, it is not only the inefficient that go to the wall; so do efficient industries which happen to be operating in areas from which the market has shifted away. Efficiency in those firms which happen to have developed at the right time and in the right place may be at the price of great waste of human ability in areas which no longer suit the market.

Efficiency matters to the poor. It is indeed one of the moral crises which Socialism must face. Poor people need a reliable service from the Direct Works Department of a local authority, and do not always receive it. If tenants on many corporation housing estates were asked to rank in order what they believed their needs to be, quick and reliable housing repairs would be at the top of many lists. It is not unusual on some estates to have to wait a year for important repairs. It is a challenge to Socialism to produce the same energy, imagination, profitability and efficiency in a public enterprise as an entrepreneur brings to his own business. The challenge should be put and successfully met; if workers feel that they can control the main directions of their work, that should lead to more efficiency, not to go-slow protection of jobs.

Efficiency in services such as housing repairs matters very much to the poor. Competition can offer them more efficiency in many fields. But that is not always the case; sometimes fair competition for the stronger denies the weaker any choice at all. Both the champions and the critics of competition have been too undiscriminating. They have too often failed to make clear just what forms of competition they object to or favour, or what bad or good effects they expect from them.[20] This leads us towards a mixed economy, examining on its merits the need of government intervention in any particular case.

Freedom of the strong

The third major argument for Liberal Capitalism is that it best protects freedom against totalitarianism. It is argued that there are close connections between economic freedom and political freedom. Decentralisation of economic power means decentralisation of political power. It is a popular argument to suggest that decentralisation is always for the good. I do not believe that is true. It is generally those who feel they have strong resources and bargaining positions, who deploy this argument. Centralised power must be prevented from being absolute. But it is properly used when it protects the interests of the weaker.

The moral test for Liberal Capitalism at this point is whether the freedom given to the strong is helpful to the community as a whole; or whether in many cases it leads to lack of freedom for the weak. In over-simplified form the central doctrine of the free market is that there is an automatic harmony of interests; this claims that the result of economic competition, conducted within the framework of fair and settled law, will be that everyone will end up in the job that he is best fitted to do, and that the economic needs of the community will be precisely identified and swiftly and efficiently satisfied. It is asserted that the free market is not arbitrary. It has its own clear criterion for the distribution of wealth. The price of everything, including labour, should be determined by the market, that is to say, by the relationship between supply and demand.[21]

It is precisely the arbitrary nature of the market which means that it must not be allowed to be our sole master. At present the market does not need the labour of 30 per cent of the labour force in many areas of Merseyside and many other cities in developed countries. It does not need the labour of possibly 30 per cent of the whole labour force of Third World countries. New technology may lead to similar figures for the whole of the older industrial countries. There is no freedom for the unemployed to end up in the jobs they are best fitted to do.

Clinging to such beliefs about the automatic harmony of interests is preventing many who are in positions of power from facing what seems to be the truth, that there will never again be full employment in the old terms. If that statement is felt to be dogmatic, it seems certain at least that many areas will face such figures of unemployment for a generation, unless real alternative work is developed. That would be long enough to leave the fabric of society in ruins.

Capitalism holds that the freedom of the strong to pursue their personal interest increases the resources available to all. Those who argue for freedom from interference in the market change their attitude when it comes to free collective bargaining. When powerful unions push wage bargaining to the limit the market will bear for their own members' interests, they may well be reducing the number of jobs available to school leavers.

During the 1978–9 Winter of Discontent Arthur Scargill, then the Yorkshire miners' leader, said that the Government should keep out of wage negotiations between the National Coal Board and the National Union of Mineworkers. He argued that it was right to push the wage demand to the highest figure which the coal industry could bear. But the price of coal affects many other industries and the standard of living of many people, who do not have the industrial muscle to push for high wages. Free collective bargaining reflects the language of capitalism about the free market. Trade unions say, 'In a free-for-all we are part of the all.' But if the employer and the union alike insist on selling their goods or their labour without interference for the highest figure the market will bear, the weak go to the wall. The weak will include those whose location or trade the market does not currently need; they will include those who—like nurses—offer vital public services. And they will include those who never sit at a bargaining table, the unemployed.

A concern for the weak, which reflects a bias to the poor, must include some way of controlling the economy and of restraining the demands of the most powerful. In such a debate the most powerful are often supposed to be the strong unions; 'league tables' are published of wages, showing one or other group of industrial workers at the top. Such league tables have an element of fantasy about them, for everyone knows that there is another unpublished table. The salaries of directors, managers and professional bodies ought to be published, if there are to be league tables which show how people's wages relate to each other. A true prices and incomes policy would have to include all of these.

A moral re-entry into the market must include policies of restraint on the most powerful. An entirely unreasonable act of faith is called for in order to believe that the free market will automatically correct itself with beneficial effects except for the strong. Concern for the needs of the weaker demands that everything is not left to chance and to the uncertainties of international market forces. The Government must take a major part in controlling the economy. Indeed every government does so. A moral re-entry must include a determined effort towards fairer distribution. That would be seen to be attempted much more by an open prices and incomes policy, which took in everyone than by indirect and hidden interventions.

Intervention is needed to ensure that investment is made in areas like Merseyside. Liverpool was once very important to the market, because the industries of the North of England and the Midlands required a great seaport through which to trade with North America and the empire. A large labour force was needed, including a proportion of less skilled workers which was well above the average. Now the market has shifted to Europe and the South East of England; without government direction or encouragement the free market is not likely to invest in Merseyside on anything like the scale that is needed.

Even supposing the emergence of the real alternatives I have argued for, each region of a country will need to have a reasonable share of the wealth-producing, high-earning jobs.

There are businesses which accept some of the moral implications of reducing their manning levels in an area. For example, the St Helen's Trust in Merseyside is an enterprise by which larger firms offer help, through secondment and modest financing, know-how, good contacts and some facilities to small businesses starting out. New capital-intensive technology is needed for a country like Britain to be competitive; there may be a place beside it for intermediate technology. Firms which have slimmed down their work force could well consider buying from such labour-intensive enterprises.

Firms which accept that they have moral responsibilities to the community face questions much nearer the heart of the enterprise than questions about how much money should go to charities in the area. Questions about reinvestment or disinvestment must not be decided simply by deciding which location gives the greatest advantage in the market. Firms and shareholders who have made money out of an area have an obligation to the people of that area.

The United States has been used to mobility in far greater measure than European countries. Nevertheless there are many casualties there who cannot keep up in the race which the great god Economics commands. During the twenty-five years up to 1968 two thirds of farming families in the USA moved away as a result of developments in machinery, chemicals and capital expansions in argiculture. Many of those who migrated to the cities wanted not simply to find a job, but in time to buy a shop. More recently small shops have been displaced through development of supermarkets with powerful capital behind them and of costly tools and corporate mergers. When industries expanded, they often moved away. Factory jobs have fled outwards from older industrialised cities at a rate more than twice that of the resident blue-collar workers.

Dick Luecke describes a flight of jobs from country to city, from city to suburb, from northern metropolis to sun belt and from domestic to foreign shops—with workers running to catch up. Among the casualties are many worker families, who find themselves financially unable or reluctant to move. At each stage of this displacement of work he observes how the casualties have been predominantly black or non-white. He also sees a racial factor in the movement of firms out of the city and in their almost total reluctance to move back, in spite of allurements in the form of public services, tax credits and abatements.[22]

The philosophy which argues that all sensible young people will 'get mobile' when an area becomes economically depressed, makes a god out of economics. It encourages the strong to use their freedom without taking note of the effect on the less self-confident, who will never move. When the get-up-and-go young people are in any substantial numbers successful in finding employment elsewhere, areas which are already vulnerable become increasingly communities of the left-behind. Thankfully many able young people in Merseyside love their community and their city enough to stay. Perhaps the value they place on family, community and pride in their city is a lesson which those who live in careers rather than in places need to learn.[23] Archbishop Worlock and I in a joint letter to *The Times*[24] challenged the call by the Prime Minister, Mrs Thatcher, in 1980 to unemployed young people to 'get mobile', and said, 'For God's sake stay.' The *Daily Telegraph* in a leading article attacked us the following day as 'Interventionist Bishops'. The final nail in our coffin, to show how foolish were our comments, was the statement that our respective dioceses of Liverpool would not have come into being but for the mobility of people in rural Ireland and England in the nineteenth century.[25] That was accepting disastrous developments such as the potato famine as though they and the movements of population which followed them were inevitable or good.

It is claimed that allowing the strong to use their freedom to pursue personal and family interests increases resources which are available to all. This is not true of 'positional goods'; these are scarce resources to which there must be an absolute limit. When people buy what they believe to be an educational advantage for their children or speedier medical treatment for themselves, a Christian critique must ask whether their action is adding to the disadvantage of the poor.

I argued in 1974 in *Built as a City* that good educational opportunity would only be given to the disadvantaged if there was a fully comprehensive system.[26] This view has been frequently attacked on the ground that it is a denial of freedom to prevent parents from buying an advantage for their children in private schools. I stand by what I wrote then, and will not

141

repeat all the arguments here. But some points are relevant to the present subject.

A discussion about freedom will acknowledge that at times a point will come when the damage to society appears too great to justify the individual freedom of action that results in such damage. I believe that time has come in respect of private and selective schools. The lack of good educational opportunity for those who start at a disadvantage damages society severely. Private and selective education perpetuates the segregation of social classes and starves the comprehensive schools of the resources they need to attain high standards; some of the reasons which are rarely acknowledged are that it removes from them a significant number of motivated children, expert teachers and the articulate, critical pressure middle-class parents can exert for improvement.[27] If they all had to use the national system of education—or the National Health Service—they would soon see to it that there was a much more efficient system.

The defence of selective schools and the assisted-place scheme is that they offer wider educational opportunities. The defenders usually have in mind making it easier for the gifted children of poor parents to get jobs carrying large social rewards (whether in money or prestige), rather than increasing the range of occupations open to everyone. This defence has been portrayed as helping a few individuals to pass through a *door* into another room, where there are better opportunities, rather than lifting the *floor* on which a whole community stands.

As in other fields the presence of black people in a largely white society has revealed processes already happening, but not previously noticed. As Bishop of Woolwich between 1969 and 1975 I visited most of the grammar schools in South East London. I doubt if I ever saw more than three black faces in any one of those schools. I asked the Runnymede Trust, with their concern for race relations, if they would consider researching this. Their reply was that they did not believe that this was the result of racial bias; rather it revealed the fact that working-class children have never got through the hoops of educational selection in proper proportions. No trustworthy method of selection has ever been devised; those children who are at ease in the atmosphere of school (and of the selection process) because of the homes they come from, have an enormous advantage over those who feel strangers in that context.

It is fashionable to play down the effectiveness of programmes for school integration in the United States. When it is claimed that they have failed, they have often been blamed for not correcting by themselves disadvantages which are caused by multiple factors and not only by schooling. Breaking down segregation needs more mixed-housing policies in every city; it also needs integration of schools. In Pittsburgh in 1979 I met a group involved in a Class Action law suit to desegregate schools. One woman was a counsellor in Westinghouse High School, which then had one white student; she said, 'I come from the South. I don't have problems with a segregated school. But black kids won't have a chance unless they sit next to white kids. It's taken me a long time to say this.' A black priest said, 'If you put fifty kids from a low economic environment together, they will achieve badly. Quality education means I must go to school with other folks not like me.'

Parents who genuinely want a less divided society are sometimes placed in a very difficult personal situation; for example it may appear to parents from the professional classes that their child will be asked to bear alone the burdens of changing a divided society if no other children from a professional family go to their local comprehensive school. That is why corporate, political action is needed. Using the argument for freedom in this context appeals to that capitalist principle of harnessing the natural instincts and affections. It is natural for parents to want the best for their children. That will not be the last word for Christian parents, if they put the Sermon on the Mount alongside these natural feelings; 'If you love only those who love you, what reward can you expect? Surely the tax-gatherers do as much as that. And if you greet only your brothers what is there extraordinary about that? Even the heathen do as much. There must be no limit to your goodness, as your heavenly Father's goodness knows no bounds.'[28]

There is an even more basic assumption underlying the

argument that economic development is the best way to give good opportunities to the poor. It is that the better off have a right to maintain their standards of living. As the phrase is generally used, it means cash and consumer goods for an individual and his family. A bias towards the poor would make people much more aware of the relatively poor standard of living many have. Then cooperative feelings might grow stronger. Rather than the appeal to self-interest contributing to the social good, we could appeal to the pursuit of the social good and the satisfaction of self-interest which followed from that.[29]

Such a motive can lead many to find zest in the much-needed work of wealth creation, and to refuse to give up the elusive goal of fairer distribution. This may lead wealthy nations to be rather poorer. Yet their standard of living in a truer meaning of the phrase would be higher, if within each nation and in the world the poor had a significantly better share of wealth and opportunity.

CHAPTER NINE

Liberation Theology

It is natural, in considering how the Church is to reflect a bias to the poor, to look at liberation theology. Many Catholics and Protestants in South America have reacted against long years when the Church benefited from or remained neutral under oppressive regimes. Now they insist that the liberation of the oppressed must always be a central part of the Gospel.

Liberation theology looks to the classic Old Testament action of God in salvation and liberation in the Exodus. God delivers His people from the oppressor. The Jews have to get rid of their own slave mentality, which hankers after fleshpots and security, and repeatedly wants to return to Egypt. The oppressed themselves need to become 'the artisans of their own Liberation', says Gutierrez.[1] The claim is not that the Exodus provides a precise and universal pattern for Christians to follow; it is that the Exodus, the Prophets, Jesus in conflict with the authorities provide us 'example-giving' memories, which nourish consciousness and provoke to action.

Much thinking is based on 'political theology'. Fierro says that political theology is a theology operating under the sign of Marx, just as truly as scholasticism was a theology operating under the sign of Aristotle and liberal Protestant theology was one operating under the sign of Kant.[2] It rejects any idea of Christendom or of a Christian politics. Segundo argues that the normal condition of the Church in society is that of a creative minority, as indicated by the symbolism of leaven. The purpose of leaven is not to transform the whole piece of dough into leaven but into bread. So the Church is meant to be a transforming ferment in humanity.[3] Bonino says that the Church does not impose a system from above—as in colonial Christianity. 'It accompanies the people';[4] that means standing

145

with poor people when their cause is just. It also means challenging them when the Christian Gospel questions the methods they use and the attitudes they hold towards others.

Liberation theology may be described as a method of studying and living. This can be worked out in the discipline of a hermeneutical circle; an example is my study of Jews and Gentiles in Chapter Six. Liberation theology writers insist that the circle is entered by a prior commitment to the poor. Theology is a critical reflective discipline which arises as a second step. 'The first book is life; the second book is the Bible.' 'Theology rises only at sundown.'[5]

A hermeneutical circle can help to attempt to interpret what the God of history is doing in today's world. He says Yes to some of its settled structures or processes of change; other evil situations cry out to heaven and to God. They receive what Jon Sobrino calls 'God's No to history'.[6] He calls Christians to be more cautious of false impartiality than of partisanship. There can be no cool, impartial theology above it all. At the conference of Latin American bishops at Puebla, Mexico in 1979, there was some discussion about ideologies and the fear of Marxism. Bishop Schmitz from Peru pointed to those who were scandalised by the possible use of some aspects of Marxism; 'Let him who is without an ideology cast the first stone.'[7] Ideologies lie as much behind keeping the status quo or economic development as they do behind liberation.

When it comes to critical reflection, liberation theology insists on 'ideological suspicion'. We must be suspicious about how much our own assumptions or other people's views are influenced by the social and economic circumstances in which we or they live. Some Christians become nervous of such study, when they realise it includes looking at the social and economic situation in which the Bible writers found themselves. Yet Christians have long taken account of the different circumstances in which the Bible writers found themselves; this has generally been in order to explain why something which they read in the Bible is not held to be applicable now. For example, usury was roundly condemned in the Bible; slavery was not. The Law of Jubilee insisted that no land could be sold freehold; it had to be returned in the fiftieth year, lest large estates be built up and the poor be left with no land.[8] In each case most European Christians have held the view that the Bible writers at these moments reflected the economic and social order in which they found themselves—so different from present-day circumstances, that it was not believed they speak to our situation. Ideological suspicion means that we ask about the circumstances of the Bible writers and the assumptions which they made. We are to ask the same questions about ourselves, for our social and economic experience colours how we understand the Christian faith.

What kind of God do we believe in—or reject? At different times in history men have looked at their concept of human authority, and their ideas about God have reflected that concept. Lord, King, Father have been among our mental pictures of God. What we feel about God has then been influenced by our human experience, perhaps of a feudal lord, an absolute king or our own father. 'The God of the white overlord is not the same as the God of the Indian labourers.'[9] Their understanding is influenced heavily by their different economic and social experiences of life.

Another example of this is how Christians understand the meaning of freedom, when they read it in the Bible. Devout Christians, belonging to a Church which gives priority always to the building up of the worshipping community or personal commitment to Christ, are likely to think first about freedom from sin.

Some old people, worried about whether it is safe to go out at night without being mugged, react against today's freedom, and want firmer law and order.

Teenagers, rebelling against rigid patterns of behaviour, argue for freedom to make personal moral choices for themselves.

Businessmen, who have worked hard to build up their own businesses, insist on the freedom of the individual and his family to prosper without interference from the State.

Those who experience urban deprivation want the freedom to find a job or satisfactory housing, or some say in how decisions are made which affect their lives.

In each case people's own economic and social experience

147

colours what they think about, when they hear, for example, the promises that Christ will set them free. That becomes plainer still with a poor Indian driven by rural poverty to a shanty town in Sao Paulo or a black man with no vote, forcibly moved to a black area in South Africa.

The Pope at Puebla

Pope John Paul II carried conflicting hopes with him when he went to the Third Conference of the Latin American bishops in 1979 at Puebla. In 1968 the bishops' second conference at Medellin, Colombia, had issued a strong call to the Church to take up the cause of the poor and oppressed. Reactions within the Church had been very different; it was not simply a division between traditional and progressive. For example, Archbishop Manrique of La Paz was described as a subversive troublemaker by successive military regimes in Bolivia, because he supported the grievances of peasants and tin miners in times of repression. Yet his approach to theology was traditional. Another archbishop in Guatemala was reported as saying that the Medellin statement was optional and that he had opted out.[10]

Those who stressed only the spiritual side of the Church's task, hoped that the Pope, who had only been four months in office, would condemn liberation theology and all its works. Indeed the first newspaper reports of his keynote address at the inauguration of the Puebla Bishops' Conference quoted extracts which appeared to do just that. But the speech was an attempt to bridge the gap between the differing viewpoints of the Church's role in Latin America.

The Pope had much to say in favour of both sides. He reproached those who denied or undervalued the divinity of Christ. He attacked those who would reread the Gospel and turn Christ into simply a political figure. In the second half of his address he endorsed the search for justice; he mentioned 'the delicate question of private property', which he said involved a 'social mortgage'. The implications of this (which he set out explicitly in a subsequent speech) are that, if the mortgage is not paid to society, then expropriation of the private property may be in order. He said the commitment to the poor was based on the Gospel: it did not have to rely on some political manifesto.

After his tour of Mexico and his return to Rome, John Paul II made a speech about the Puebla Conference which had now ended. His subject was evangelisation; it meant doing everything possible in order that man may find himself again in Christ. This finding again was the deepest source of man's liberation . . . Liberation meant man's inner transformation, which came from the knowledge of truth. Truth also had a prophetic significance and power, which involved opposing non-truth.

'It is necessary to call by their name injustice, the exploitation of man by man, or the exploitation of man by the State, institutions, mechanisms of systems and regimes, which sometimes operate without sensitivity . . . Liberation also in a social sense begins with knowledge of the truth.'[11]

The conclusions of the Puebla Conference include a message to the peoples of Latin America. A main heading is 'A Preferential Option for the Poor'. The whole Church needed conversion to this option. The vast majority of our fellow humans continued to live in a situation of poverty and even wretchedness, that had grown more acute. This was in contrast to the accumulation of wealth in the hands of a small minority, frequently the price being poverty for the majority. The poor did not lack simply material goods. They were also denied the human dignity of a full participation in social and political life. The bishops referred particularly to the indigenous peoples, peasants, manual labourers, marginalised urban dwellers and especially the women of these social groups. They said that the women were oppressed and marginalised.

The Puebla Conclusions recognised tensions within the Church itself. On the one hand these were provoked by groups that stressed the 'spiritual' side of the Church's mission and resented active efforts at the improvement of society. On the other hand they were provoked by people who wanted to make the Church's mission nothing more than an effort at human betterment. They said that fear of Marxism kept many from facing the oppressive reality of Liberal Capitalism. Faced with the danger of one clearly sinful system, Church people often forgot to denounce and combat the established reality of another equally sinful system. They should look critically at capitalism, without overlooking the violent and atheistic historical forms of Marxism.[12]

It is not illuminating or truthful to transfer unexamined all the ideas and categories of liberation theology from South America to countries like Britain and the United States. Liberation theology insists that if Christians want to discover the Word of God in their circumstances they must examine very carefully the particular historical situation which they experience. If we ask where Britain stands in relation to liberation, we are asking a more complex question than in South American military dictatorships. We cannot say that every nation can be explained in terms of oppressors and oppressed. We cannot assume that every country needs a liberation movement and the overthrow of the system every century.

Of first importance is the existence of a rule of law, to which government and police are answerable. That is why we must examine with particular care allegations which suggest that the law is not administered even-handedly. The majority in developed countries like Britain have good opportunities. That does not mean that gross lack of opportunities experienced by a minority can be shrugged off. One revolution which brings about relatively good institutions does not produce a perfect system once and for all.

The experience I have described in Liverpool and in the black community in Britain shows that disadvantage has obstinately persisted from generation to generation. A. H. Halsey said in the 1978 Reith Lectures that we had offered citizenship to all, but that class and citizenship were at war in the twentieth century. The development of the social rights of citizenship led those who were told they were citizens to expect a more equal deal.[13] But obstinately class lines hold many back; in a subsequent study of social mobility in relation to education, Professor Halsey and his team concluded that there had been no significant reductions in class inequalities since the Second World War.[14]

It is the argument of this book that the Church is called to a bias towards the poor in the Western democracies as well as in Latin America. Liberation theology reminds us that our materialistic, comfortable and selfish community pushes those on the margins of society to the edges of its consciousness. It would not be enough to reach out to the poor in occasional charitable works, if the concerns of the Christian community are to reflect those of its Founder. It must put the needs of the poor at the centre of its worship and of its study and activity.[15]

Christians and Marxists

It would be impossible for a Christian in the twentieth century to consider the situation of the urban poor without taking a careful look at the Marxist analysis and philosophy. Christians have important common ground with Marxists, which should be affirmed wholeheartedly before we examine our disagreements. The common ground includes:

The belief that man is a social being, with longings that his gifts should be used for the community and recognised by the community.

The realisation that the economic and social structures of society can form the minds and shape the destinies of those who are subject to them.

The questioning of who controls the means of production, and to whom they are accountable.

An indignation at unequal distribution of wealth and opportunity.

A belief in a better future order.

A longing for a realistic programme, which the poor especially can strive after.

I offer three criticisms of Marxism here, which I hope may help in the dialogue between Christians and Marxists.

Belief in God

First I believe in the reality of God as the centre of human aspiration and history. What I believe about man, made in the image of God, derives first and foremost from what I believe about God.

Some liberation theology writers have followed Marxist thought in saying that any idea of a transcendent God will inevitably lead to a society in which there are dominators and dominated—to the servility which Marx thought was the worst of all human attitudes.

The point is about what kind of God we believe in and worship. It has been well argued that in a country with a monarchy, Christian worship and belief often reflect our greatest idea of a king, only more powerful. The connection then is very likely to be made between bowing down unquestioningly before such a God and believing that we must also bow down before other authorities which such a God deputes to keep us in order. So it has been in Britain. So it was in Holy Russia before the Revolution. But Archbishop Anthony Bloom speaks of his generation of five million Russians, who after the Revolution found themselves barred from their country, not needed, helpless, unprotected; 'we discovered a God we had not known in the time of the great Cathedrals—a God who had become of His own free will, what we had unwillingly become. It would not have helped, had we met a great God in His Cathedrals, the overlord of the land. It is not enough to recognise Him as the Lord and Master of all things, unless we can respect Him because He is with us in our agony.'[16]

We have generally thought about God's transcendence as coming from outside. That is part of what has made some turn away, believing that the authority of such a God is handed down from altogether outside our situation. However, in our own experience we meet acts of self-sacrifice within very human situations; we know that such acts transcend those situations. Transcendence sometimes comes from within our hurt human situations. We give authority to Jesus Christ because He showed us transcendent love within the most hurt and powerless state; He took upon Himself the nature of a slave, and in obedience accepted death, even death on a cross. 'Therefore God raised Him to the heights and bestowed on Him the name above all names, that at the name of Jesus every knee should bow.'[17] Here was self-giving love and obedience to truth from within a situation of total powerlessness. The understanding of God's authority was—or should have been—irreversibly shifted by the coming of Jesus Christ.

Jürgen Moltmann wrote about the Crucified God. He saw in the God and Father of Jesus Christ the God of the poor, the oppressed and humiliated. He argued that the rule of Christ could only be extended through liberation from forms of rule, which make men servile and apathetic, and the political religions which give them stability.[18] Segundo argues that the Church must put away the ambitions of such political religions. In Latin America there is mass Christianity and minority Christianity. As a result of his commitment to 'minority Christianity' Segundo disagrees with Marx's view of religion. Over against Marx he affirmed that religion could perform the function of unsettling people. A mass religion could not be a disestablishing religion at the same time. It could not appeal to the whole population and unsettle the existing order simultaneously.[19] A Church such as the Church of England is wedged very uncomfortably, but perhaps creatively, between these two positions. It sets out to be a Church for all the people, yet bearing a Word, which will be unsettling to the existing order, if it is faithfully lived out.

Many Christians have sought a clear-cut relationship between Christ and culture. And many Anglicans today long to be released from this often ambiguous relationship with the nation and the Church embedded in the fabric of society. The issues would be clearer if the Church of England became more like a sect, with clear lines drawn between those who belong and those who do not. The insight which comes from trying to hold a bias to the poor does not suggest that it would help the poor to believe they could belong. Articulated, tidy systems of belief and Church order would remove the many stepping stones on which the poor need to be able to meet the life and members of the Church. The Church is called to express solidarity with the culture around it; but it must insist on unsystematic relationship. A critical solidarity must allow the Church to encourage and enter into genuine counter-cultures, which challenge the accepted order of society.

Christ's authority unsettles and transcends all our human systems of every generation. In the USA James A. Joseph

153

argued for an approach in which no creed should be treated as final, no institution as closed, and no ideology as absolute. He described the American Revolution as not simply an event in the nation's past, but a process of fulfilment, which continues into the nation's future.[20] The transcendence seen in the God and Father of Jesus Christ does not lead to a society of dominators and dominated. Indeed it has a continuing critique built in. It delivers us from the worship of the State or the party. The person who believes in nothing transcendent rests all his hopes and fears with the party, the cause, the class, the State. He cannot bear to hear criticism of them, cannot tolerate any nonconformity or opposition. The transcendent God dwells within our life; He also speaks from outside. The worship which lifts up our hearts to Him allows us to make a critique of the society in which we are involved.

In rejecting belief in God, Marxists have often put up an Aunt Sally of a God, whom many Christians would also reject. Do they really disbelieve in the Crucified God? Or have they never asked that question?

The human factor

My second criticism of Marxism is that it underplays the importance of the human factor in all economic and social planning. The enemies from which we need liberating are not all outside us. When political liberation has come, there will still be inside people's hearts and minds greed, the will to dominate, irresponsibility. If Christians talk about liberation, they must show the need to be liberated from sin both at a corporate level and at a personal level. No doubt Christian preachers have been rather selective in the sins they have labelled. At the Lausanne Congress of Evangelical Christians in 1974 Samuel Escobar spoke of those Christians who condemned all the sins that well-behaved middle-class people condemned, but said nothing about exploitation, intrigue and dirty political manoeuvring done by the great multinational corporations round the world.[21] Sin has to do both with those corporate actions and our personal dealings. Gutierrez speaks about liberation from sin as the ultimate root of all disruption of friendship and of all injustice and oppression.[22]

Christian liberation should be concerned about a political Exodus, such as set the Jews free to make their own choices about the society they wanted to live in. It is not only concerned about such freedom for those who accept that they are called to be the people of God. The prophet Amos reminded the Jews that God did not only bring Israel out of Egypt; He also brought the Philistines from Caphtor and the Aramaeans from Kir.[23] But it would be a lie to pretend that only bad economics and systems corrupt people. Jesus said that sexual greed, envy, slander, arrogance come from inside, out of a man's heart.[24] Self-sacrificial love cannot be planted in someone's heart simply by bringing in a new economic order. Christianity is both about justice and about Christ changing people from inside out.

Capitalists and Marxists have both treated economics as though it has autonomy; Christians believe in one God and one world, in which no subject has autonomy. All disciplines—economics, law, theology, social and family life—are interdependent, because life is one whole. Marxism has not believed that social and political changes must go hand in hand with people being changed from inside out.

As long as people refuse to locate sin within themselves, they will look for an enemy to blame. But when the class enemy or 'the system' has been destroyed, evil will still be there in us. The new structures of society which are then developed will also be penetrated by sin, and will constantly need to be criticised and reformed.

The class struggle

My third criticism of Marxism has to do with romantic and often dogmatic views about the proletariat. Marx believed—with a remarkably blind faith—that the proletariat alone, the most alienated group, would destroy one type of society deliberately in order to put another in its place. He said that they alone would put an end to alienation by making men for the first time masters of their social environment. They alone were the redeemers of mankind.[25] Liberation theology writers like Fierro have followed this belief; only by identification with the class that is destined to be the whole could Christians help towards a society in which the divisions are finally broken down.[26]

All this takes a very dogmatic view about the proletariat. Marx saw the proletariat as an economic concept, defined by workers' relationship to the means of production. The reality of inner city life in Britain today does not reveal one main stream of working-class life. Different groups who would claim to be working class have different attitudes which are greatly influenced by their particular local situation. In particular minority groups frequently do not respond to those who speak of them as being involved in a class struggle.

Marx believed that evil was in the system and in the class enemy. He said that class interests are irreconcilable and that class conflicts had to be fought out to the end.[27] Christians must reject this. Groups of people, who are part of God's creation, are not evil. Nor are other groups all good. The world is not made up, like some Western film, of goodies and baddies. All of us are made in God's image. All of us have potential for good. All of us are infected by evil. All of us can be reconciled to God and to one another.

At different points I have written about some of the crises for capitalism and for socialism. One of the moral crises for all who seek the liberation of their class or race or nation is how they behave, once they are liberated, towards those who are weaker. It is one of the bitter facts of history that those who have suffered greatly, and know what it is like to be victims, so often behave only with self-interest. Christians, following Bonino's phrase, 'accompany the people', listening, respecting, joining hands, when we believe the cause to be right. As we accompany the people, there will be moments when we must offer a Christian critique. We shall only be heard if we have stood with the cause.

Criticisms are still more likely to be heard when they come from those who themselves belong to the disadvantaged group. A black American can say to black people that to try simply 'to get your piece of the pie is idolatry'. A black leader in Britain can say to the black community, 'A basic canon in all teaching is never to teach anything it is necessary to unteach later. However much self-respect must grow for your own group, it must never be exclusive.' A Socialist leader in Britain can say to his comrades, 'Damn it! They've beaten us,' when he finds trade unions pursuing the same selfish interests of personal standards of living, which they have condemned in bourgeois people, and ignoring groups like the unemployed. A Jew can remind Jewish people in Israel that they of all people should know what it is to be a victim, when they deny rights to Arab communities.

At times there must be a voice which challenges the appeal to self-interest within the group to which one wholeheartedly belongs. The Jews had been repeatedly told that they should remember that they had been slaves themselves. It was to colour all their dealings with other people.[28]

Liberation simply means replacing one tyrant with another, if it only leads to the revolutionary group becoming top. A more fraternal society can only be built, if we learn the lessons of fraternity all the way along the journey. Jesus's theme of the Kingdom of God always involved the others, not just those who belonged to your clan, your movement or your Church. He talked about loving your enemies, forgiving those who sin against you.[29]

Those who work for a better society and for their own group need to admit that sin is within them personally and corporately as well as in 'the others'. Jesus pointed out the hypocrisy of a man trying to take a speck of dust out of his brother's eye, with never a thought for the great plank in his own.[30] We do not have to wait for God's liberation to be complete before we can see it working out in our midst. Liberation is indivisible. A revolution which believes that liberation is only concerned with socio-economic forces, and not with the hearts of people, simply replaces one tyrant with another. Christians, who believe that God's perfect Kingdom will one day be brought in, know that they are called to start living as citizens of that Kingdom now.

It follows from these criticisms of Marxism that I also criticise liberation theology at these points. It is not always as suspicious of Marxism as it is of other ideologies. As often happens in the Church, the pendulum swings too far; some liberation theologians react against a Gospel in which all the emphasis is placed on the response of the individual. They swing to placing all their emphasis on changing the system. The argument of this book is that these are not opposites. The Christian must work and pray for the change both of the individual and of the system.

Liberation theology performs a most important service if it makes Christians aware that God is the God of today's history, and that political processes matter to Him. Often it assumes that those who hear its words already know and understand the Christian faith. That might be true in Latin America, which has never really been through the process of secularisation; but no such assumption can be made in Britain. The Gospel must include at its heart the good news about Jesus Christ.

Liberation theology presents some challenges to the Church of England; it has not shaken off its preoccupation with the personal encounter with God. It recognises a role for the Church in society; but the terms in which it understands and discharges its social responsibility are those set by the world, not by the Gospel. Specifically it takes its cue from the powerful, those at the centre, and sees the poor as a problem and potentially as a threat. But God is to be found among the poor and powerless, those at the margins of society; a Church which seeks to be faithful must learn to listen to such, admit them to its decision-making, and then face the implications for its life as an established institution in society.[31]

Bishop Ted Wickham spoke of the Christian calling to 'influence the influencers'.[32] We must then go on to question our assumptions about where we shall find the influencers. Liberation theology is a sharp reminder in any society that change is often brought about from the bottom up, rather than through the actions of the influential, 'top' people.

CHAPTER TEN

Human Hearts and Social Structures

Joining the public debate

Christians are often warned to keep off the grass if they comment on the worlds of industry or politics—some of the structures of our society. A discreet word in private to the powerful has always been thought to be right and proper. But it is widely regarded as stepping into other people's territory for Church leaders to take sides in public debate. They are then told that they should stick to their spiritual task; it is assumed that this is concerned with human hearts not social structures. Politely or impolitely we must refuse to keep quiet. Christianity is rightly concerned with wholeness of life. That includes both human hearts and social structures. We do not accept that life is made up of a series of compartments, each having its own autonomy.

This is not to assert, as was done in the Middle Ages, that theology is the queen of the sciences. Theologians are not authorities about everything. A friend looked in a large book-shop for a copy of my book, *Built as a City*. After a long search she found it under the heading Constructional Engineering! I readily acknowledge that I do not have the qualifications, experience or the calling to speak about the technique of engineering or the technique of any other part of industry and commerce. But I am in the 'People Business'.

A distinction needs to be made between intruding into matters of technique and of offering a Christian critique about the effects of policies on people. In an editorial article the *Daily Telegraph* supported Margaret Thatcher in rebuking 'those churchmen who identify the teachings of the gospel with the discredited interventionist policies of the past . . . The Church must respect what Archbishop William Temple called "the autonomy of technique".' It said that it was proper for the Church to be concerned about unemployment, but 'how unemployment is to be reduced is a matter outside the province of moral theology'.[1]

There is a difference between acknowledging technical know-how in its field and insisting that Christian insights should have their place in matters which affect the whole lives of people. How unemployment should be reduced is not a narrow subject in which economists alone are competent to have opinions. Value judgments have to be made about the effects of different policies; in making these a nation needs the widest possible participation in the debate, and moral theology has a contribution to make along with other disciplines.

William Temple was rather a remarkable choice to support that line of argument: it was also a remarkable quotation to select. In it William Temple certainly warned Christians not to ignore the autonomy of technique in various departments of life. But his warning was lest the right of the Church to be heard in relation to political and economic problems should be compromised. He went on immediately to say that religion may declare the proper relation of the economic order to other activities of men, but it cannot claim to know what will be the purely economic effect of particular proposals. 'It is, however, entitled to say that some economic gains ought not to be sought because of the injuries involved to interests higher than economic: and this principle of the subordination of the whole economic sphere is not yet generally accepted.'[2]

William Temple is held up as a blind guide in leading the Church astray in Edward Norman's book *Church and Society in England 1770–1970*. His social thought was said to be inept and second-hand, resulting from a guilty moralism.[3] In that book Norman repeatedly expresses his own preference for laissez-faire political economy; in one of many similar comments he claims, for example, that most ordinary people in late nineteenth-century Britain believed in the self-help ethic and competitive principle, and the belief that those forms of government were best which least interfered in social or economic relationships.[4] He made it clear that this is what he believed in.

Norman moved on to rather different ground when he delivered the BBC's Reith Lectures in 1979 on *Christianity and the World Order*. He now said that the true Christian position was to be sceptical of all versions of Christian politics, including conservative ones. These lectures were widely publicised and welcomed by those Christians who believed the Church was becoming too involved in social and political matters. Sometimes these critics fall into the trap of accusing those who call for corporate change of being political, without acknowledging that allowing things to remain as they are, laissez-faire, is also being political.

Norman's lectures had an important word for the Church to hear, fighting for the uniqueness of the Christian revelation; he feared for Christianity that its distinctive content was being 'drained away into the great pool of secular idealism'. But his lectures were misleading, because he repeatedly set up opposites. Spiritual Christianity was true; politicised Christianity was false. True religion pointed to the state of the inward man; the Gospels spoke about a personal rather than a social morality. The privatisation of religion was good; only a man with such a private religion could perhaps help his brothers.

A proper Christian spirituality, said Norman, leads to an awareness of the relativity of all human values, not the espousal of human causes. Christianity was once about human fallibility, about the worthlessness of all earthly expectations. Now it was seemingly preoccupied with human capabilities. The wise man knew that there was no hope of a better social order, and that he should take no thought for the morrow. True religion was an education of the soul to see the shadow of eternity. He said that the visible and the unseen world were briefly joined in the Incarnation.[5]

They still are. What began in the Incarnation, when God took human flesh, has gone on. God the Creator and the Sustainer is the God of history; history includes what is happening now. That does not mean that there will be smooth progress to a perfect society. That is promised only by God's action beyond this world. But in the light of that promise Christians cannot be indifferent to those corporate structures of society which contradict God's purpose. The question is asked of the Christian, who is involved in secular life, what will happen to his spirituality. His reply should be that unless he follows Jesus into the thick of life, he will not know what the pressures are which he is called to face. And he will not discover the interior spiritual resources needed to face them.

It is not true Christianity to dismiss all earthly expectations as worthless. There is a light which enlightens every man; John claims that it was this true light which was coming into the world at the Incarnation.[6] Nor, if all human values and earthly expectations are worthless, is there any starting place for debate about morality. The Church is then left saying, 'Unless and until you accept the whole of our Christian package, we have nothing to say to you, except that everything you are doing is worthless.' If all human values and expectations are worthless, we should not argue with the Christian who withdraws from any true engagement with the world and who leaves his mind up in the heavens, while he goes through the motions of daily work.

Edward Norman is right to say that human ideals are relative. He is wrong to imply that God is not concerned with making conditions relatively better. Christian morality begins where people are. Where they are is greatly affected by corporate attitudes and actions as well as by individual attitudes and actions. So we must enter into debates about corporate ethics. Every businessman and every trade union official wrestles with such corporate choices every day. The Church does not help them if it simply pronounces great principles from on high. We must stay with them as they face the pressures of conflicting interests and the lesser of evils, and try to find a right way through. The Church doesn't have authoritative answers in such situations, and we must say so; but we can help a great deal by encouraging people to think through the ethical questions of work in a Christian context.

Often Christians are silent or paralysed in vital human situations because they feel so alone. The role of the clergyman may be simply to organise the possibility of lay people's meeting to think through issues of their world of work. If it is right for him to be present, he may have to say words to the effect that 'I'll hold your confusion for you, so that you can go back into your work place'.

Sometimes it is a proper calling to Christian leaders that they should go and join the debate in the market place. They should go in fear and trembling, having been carefully briefed by those who are well informed. They should bring distinctively Christian insights. In particular Christians should be able to bring a mixture of passion, because they care deeply about the needs of people, and of respect for the opinions of those with whom they disagree. They do not claim that there is a Christian economics or a Christian politics.

Industrial mission and sectors of urban life

If they go into the market place, Christians will disagree in public. Often the Church has shrunk from that kind of conflict; thereby it has withdrawn from so much of the working out of corporate ethics. Then debates which have far-reaching consequences in shaping people's lives are carried on without a Christian voice. As the urban and industrial world developed, the Christian Church shrank from bringing these matters on its agenda. So whole areas of life in industry, technology and scientific thought slipped out of reach of the prayers and understanding of Christians. Alan Ecclestone writes, 'Neither with penitence nor with joy could men grasp the spiritual implications of the world which they were so swiftly building.'[7]

The Church needs to attend to that sense of being alone which many Christians have at work. To speak of a bias to the poor invites some sharp questions about what God's good news may be for the relatively rich and powerful. It would be good news for those who carry heavy responsibility at work if the Church made it possible for them to think through some of those responsibilities with other lay people of all denominations, who carry similar burdens.

It is part of the calling of industrial mission to offer some experience of holding together Christian understanding with the reality of the world of work. Industrial mission does not simply mean the relatively small number of industrial chaplains who live out their ministry in the world of industry. It means whole networks of lay people from management and shop floor and from all denominations, who have been helped by

BIAS TO THE POOR

industrial mission to do some thinking about their work in the company of Christians. Such groups may sometimes meet in the suburb where many live; or they may meet in a particular factory, or bring together people from different works on an industrial estate or in the city centre, where some Churches will also offer this kind of group.

A city is not simply a series of small towns or villages, where everyone experiences work, leisure interests and family life in the same one parish. There are sectors of life in a city. The sector where someone may have the greatest possibilities of influence and face the greatest strains is as likely to be the work sector as the family one. There are other sectors too; for example, where leisure interests bring people together, or community and political life. The Church does not offer much support to Christians in sectors other than where the life of family and immediate neighbourhood takes place. When people face strains, joys and crises in those vital personal areas of life, we expect the Church to be organised to serve them. Yet the Church does not generally think of organising itself to support Christians in other sectors with their opportunities and pressures.

When we think of the Church in a city, we are inclined to think of flags in the map where people have their homes. We need that expression of Church life. In addition we need to find ways of providing what might be described as a chain of support groups in the different sectors of life, where neighbours and colleagues can come together. Such a group may meet four or five times and then disperse. It may take on a particular project; for example, sponsoring a project for unemployed people or a project to think about the future of work. It may have a continuing life. A clergyman, stipendiary, or perhaps non-stipendiary in his own field of employment or interest, may have to do with bringing the group together and finding 'resource people' who have already done some thinking about the matter in hand. He will not necessarily expect to be the leader of such a group.

Some resent such matters being tackled in the Church fellowship. There is a tunnel in East Surrey. Commuters to London used to tell me, when I was Bishop of Woolwich, that they breathed a sigh of relief when the train came out on the Surrey side of the tunnel. They were relieved that they had left London and its business world behind. If questions were raised in their Surrey parishes about issues in their working life or about unequal opportunities in London, two conflicting emotions were at war in their minds. On the one hand there was a defensive, angry voice; 'Don't you dare raise those complex questions! Why do you think we live out here? And what do you know about such questions anyway?' On the other hand there was a cry from at least some hearts. 'For God's sake help me! I don't want my Christian faith to be divorced from these ambiguous demands my work lays on me every day.'

It would take a major change of heart in many congregations to allow questions about the world of work on the agenda of sermons or discussions. But such subjects need to be tackled within the Christian circle. There is an assumption which should be overturned. It assumes that, if someone is a deeply committed Christian, he will know by himself how to behave when he is confronted by issues at work. That assumption is made because Christian ethics have been limited to personal behaviour, being reliable, honest and a good friend to colleagues. The moment it is admitted that corporate ethics are the proper concern of the Christian, and that it is sin to walk away from them, the realisation follows that we need all the help we can get to wrestle intelligently with them. Indeed the more common cry, once Christians do begin to face such questions, is that they are too big for us to understand.

Theological slogans often cause Christians to rush into opposing camps without pausing to think what truths may be at stake. It has been like this with the slogan 'Let the world set the agenda'. On the one hand it has been taken to mean that the Church simply goes wherever fashionable thinking will lead it, accommodating Christian theology to the fashions of the day. From that point of view the slogan has to be opposed as selling the pass. On the other hand it reflects the truth that God is present in the whole of His universe, and does not speak only through the Church.

Reaction against the assumption that truth must always

come through the movement God–Church–World can produce an equally misleading idea: the proposition that truth must always come through the movement God–World–Church. God will not be tied down to one formula or the other about how He makes us aware of His truth. To say that He sometimes sets the Church's agenda through events and ideas in the secular world is to reassert that we believe in the God of history. This does not mean that we take the world on its own terms, but that we must take the world absolutely seriously.[8]

In the world of work or community Christians are called not simply to fit in as individuals, but to change the course of events if they block God's purposes. We must reject Edward Norman's way of setting up opposites over against each other. It is not a question of either being for personal conversion or for changing the structures of society. I am for both. The prophets of the Old Testament (who were never mentioned in Norman's lectures) returned repeatedly to two themes. They were not opposites. They marched hand in hand. One was the commitment to social justice; the other was the knowledge of God. The Biblical basis of social concern was the revealed character of God. We are called to reflect that character; we shall not do that unless worship and prayer are central to our lives.

Sin is to be found both in the human heart and in the social structures which prevent people from developing God-given possibilities. Edward Schillebeeckx writes that Christian redemption is certainly not something that takes place only in the hearts of individuals. It has personal and social and political aspects, because it is man who is redeemed. 'It would, however, be simply a new ideology to expect the redemption and improvement of the world to come about automatically as the result of structural changes, which would remove all elements of repression and violence from society.' Human freedom is situated in a context of external factors which influence that freedom. The story of redemption calls the individual to a change of heart and to follow Christ. It would however be a fiction if it did not also attack the objective social structures which determine our lives.[9]

If we want to change the course of events in urban and

industrial life, we must pay attention to the institutions, the realities and the powers of our day. The great temptation is to withdraw. Sin is to come short of the glory of God, not to go far enough. It is to know that it is possible to commit yourself to Christ and His Kingdom, and yet to hold back, whether out of selfishness or out of fear of becoming involved in something too big to handle.

There is an alienation for which we ourselves are responsible. Today's Christian knows that urban and industrial life cry out for those who will make the first move, and join hands with others in dealing with complex structures—some of which need changing and some sustaining. We know that we remain willingly in our sin, if we do not join all those people of goodwill who want to work for a more human shaping of the institutions and structures that affect our life together. God has given each one of us gifts which match our calling. To repudiate that calling is to make our decision for alienation. God calls each of us to share responsibility in all that is good. Bernard Häring says, 'It is impossible to separate individual conversion from our commitment to a more just, more fraternal and peaceful world and to better structures and institutions.'[10]

Alienation is a powerfully descriptive word in urban and industrial life. In Marx's writing it is not primarily the worker himself who is responsible for his alienation. Alienated man is afflicted by society. The proletariat is the most alienated part of mankind; this is because they are at the mercy of an uncontrolled and quickly changing economy. Nobody wants unemployment, but it happens as a result of a system which is out of the control of those who have promoted it.[11] The capitalist is in this sense as much a victim as the worker. So Marx believed that the system must be destroyed. He never spelled out how society should be reconstructed; that could only be seen once the institutions which bound men's minds in false consciousness were broken. Only then could reconstruction on a true basis begin.

In the Gospels there were moments when Jesus shook the dust off His feet against someone or something which rejects what makes for peace.[12] Marx would encourage us to do this against all the institutions of a capitalist world. But most of the institutions which affect people's lives are ambiguous in their effect. Suggest that much-criticised institutions like the Port of Liverpool or Ford's, Halewood should close, and there would be furious protests. Before we talk seriously about shaking the dust off the feet against institutions, we need to examine carefully whether they can be called back to being the kind of good structures on which people can rely.

Reconciliation of persons and institutions

In searching for a way to offer a Christian critique on institutions which influence people's lives in this ambiguous way, I turned to Paul's use of the word reconciliation in the New Testament.

The reconciliation is first between man and God: 'God was in Christ, reconciling the world to Himself, no longer holding men's misdeeds against them . . . He has entrusted us with the message of reconciliation . . . In Christ's name we implore you, be reconciled to God.'[13] Men and women have turned away from God; they have broken the relationship with Him, so that they are alienated from the intended and purposeful life He planned for them. In Christ He has made it possible for them to be reconciled; now they are called to come back into the positive relationship He intended for them.

Paul also says that God has made reconciliation possible for the powers which influence our lives; 'Through Christ God chose to reconcile the whole universe to Himself, making peace through the shedding of His blood upon the Cross—to reconcile all things, whether on earth or in heaven, through Him alone.'[14] Just previously Paul described the 'all things' which God chose to reconcile; they are 'not only things visible but also the invisible orders of thrones, sovereignties, authorities and powers'. There has been some recent debate about what Paul meant by 'the powers'.[15]

Paul borrowed these terms from both Jewish and pagan realms of thought, which many of his readers would have known. He did not invent them; nor did he necessarily endorse all their previous meanings. Jewish apocalyptic writings

168

thought of powers, thrones and the like as classes of angels who had great influence on earthly events. Many Gentiles in the Middle East had been brought up believing that demonic powers controlled the stars and through them the destinies of people.

That is the background. It does not follow that Paul believes in a universe controlled in that way by demons and angels. He means to name a number of realities in people's experience. He talks about 'elemental spirits', 'cosmic powers and authorities'. At the same time he describes the solid structures—thrones, sovereignties, authorities—which dominate human lives. These might be the authorities of the Roman Empire, or the literal observance of the Jewish law or the pervasive influence of traditions handed down. There is an ambiguity about them; they make a powerful framework, which influences people for good or ill. He goes on to say that 'On the Cross Christ discarded the cosmic powers and authorities like a garment; He made a public spectacle of them, and led them as captives in His triumphal procession.'[16] It is hard to avoid the conclusion that he was thinking of Pontius Pilate, representing the powers of the Roman Empire, and of Herod and Caiaphas and their powers of Church and State.

It appears that at times it will be God's will to discard some of the powers. But not before the possibility of their reconciliation has been determinedly and patiently pursued. King Herod was glad that Jesus was brought to him; he questioned Him at some length. He received no reply.[17] When someone has consciously and steadily turned his back on truth, goodness and self-sacrifice, as Herod had done, he may find only silence when he approaches God.

With Pontius Pilate it was different. At first there was silence. Then, 'Surely you know I have authority to release you and I have authority to crucify you?' 'You would have no authority at all over me,' Jesus replied, 'if it had not been granted you from above; and therefore the deeper guilt lies with the man who handed me over to you.'[18] Perhaps here there is a reaching out to a man who was like a manager in a very large industry telling an industrial chaplain that he was conscious both of the power he wielded and of the powers to which he was subject. It suggests that Jesus had not written off Pontius Pilate and the institution he stood for: His understanding of the dilemma of power amounted perhaps to an appeal to his conscience, not an appeal in the sense that Jesus was appealing to His judge to let Him off, but an appeal to the man in authority to face truth in himself.

In our day there are those who want to discard all institutions and structures. The Establishment, Big Business, the Bureaucracy and Laws are seen as enemies to human development, preventing moral freedom from being exercised. Anarchists do not explain what they would put in the place of these powers; sometimes they suggest we would be better off if 'the state' and law and government disappeared. Disputes would be settled by ordinary members of the community without coercion. Such theories brush aside two objections which seem to me to be unanswerable. The first is that an urban and industrial society is complex. It is not made to work effectively simply by individuals relating to individuals. The second is that sin and evil are to be found in the human heart and not only in the structure of society.

There is, for example, a need for a rule of law in society to restrain evildoers. If I attempt a Christian critique of the police/community relations, I am not in any sense arguing that there is no need for a police force. Rather the attempt acknowledges the fundamental importance of a rule of law which is administered fairly and firmly.

The human heart will not be changed either by law or by good institutions, though it may be reformed and stimulated by both. Beneath all this is our need to be reconciled to God Himself. We have gone after other gods—be they economic gain for ourselves and our family, blind worship of our nation or selfish defence of the self-interest of our class. When we make a god of any of these, we turn our backs on the living God. Always, when Paul speaks of reconciliation, the one who makes the first move is God Himself. God was in Christ, reconciling the world to Himself. Christ's death on the Cross was not simply a demonstration of God's love at all times. It shifted the ground between us, and made a new relationship possible.

C. F. D. Moule says that for every human reconciliation to take place, there has to be a giving out of energy; for the one who makes the first move, there is generally a costly giving away of self. There is then an answering giving out of energy from the other person, in response and change of heart. This too is costly, because it brings the admission of being wrong and the surrender of pride. The streams of energy from both parties come together into a kind of pool of energy. The act of reconciliation therefore makes available 'energies of repair' which enables them not to go back to how things were before; they can now repair the broken relationship and go forward to new possibilities. So it is with the sacrifice of the Cross. The language of sacrifice speaks of costly self-giving. The energy of the self-sacrifice of Christ calls out energetic response from each person in a change of heart. The resulting pool of energy enables us to go forward to a new relationship with God and to new possibilities—not back to the way things were before.[19]

The word reconciliation has often been taken to be a soft word: in personal and group relationships it has led us to try to calm people down, to avoid conflict. To do that can actually prevent reconciliation: for if we avoid conflict, which is genuinely there, we only go back to the way things were before the breakdown of relationships. A commitment to true reconciliation is tough enough to face conflict. I am not here discussing violence. Often it is only through conflict that the true issues emerge, and the way is opened for reconciliation and new possibilities.

In the name of a soft reconciliation Christians have often taken the stance of neutrality in politics or industrial relations. Such a stance of neutrality assumes that both sides have an equally valid point of view. Justice calls us on many occasions to take sides; all points of view are not equally valid. There is a natural longing that Christians could stay in a serene world above conflict and dirty hands. In a consultation on urban theology in New York there was a presentation on the Trinity. A comment was made to the effect that the doctrine of the Trinity seemed serene, whereas the Incarnation was not serene. In the Incarnation there was energy, conflict, un-sereneness.[20] The Methodist Conference deliberately took up the position of neutrality at the time of the Luddites and the Chartists, among whom were many Methodists. Keeping silent seemed like neutrality, but in effect it was not. The powerful figure of Jabez Bunting was Secretary of the Methodist Conference. His favourite text in public matters was, 'Meddle not with them that are given to change.' In his case neutrality meant maintaining the status quo.

When conflict turns into violence, many Christians believe that they can have nothing to do with it. In recent years liberation theology has encouraged some Christians to believe that they are called to march with the Revolution. Europeans should not condemn this out of hand, while for example honouring Dietrich Bonhoeffer for his revolutionary act in joining the assassination attempt on Hitler's life. Bonhoeffer would have argued, as would many Christians in South America and Southern Africa today, that every peaceful means of changing an evil system had already been repeatedly tried. Oliver Cromwell, with the Independent and Presbyterian Christians who marched with him, the Americans who rebelled against King George, and Bonhoeffer believed that there is such a thing as a doctrine of a just revolution, just as many Christians have long claimed there is a doctrine of a just war.

We should not assume that every country needs a liberation movement with the overthrow of the system. That is an extreme solution which should only be contemplated when every peaceful means of developing a more just society has been determinedly worked for. I do not believe that revolution is the way forward in a society like Britain, where there are many channels available for bringing about peaceful change. Bringing the whole system down would not automatically bring a better order. Human society is a fragile structure. A new Dark Ages would bring joy to very few. In the end, after a revolution has been successful, the long slow business of building up good structures and good relationships has to begin again. Christians should work with a will at reconciling institutions and groups, before we can seriously consider that the time has come for shaking the dust off our feet against them.

To say that the powers can be reconciled is to challenge us to call the institutions back to their proper place in God's purpose. Institutions of government, law, education, Church, commerce and industry can be used for good or evil, like the rest of creation. In an alienated world institutions and structures are often jolted out of their proper place. Sometimes they become enfeebled monuments to out-of-date needs. Sometimes they become gods. Then they will be tyrants, any or all of them— for example, the State, the party, the company, the trade union, public opinion, accepted morality, tradition, religion. The needs of human beings who serve them, or are served by them, are lost in the pursuit of the institution's authority or success. A Christian critique will try to understand their history and the present needs they exist to serve. We may be allowed to hold up a mirror to those with responsibility to see how much the organisation is serving those needs, rather than its own ends. When powers and institutions are reconciled to God, they become more modest, and take on their proper place in His purposes.

Finding the proper place for an institution in relation to God's purposes will always imply helping other groups and other persons to find their proper place in relation to ourselves. Paul wrote, 'Gentiles and Jews, He has made the two one . . . This was His purpose, to reconcile the two in a single body to God through the Cross.'[21] So a trade union or a school or a firm does not exist simply to serve its own members or shareholders. The call to be reconciled involves its relationship with other bodies and to enable people who are affected by its life to find a valued place in the world.

Christians are called to be reconcilers, bridge people. That will mean repeatedly making the first move towards understanding and staying with those who feel deeply alienated; that will often mean being refuted by suspicion or anger. It may also bring harsh criticisms from those who lay the blame entirely upon the alienated themselves. We shall be accused of being soft and of undermining society. Some may see that as would-be reconcilers they will be attacked from both sides, yet refuse to give up the attempt; they may come to perceive that beneath the will to bring about reconciliation lies the deep experience of the human heart of knowing what it is to be reconciled to God.

CHAPTER ELEVEN

Attitudes to the Poor

Harsh judgments in Britain

A bias to the poor cannot be taken for granted either in the population as a whole or among Christians in particular. In 1977 a report was published by the Commission of the European Communities, following a public opinion survey on attitudes to the poor. The report set out a spectrum of attitudes; it described three categories among those who claimed to have had the opportunity to perceive poverty directly:

Militants for Justice : 10 per cent
Optimists : 11 per cent
Passive : 13 per cent

It then listed four categories of those who did not have the opportunity to perceive poverty from first-hand experience:

Well-intentioned : 39 per cent
Pessimists : 7 per cent
Egoists : 6 per cent
Cynics : 14 per cent

The British had far and away the highest proportion of those categorised as cynics—27 per cent. Those whose opinion was asked were shown a list of nine factors which might lead to poverty, and were asked to choose what were in their opinion the three most common causes; top of the list of British answers were laziness (45 per cent), chronic unemployment (42 per cent) and drink (40 per cent). This was by comparison, for example, with the French answers, which listed old age and loneliness, deprived childhood and ill health, or the German answers, which were deprived childhood, ill health and lack of education.[1]

It may be reasonably supposed that the 'cynics' would not have bought a book entitled *Bias to the Poor* or, if they have borrowed it, that they would not have read as far as this chapter. Nevertheless many Christians are among those who believe that the poor are themselves primarily to blame. Before we go on to look at how good intentions may be translated into effective actions, it is necessary to examine the attitude which blames.

One expression of this attitude came in a letter chiding me for arguing for more resources for the poor; 'I came from the bottom of the pile. By working hard, I have pulled myself and my family up. If it was possible for me, it must be possible for anyone. It's all a question of priorities.' Often the conclusion to a discussion about areas, such as I have described in Liverpool and elsewhere, is 'I blame the parents'. In some cases that would be right, though we should still need to consider what should be done for their children. But in many cases it would be much too shallow simply to blame parents.

A community worker told me that a head teacher said to him one afternoon, that a particular girl's mother just didn't care; 'As it happened, that mother had been in my office that morning, saying, "I can't cope".' A brassy exterior often hides deep feelings of inadequacy. It is unreal to talk about taking responsibility, unless a person has enough of the fragile human commodity which we call self-confidence. If someone has the self-confidence to 'pull themselves up', they should thank God for it, and not blame others who, for varying reasons, have failed where they have succeeded.

This is not to say that poor people are no more than cases with no responsibility for their actions. 'Where a man has been given much, much will be expected of him,' said Jesus.[2] The implication is that where a man has been given little, little will be expected of him. But it would never be right to go on and say that anyone has been given nothing. No one is to be treated as a 'case', as though nothing could be expected of him. The good news for the poor is that Christ meets people where they are; He understands the place where new beginnings are possible. His call to follow Him from that place may be difficult, but it will be realistic.

Blaming, scolding, washing our hands of any responsibility for the poor—these are all ways of avoiding taking a hard look at the kind of society of which we are responsible members. Robert Holman describes the consensus in views held by British governments of different political persuasions; on the whole the economic and social machinery of society is assumed to be working well, providing a tolerable standard of living for most people. A minority of certain families are regarded as the grit in the machine, being unable to use it themselves and causing trouble to other people.[3] Attitudes like this add to the hurts of being poor and its sense of powerlessness; 'People look down on us. A neighbour had a go at me for being on social security.' 'We have to spend so much time going to see officials, DHSS, housing, asking for help, asking for advice. They ask you the same questions over and over again. We feel so ashamed, so low, as if we are beggars.'[4]

Many in Britain object to priority being given to deprived urban areas. Some say these areas should be described as depraved rather than deprived. In the United States there is much antagonism expressed by town and rural America against the big cities; they feel that the streets of the big city are not safe. Urban life seems to offend against all the country's values. Illegitimacy is assumed, not always correctly, to be higher in cities and family life not to be valued. It is alleged that ethnic minorities have been attracted to New York for political advantage by the promise of over-generous welfare benefits. So if New York became bankrupt, it deserved to sink. The truth is that rural America was much more responsible for the landless poor moving to the cities than it cares to acknowledge. Each fresh development of agricultural mechanisation made very large numbers unemployed, especially of black people. Frequently they were given their fare and told to go north to the big cities.

The inner city and the outer estates which developed from it did not create themselves. Its first population was driven there by rural poverty. Then those who achieved well moved out to the suburbs or beyond. Others travelled in to work and took their wealth out of the city. All these are as responsible for what the inner city is today, as are those who now live there. Its needs are a proper charge on national wealth.

The harsh attitudes of the British revealed in the European opinion survey may in part reflect a backlash against the Welfare State. It has been blamed for turning people into scroungers. But that depends on how history is interpreted. Urban and industrial development took place earlier in Britain than in other countries. The older the city, the longer is the history of haphazard charitable relief. I have described elsewhere[5] the pauperising effect of erratic charity at the turn of the century. Relief tickets were available from different committees; Churches, missions and settlements all offered small sources of help if you could argue that you were poor and preferably deserving. The whole degrading process encouraged adults and children to beg and to lie, and cumulatively helped to make the poor believe there was nothing they could do to affect their destiny. In 1945 the concept of National Insurance put the matter of how to offer help without pauperising people on to a healthier basis, so that poor people knew what they were entitled to.

Indifference to the poor or blaming them were attitudes to be seen long before there was a Welfare State. Lord Shaftesbury did not always find that practising Christians were allies in his campaigns on behalf of the poor. He wrote in his diary in 1842, when he was pushing through Parliament the Mines and Collieries Bill, ' "Sinners" were with me, "saints" against me. Strange the contradiction in human nature!'[6]

For Christians the idea of the body is a natural way to think of society as well as of the Church. When Paul spoke of the Church as a body, he was using an analogy which had already been widely used of the body politic by Roman writers. We are 'members one of another'. 'God has combined the various parts of the body, giving special honour to humbler parts, so that there might be no sense of division in the body, but that all its organs might feel the same concern for one another. If one organ suffers, they all suffer together. If one flourishes, they all rejoice together.'[7]

This is the basis on which Christians should give a lead

to a programme of education which would alter attitudes to taxation. To earn all the wealth that can be created, the market economy will not need considerable numbers of the population. Those who are fortunate enough to have demanding and well-paid jobs need to turn away from attitudes of resentment against paying taxes to support the unemployed. Instead they should resent the way in which the poor are given barely enough to survive. The cost of Supplementary Benefit and Family Income Supplement is already very large; it would be an economy to pay more for a sufficient social wage or better for a reasonable wage for alternative work. Then people would be able to help themselves and their neighbours to stand up. The long-term costs to the State would very probably be less.

There is an ambivalence about public attitudes, which is reflected in media campaigns. When there is a tragedy of child neglect or cruelty, the social services are bitterly attacked for not having followed the case more thoroughly. Within a matter of weeks the same newspapers are campaigning against too much public expenditure. The result of public expenditure cuts is to reduce efficiency of the social services.

When Secretary of State for Social Services in 1972, Sir Keith Joseph introduced to the political debate in Britain the idea of 'a cycle of deprivation'. He pointed to a process by which problems reproduced themselves from generation to generation. Some children were doomed to an uphill struggle against the disadvantages of a deprived family background. Many would not be able to overcome the disadvantages, and would become in turn the parents of deprived families.[8]

There are different ways in which a cycle of deprivation is understood. The 'culture of poverty' thesis was first developed by Oscar Lewis in the United States in 1966. He argued that the poor formed a sub-culture with its own values and expectations. These were often at odds with those of the rest of society, and combined to keep them in their impoverished state. Lewis said that such a sub-culture was distinct from people living in poverty; it was 'both the way poor people adapted themselves to, and reacted against a class-stratified, individualistic society'.[9]

Oscar Lewis's books are full of vivid accounts of the lives of individuals and families. He did not look at the effect on the poor of economic and social systems. His writings may have had some influence in directing policies towards low-cost social work, individual training and character reform; the theories about the cycle of deprivation have often turned governments away from more costly programmes of economic and social redistribution.[10]

Anti-poverty programmes

When theories about poverty had to be turned into policies for Government or charitable intervention, a large emphasis was laid on area needs. In the United States the Ford Foundation launched a 'grey areas' programme early in the 1960s. This was the approach of the US Government's War on Poverty, through the Community Action Programmes later in the 1960s. In Britain Educational Priority Areas, the Urban Aid programme, Community Development Projects, Housing Action Areas and Partnership Areas have all attempted to direct aid at areas of multiple deprivation.

Joan Higgins examined the relatively small results of these anti-poverty programmes in the United States and Britain in her book *The Poverty Business*. She argued that the emphasis on pockets of poverty helped create the impression that poverty was not an issue for society at large, but could be confined to these areas and eliminated. Areas of deprivation may certainly be identified, but they often become impoverished as a result of economic forces outside them rather than through the failings of those who live within them. At the same time poor people are to be found in a great many areas in America and Britain. The objective became one of giving opportunities to individuals rather than the guarantee of a minimum income and standard of living for all. Positive discrimination towards strictly limited areas was in effect a way of limiting the amount the State must pay.[11]

The reality of relative poverty has already been described. We manufacture new forms of poverty as the affluent majority constantly drives forward its standards of living. Few people realise what they are doing to those who see them, but cannot keep up.[12]

In terms of job opportunities or the housing market the success and growth in areas which are already wealthy keeps investment away from areas of deprivation.[13] The strong grow stronger and the weak grow weaker unless there are deliberate and tough government policies to redirect resources towards the neediest areas.

President Reagan has stressed that his economic policies have been aimed at making the whole country wealthier. He told black people that his economic package would help to achieve black economic freedom, because it was aimed at lifting an entire country and not just parts of it. But areas of deprivation soon discovered they were only to benefit in the long term, and if dogmatic theories of the free market worked out. The package included huge cuts in Government spending, aimed largely at welfare and social programmes and at a reduction of 25 per cent in taxation over three years. President Reagan said that black people had become progressively worse off during the 1970s despite all the Government programmes designed to uplift them. He claimed that a strong economy returned the greatest good to the black population. It would return a benefit greater than that provided by specific federal programmes.[14]

That would depend on black people's having a full share of opportunities in the most successful parts of the economy; whereas a disproportionate number are unemployed or are in areas where the economy is growing weaker. The history of Britain and the USA does not show that the poor received a sufficient share when either country was the most prosperous in the world with a booming economy. Not surprisingly the President's speech to the black audience of the National Association for the Advancement of Coloured People was not received with any enthusiasm. There was politeness and occasional scattered applause.

The assumption is widely made in both countries that we have poured money into deprived urban areas. This is usually claimed about money for welfare benefits, which ignores the massively unequal opportunities provided for the successful in higher education and skills training in more flourishing areas. These have decisive influence on whether people stay poor or not. The long-term target is not to have generous welfare benefits, but sufficient resources in each community for it to develop its own strengths. Policies which brought that about would be very much more costly to the affluent.

The most dramatic attempt to use public money to help the poor was President Johnson's War on Poverty, declared in 1964. Its history shows up some of the problems involved in government funding for needy areas. The Community Action Programme had been intended to be confined to ten or twenty urban and rural areas. Federal money would make a significant contribution to the total available resources of the community. The idea of such a pilot programme was swept away by the 'total war on poverty' of Sargent Shriver, the Director of the Office of Economic Opportunity. Shriver spoke of the objective of abolishing poverty within a decade. He reflected President Johnson's great expectations. The President wanted action not planning, wanted nationwide scope not pilot schemes. He wanted black people to get something fast, without in the process alarming white people. There was soon very little life left in the plan to pick ten cities and spend several years preparing for the experiment. [15]

Political reality had much to do with this. Outbreaks of violence occurred in 1964 in eight cities. They were followed in 1965 by the riots in Watts, Los Angeles, in which thirty-four people died, hundreds were injured and four thousand arrested. The relationship between which cities had riots and which received Federal Government money has been a matter of dispute. But it made it even more difficult to concentrate large public funds on a strictly limited number of areas. Whatever the reasons, the money was spread very widely. One example was that Sargent Shriver wrote 35,000 letters to local officials concerned with children, inviting them to encourage needy families to enrol their children in Operation Head Start. The demand for places far outstripped the number available. The response from the supposedly apathetic poor was over-whelming and Head Start's budget was quickly increased from $17 million to $103 million for 1965.

Even this scale of expenditure was scanty in proportion to the problems they were tackling (though it was much greater than all previous public spending) and it was not sustained for very long. Of the two large programmes the Community Action Programme had its budget substantially reduced in 1967 after only two years of operating. By 1974 both it and the later Model Cities Programme were being phased out. Those expecting immediate results became disillusioned; the advent of the Nixon Administration in 1969 with less sympathy for 'participation of the poor' and the escalating war in Vietnam both influenced the rundown of the programmes, though some resources were transferred with continuing programmes.

The programmes were allocated sums of money which were not equal to tackling the grandiose objectives which were spoken about. The US Government spent far more on the poverty programmes than did the British Government. But, when they began, the United States was spending a considerably smaller proportion on social welfare than Britain and the rest of Europe. Even so, when compared with other priorities in spending, the resources were not large, and should never have been described as pouring money into deprived areas. The 1967 budget of $1.7 billion for the War on Poverty should be compared with annual expenditure of $3.2 billion on cosmetics, $17.4 billion on tobacco and alcohol, $2.8 billion on TV commercials and $75 billion on defence.[16]

In Britain the Urban Programme, including the Community Development Project, was launched in May 1968. There has been dispute about what led to its launching at that moment. The Labour Government was having a bad year. Four by-elections were lost in March. On 9 April the controversial Race Relations Bill was published, and on 20 April Enoch Powell made his 'Rivers of Blood' speech about dangers of coloured immigration. It is almost inconceivable that, when the Prime Minister, Harold Wilson, made his May Day speech in Birmingham, he did not have some of these difficulties in mind. He announced the Urban Programme with the Community Development Programme as one of its parts. Here were some positive steps to tackle urban problems, which were associated in many people's minds with coloured immigration.

The Urban Programme has continued as an extremely useful way of giving capital sums to statutory, voluntary and community organisations. In terms of national budget it is a modest programme. Other projects such as the Community Development Project, Educational Priority Area Programme and the Inner Areas Study were action research programmes. They were based on the hope that, if the facts about poverty were made widely known, change would follow. This hope is a fundamental misconception. It assumes that governments have failed to pursue change, because they lacked the essential information upon which to base their actions. We know a great deal about poverty, but have lacked the will to eradicate it. The point has been well made that governments should consider acting upon the research evidence they already have, before commissioning more.[17]

The claim that money has been poured into particular needy areas has often been asserted about Toxteth. Surprisingly the evidence does not support the assertion. A very careful study was made by the Inner Areas Study, set up by the Conservative Secretary of State for the Environment, Peter Walker. The Liverpool part of the study was in Area D (part of Liverpool 7 and part of Liverpool 8), including the areas where the 1981 riots later took place. The Inner Areas Study team made a careful study of the possibilities of area management within the city. They therefore examined revenue and cost very closely. They did not discover that any disproportionate funds had been poured in; the final report in 1977 showed that the resources put into the area were about the same as the average for the whole city.[18] Those figures are extremely surprising and disturbing, because it has never been disputed that this is an area of multiple and extreme deprivation.

In spite of the criticisms which can be levelled at lack of progress, the continuing involvement of central Government in inner city areas has been good and important. One of the problems is that concentrating on areas of particular deprivation may starve other areas, whose needs are very great, of resources. As this book has set out to show, the needs of outer area corporation estates, in which many inner city people live, are often quite as intense as those of the inner city itself. Their

183

more modern housing should not prevent them from being included in urban priority areas. Richard Titmuss in 1968 defended area policies of positive discrimination; they should not be a substitute for universalist social services. A more adequate safety net should be consistently provided for the many, while giving extra help to the few.[19]

Looked at from within such areas, Government funding has often seemed very erratic. Policies which will help lastingly in a city need ten years or more. Three-year projects (the time limit often placed by Government or charitable trusts) are sometimes only long enough to raise hopes and emphasise the letdown when they come to an end. Changes of administration in local or national government have added to changes of fashion in the kind of projects which are favoured. Frequently one party insists on reversing what its opponents had just got under way when they left office.

Government departments are often out of step with one another. For example, when the 1981 riots in Toxteth were the subject of a government announcement the following day, attention was drawn to the Inner City Partnership arrangement with Liverpool, costing £17 million a year, and the newly established Merseyside Development Corporation, costing another £17 million a year. This sounded like substantial money. To make clear what was happening between national Government and Liverpool, another figure should have been included. Cutbacks in the Rate Support Grant given to local authorities, and adjustments in how it was divided between cities and other areas, meant that in 1981 Liverpool received £14.5 million less. One hand seemed to be taking away what the other was giving.

The Secretary of State for Health and Social Services had fought in the Cabinet to prevent cuts in the social services. It was claimed that nationally there was no reduction of social workers in the field. But Liverpool City Council had to make cuts somewhere in order to stay within Government spending limits. The result was that over two years Liverpool had effectively abolished fifty out of three hundred field posts. This meant that social workers increasingly had to concentrate on emergencies rather than preventive work; for example, adoption cases were delayed for months, and rehabilitation of children in residential care was put off. That could mean a child deteriorating mentally; and it could lead to a great increase in cost both in paying for longer residential care and in human suffering.

Different parcels of Government money are earmarked for different purposes. For example the Liverpool Inner City Partnership Committee decided to concentrate its resources largely on efforts to regenerate industry, as it is likely the Merseyside Development Corporation will also do. The Inner City Partnership aims at long-term benefit; it is right though to question whether this programme is tackling structural factors. Preparing sites for manufacturing industry, building advance factories for small firms and providing seed money for firms to set up and expand are marginal to the processes of the national economy; such processes involve the decline of traditionally important industries, the impact of labour-shedding technology and the search by capital for more profitable investment in other areas.[20]

Even if it is not going to change the structures of the economy, help in the regeneration of industry is a proper medium-term Government intervention in an old city like Liverpool. But cutbacks in the Rate Support Grant mean that some of the needs, more immediately felt by inner city people, are not being met. Renewal of the inner city should ensure that there is adequate housing for the many young families, who want to stay in the areas where they have grown up, to be able to do so. The continuing drain away of young people from many inner city areas is tragic. They feel that new factories are more likely to import their existing personnel, and because of new technology to employ fewer but more skilled workers.[21]

Those who work in inner city and outer corporation estate areas have to spend quite an amount of energy in keeping services steady in the face of some erratic changes in fashion and policy. It would be possible to write an underground history of the city; this would show the same workers continuing to serve the same people; in response to fashions of Government funding some would be settlement staff, then youth workers, youth and community workers, community

185

development workers, neighbourhood project group workers, supervisors on Manpower Services Commission temporary programmes. Some would go on Social Security and continue to serve the same people, until new funds and jobs emerged.

Three-year funding for a project, arbitrary changes in policy with a new administration, cutbacks or threats of cutbacks in times of recession, sudden expansion requiring funds to be spent within two or three months before the financial year ended—all of these drain the energies of the staff in both statutory and voluntary organisations; they often reduce morale to a very low level. The philosophy of one city's chief executive is that of a man with a surfboard. He waits for each new wave, and gains as much momentum as it will give him. As soon as it has run out of force, he looks out for the next wave to catch.

Self help in family and community

Help from outside fails if it simply gives adequate welfare benefit. A floor of support for the poorest needs to be firmly provided. Then resources should be directed to enable family and community to help themselves. Some have enough self-confidence to lift themselves whatever their surroundings. But most human beings need support and have always needed it. In Bible days and in rural and town society that support has been found in the family. Before the twentieth century the family was nowhere thought of simply as two parents and their own children. The extended family accepted obligations, especially when death or disaster struck. Just round the corner there was someone to come to the rescue. In the large Corporation estates built round the edge of a city like Liverpool grandmothers and other relations are no longer there. Costs of public transport make it harder to maintain close links.

The extended family not only came to the rescue in times of death or disaster but also in finding a job or helping to bring up the children. In many estates today the proportion of single-parent families is very high; often they have no family support within reasonable reach. The extended family often contained trouble; for example, it is doubtful whether there is more wife-battering than there was in previous generations. Only previously there were relations near enough to turn to. Now professional social workers are summoned. Instead of being dealt with within the family, it becomes a statistic. The terraced street in some urban areas was a kind of extended family. In Garston, Liverpool, it is claimed that there was in every street 'a woman who knew', to whom you could turn for advice. On estates like Speke, to which many Garston families moved, that kind of support has often disappeared.

The State provides a comprehensive level of services for those in need. But there are families who have very complicated and tangled problems. Individuals within these families become candidates for help from all the social and welfare authorities. Only a very inadequate family needs contact with so many people; only an adequate family could cope with all those visitors and agencies. This is the point at which more specialist voluntary bodies such as the Family Service Unit can offer extensive time, serving the neediest as family units.

It would not be possible to bring back the whole pattern of the extended family. Nor is it truthful to be entirely romantic about it. Many have left small towns or villages, in order to escape from the sense of being suffocated by what the extended family expected of them. Indeed the dependence of rural people on the family just round the corner has often left them very ill-equipped, when they have faced the bewildering pace and complexities of a big city largely on their own.

Instead of lamenting a pattern of life, much of which has disappeared from city life, we need to ask what God's best purpose is today for the family and its support. Some claim that the basic unit of society should no longer be the small nuclear family, but the individual. It is a proper Christian instinct to launch a counter-attack on behalf of the family. Individuals carry deep wounds and insecurities within them. Most of all it is in the atmosphere of trust fostered by life-long commitment of married partners that personal healing and growth can take place.[22] Such a partnership offers the firmest base to children.

One in three marriages breaks down. That reality must be faced along with determined support for marriage relationships. Partners are widowed or deserted. They need the kind of support which the extended family offered for thousands of years. So do the most loving of married couples. The small family often attempts to carry burdens and pressures which God never intended they should bear alone. We must re-establish the obligations which the extended family itself can still fulfil. And we should go on to ask what is God's counter-part to the extended family, where that no longer exists. In a modern city we can find supporting networks in community groups, groups at work, leisure interest groups, Church groups. We must refuse to join in the fatalism of remarks like 'There's no sense of community round here'.

Community spirit has to be worked for. Some important skills have been learned in community work. It was a true instinct which led anti-poverty programmes to look for 'maximum feasible participation' in the United States and Community Development in Britain. Joan Higgins questions whether this had any useful place in anti-poverty programmes. She says that it raised expectations that would not be fulfilled and, for example, told the homeless they could not have a house, but could sit on a committee which hoped to liberalise local housing policy.[23]

Attempts at community development have been criticised for frustrating and threatening these practical schemes of help. The pressure to get things done frequently brushes consultation on participation on one side as a luxury which cannot be afforded. But if the professionals treat others as peasants, they must not be surprised if they fail to take up what is provided, or oppose good plans because of irrational fears. The vicious circle of 'we' and 'they' defeats many good plans. It will only be broken down if people come to believe they have some stake in what is being decided.

The real change agents in inner city areas, as anywhere else, are going to be local people. They will not immediately possess some of the organising skills which have become associated with leadership. Some clergy and head teachers in an area undergoing clearance and renewal said that there were no leaders there. The response of a community work organiser was, 'What a cheek saying that.' Out of a public meeting came a group of twelve local people prepared to take on responsibilities; the organiser stayed with that group for a year.

Government programmes to provide training in areas of long-term unemployment bring together two worlds. This was highlighted in a conversation between a very able manager, determined to offer what help he could, and an equally able leader in the black community. His approach could well have been that of a leader in white community groups in areas where those who are successful in the brisk world of business have long since moved away. It was an honest attempt at meeting; on one side stood a world in which managers have been trained to move quickly and efficiently from A to B. On the other side was a world in which experience has taught community leaders to keep moving on a roundabout, determined to see that as few as possible fall off. Both groups need each other if the whole community is to develop as it could.

The manager described his frustration at a meeting he had attended; he had arrived five minutes early. Others went on arriving until an hour later. He immediately asked who was to chair the meeting, and who was to act as secretary. The black leader chuckled at the description and in turn described many meetings he had attended. At the first meeting of a group people would be asked what they wanted to talk about. Everyone would express their particular concerns. Perhaps it would need several meetings before a consensus emerged, for example, that they wanted to look at the possibility of sponsoring a project for unemployed people. No chairman would be appointed immediately. Perhaps he or she would emerge as the person who insisted that the group gave a hearing to those whose voices were repeatedly drowned. He said that if a vote was taken too quickly, there should be no surprise if those who felt their opinion had not been heard failed to turn up at subsequent meetings. If the subject was approached unhurriedly, the need for a disciplined approach and the inclusion of those with business skills would emerge from within the circle.

How to bring into partnership the drive of those who are determined to get from A to B and the patience of those who keep as many as possible on the roundabout of debate and decision-making is one of the central arts of city government.

To take community development approaches seriously will mean approaching many projects more slowly. But it is not some modern gimmick. It sets out to correct some of the mistakes which have been made, especially in big cities. There has been too much dominant leadership from outside the local community, providing people with facilities they did not ask for.

Professional and local leadership

Professionals still have some very important roles to play. They can help to arm emerging leaders with skills; they can hold a group to the task which it has agreed to tackle, when there are delays and disappointments. They can give the encouragement which helps people over the hurdle of self-confidence. If some organisation is appropriate, they can stimulate people to consider how best they can set it up; they can remind a group of the need to review both what has been done and what are present needs.[24]

Non-directive leadership stands for an important truth—respect for people's ability to think and act for themselves. It should not mean that such a leader never offers his own convictions, or that in all circumstances he refuses to take a lead himself. That can cause bewilderment to those who have been used to a firmer lead. The long-term objective must be to enable local people to develop enough self-confidence to take much greater responsibility for their own destiny. The greatest temptation to the professional leader will be to cut the knot and run things himself. But he does not have to become simply an enabling eunuch with no opinions of his own. Staying a long time in a situation helps the professional leader to learn when it is right to respond to what he is asked to do, and when it is right to insist that local people work matters out for themselves.

A community work organiser in Kirkdale, Liverpool was faced in 1969 with an area about to undergo clearance and renewal over a ten-year period. The main objective she set herself was to help maintain morale in the community, and to promote all that was possible to minimise the effects of uncertainty and change which demolition and new development bring. She stayed for most of the ten years; that continuity, when so many other local authority workers, local leaders and volunteers were on the move, was an important factor in achieving a substantial part of the main objective. At first ten years seemed an eternity. The whole programme had to be broken down into day-to-day activity; then the idea of monthly cycles of meetings of all kinds was followed by an appreciation of planning for the future. Relevant information had to be discovered and made known in comprehensible terms. There needed to be effective negotiation between residents and Local Authority officers and politicians for an acceptable style of programming for change.[25] Some local people at last began to believe there would be a future, and that they could have a stake in determining what sort of future that would be.

Liverpool Diocesan Synod set up a working party on Urban Priority Areas to make recommendations for strengthening the Church in these areas, that they may worship and witness more effectively. One of the recommendations the working party made in its report in 1982 was that clergy should be trained in awareness of different styles of leadership; they should learn to identify potential in terms of what people have to offer, rather than what Church structures demand.[26] The working party recognised that clergy must take their share of the blame in denying responsibility to local people in Urban Priority Areas. This change was put vividly by Ian Fraser: 'All over Europe we ordained are like a vast oil slick, persuading ourselves that we keep the seas safe for the traffic of humanity, but in fact keeping the sun from the fish.'[27]

This charge has to be taken seriously. But it should lead us to say that clergy should be more and not less professional in the best sense of that word. For example, some do not want to see chaplains in industry, because they believe their presence will deny responsibility to lay people. Such critics may have seen clergy failing to understand their professional role. God gave gifts and callings to be 'apostles, prophets, evangelists, pastors and teachers, to equip God's people for work in His service'.[28] There was always the danger that clergy would keep all the work in God's service in their own hands. But the task they were given was to equip God's people to do the work in God's service.

Bernard Shaw said that all professions were a conspiracy against the laity. There is a special danger of entering into this conspiracy for clergy working in areas where they are the only resident professional people. It follows that they need to develop highly professional skills and attitudes to know how to enable and support local responsibility. That sort of ordained person is not going to keep the sun away from the fish. To argue that Church and community would flourish in inner city areas if only all the professional workers went away, would be to accept that the human race was irredeemably divided by class barriers. Earlier in this book I wrote about clergy of different denominations who firmly believe that local leadership can and should emerge. Local people have been encouraged to tell their own story, to share in decision-making, and to take a lead both in Church organisations and in the life of the wider community.

Old attitudes expect that a Church presence or a Christian involvement necessarily means a clergyman being there. A Neighbourhood Council held its Annual General Meeting in inner city Liverpool. A young Roman Catholic priest was present; it was the first time he had been to a meeting of the Neighbourhood Council. Old attitudes went into action, and he found himself elected chairman. A priest who had known the area for many years told me, 'We got to him the next day and persuaded him to withdraw.' They had been working for years to encourage local people to take charge of their own organisations.

Community development has come under fire in recent years. It is said, often by city councillors who feel unfairly attacked, that community groups make false claims that they alone represent local feelings; they are accused of being self-appointed leaders. It is asked how 'grass-roots people' can be expected to understand complex planning matters. In addition community development is accused of raising false hopes and of promoting false conflict.

It is foolish for any community group to claim that they alone speak with an authentically local voice. For how local is local? A Member of Parliament is a local representative; so is a county councillor or a city councillor. And so is a spokesman of an action group or a tenants' association.

A city both is and is not a chain of villages. Decisions about roads, for example, intimately affect particular neighbourhoods through which they pass. City planners and politicians can ignore needs for a good environment of a neighbourhood which has no political muscle, while concerning themselves with the transport needs of businesses and commuters. But it is not as simple as if the neighbourhood was a village standing by itself. It is in the interests of the whole 'travel-to-work area' of a city and especially of inner city people to see jobs regenerated in the inner city. Good access on fast roads is going to make a significant difference to whether firms stay or leave. No neighbourhood group is likely to vote for a motorway going through its streets: a city or county council is better placed to balance the conflicting needs of industry and of each neighbourhood, provided it gives proper weight to the local arguments.

Decisions have to be taken at the appropriate level. When that is the level of city or county, politicians and officers need to make sure that they have listened in all possible ways to those who have less muscle. City Council chambers should be places where the language of a bias to the poor is not forgotten. There are genuine difficulties about discovering who are the most authentic representatives of a community and what method will be the best way of hearing what is felt.

Following the Toxteth riots in July 1981, Liverpool City Council delivered a questionnaire to every household in the area. It asked for written answers about what local people most wanted. The method of written answers to a questionnaire is familiar to those who have some confidence in the powers-that-be and are not daunted by filling in forms. It is a good way of communication for them. For those who are more alienated from the world of offices and town halls it is a method of communication which was bound to be dismissed as window dressing. The response rate varied greatly. In the sub-area in which elsewhere in this book I characterised many people as 'good working-class', the response rate was

68.9 per cent. In the sub-area where alienation might have been expected to be greatest, the rate was 35.4 per cent. It was rightly agreed that other methods were needed in addition, where groups could be listened to on their own ground and in their own way.[29]

The actions of some hotheads should not discredit community or neighbourhood groups. A city which is alive and sometimes boiling with indignation is healthier than one in which dumb apathy sits down under decisions which others have made at a distance. Dismissing those who have not been elected through the ballot box as self-appointed leaders ignores the problems which all minority groups have about making their voice heard. So long as they remain in a minority in a district, they can never expect their representatives to win in 'first past the post' elections. But their voice needs to be heard. Community groups can help those who have long felt powerless and voiceless to find a voice. It is not to be wondered at that the first response is that of an angry and negative voice, blocking city council plans.

Moving from negative criticism to acting as those who have a stake in the decisions of a city is a difficult and sometimes frightening step to take. The pressures on local leaders who are new to public responsibility are intense.[30] If they don't deliver the goods quickly, which a protest demands, they become the objects of opposition and gossip. Resignations occur frequently. When some people start to be consulted by 'the establishment', because they seem to be more responsible, they are quickly outflanked by other leaders who make tougher demands. Some put so much emphasis on having a mandate from their own community that they shrink from ever standing up to their own people. Rivalry between different community groups, often because they are competing for limited grants, has taken too much of their leaders' energy. Significant steps forward have been taken when different community groups have combined to sponsor a project.

The greatest enemy to both town hall and community leaders is the apathy of so many urban dwellers. They criticise city councillors and community leaders alike as 'them', and at the same time resent any claim that is made on them to enter into sharing some responsibility. If some are willing to risk sticking their necks out, the prize of an increasing community involvement is worth the price of lengthy consultations by local government officers and councillors. Adult education can provide one of the vital links in the chain by helping local people to develop skills which are needed to take an effective part in consultation.

The Community Development Programme in Britain and the Community Action Programme in the United States were both attempts to act as go-betweens for the town hall and local residents. Many who served in these programmes felt torn in half, wanting on the one hand to be a spokesman for the poor, and on the other to be a servant of established authority. The attempt to build such a bridge was painful. But it was a proper attempt; disaffection between those who are governed and those who govern spells serious danger to democracy.

Some looked to Community Development or Community Action as a central way of salvation for cities. They have been deeply disappointed. Others have seen these programmes and philosophies as letting loose dangerous and anarchic forces. My attempt at a Christian critique is that we should always have been more modest about what they could have been expected to achieve; but they stand for ideas about the ordering of society, which Christians should support. All people are made in the image of God; all should be able to share in making choices which affect their destiny.

Different objectives are looked for from community development; generally they have one of two purposes: the first approach sees participation in community groups or self-help schemes as a contribution to social health, by restoring a lost sense of community involvement and belonging. The second approach sets out in addition to that first objective the strengthening of the voice of the local community; it assumes rightly that deprived communities are ultimately the product of the competition between different interest groups in society for shares of scarce resources—houses, jobs, education, social services. When there are fears that this is revolutionary talk, it is worth recalling that when people know they have a stake in society they are more likely to work for order in that society.

Enabling participation to happen in a large city is a skill which will take a great deal of perseverance on all sides to master. The experiment of democracy is to bring about change by consent, and not to give up when it is realised that it involves complexity, conflict or delay. When planners or city councillors go with a genuine intention to consult, they are often taking the lid off a cauldron, boiling with frustration, that is sometimes generations old. They are also confronted with disillusionment, because people feel they have previously been offered participation, only to discover later that this was never being offered.

Politicians should not shrink from the conflict of a lively debate. It is true that some community groups have become locked into attitudes which always take up conflict positions. That has sometimes prevented any plans from emerging. But we risk far greater conflicts than we have known for centuries, if large groups of the population continue to feel totally left out of planning which deeply affects their futures.

If people in urban priority areas are led to believe that the sky is the limit for changes they can help bring about, they are victims of a cruel hoax. God's way of bringing about change was and is through the Incarnation; taking flesh in a particular community at a particular time, accepting that limits were imposed by the realities of that situation. At the same time the way of Incarnation does not sit down under the forces which dehumanise; it takes firm hold of the potential for good in a community as well as acknowledging the realities of evil. The way of Incarnation does not promise majority movements rolling forward in triumph; it faces apparent failure, real suffering. But failure and suffering become the raw material out of which lasting values in individual and community life can be fashioned. The way of Incarnation brings with it the promise of resurrection beyond the suffering. That is about a world beyond this one; it is also proper for the poor to ask for some signs of resurrection now. Flickers of hope help to keep Christians from giving up; they should also make us tough advocates in insisting that better opportunities actually become available.

This way of Incarnation has a highly realistic message for

196

urban communities. Many children at school now will live out their lives in urban priority areas. All the limitations which those areas impose will not be swept away in their lifetime. But education should inspire young people to understand their own potential and to think boldly about how to bring about change, rather than lapse into resigned apathy.[31] It should be about enabling people made in the image of God to be transforming rather than adaptive beings.[32] Community action needs an approach which does what you can with what you have.[33] Those community programmes which recognise the limitations of their surroundings—the resources available, the numbers of people willing to be involved, the size of the problem—have had the greatest successes.

There is a sense in which we have to cater for failure, while insisting that the vision of the City of God, which is to come, is not lost. Catering for failure would include accepting that:–

There are not going to be enough high-earning and interesting jobs for everyone.

There will not be sufficient resources to build the best housing for everyone in one five-year plan.

There will not be active participation of the majority in community, political or Church groups. (To put it another way, Apathy Rules.)

There will be bad managers; the poor will always be with us, but need not be treated as criminals.

It is easier for community groups to raise support for negative protest than for joining in making positive plans.

Good information about bad experiences of poverty will not be enough to bring about action. The conscience of the nation has often been stirred momentarily by a shock report or by riots, only to be lulled to sleep again within weeks.

Beside that list, some achievable objectives should be set out; it would be a worthwhile achievement if

The Government determined to intervene, to prevent investment in areas which are already more affluent, until and unless firms invest in priority areas; and provided nationally an adequate social wage; this should include the provision of genuine tasks to be done in the community when the market has no jobs to offer.

Housing repairs and transfers were efficiently done.

Authorities, whether housing, transport or police, regularly and normally consulted in the most appropriate way with as many local people as were willing to participate.

There were access for poor people to receive the best available legal advice and service.

Those living on social security payments had more clearly understood rights.

Community groups had sufficient funds for the training of leaders and for making their views known.

Schools and adult education encouraged people to learn how to use all the existing channels of democracy. Sufficient political will to bring about long-term change will only be generated by determined and persistent campaigning.

Such limited objectives can easily be portrayed as falling far short of the vision of the City of God. But if they were achieved, inner city people would know that a great deal had changed and that they had played an important part in it. Meanwhile the day of small things must not be scorned. Community festivals offer local people the opportunity to celebrate the talents and the sense of belonging which is theirs. When opportunities to take responsible leadership are genuinely offered to local people in community groups, parents' bodies, youth clubs, Churches, some dare to step forward from communities who feel they have been denied any say for generations. A parish priest said of such emergent leaders, 'I'm watching people painfully trying to work this out, willing to make fools of themselves. There is frequent failure. Groups fall apart. But, for example, instead of seeing the local councillor as a saviour (and blaming him for every failure) they see him as an individual strictly limited by his circumstances.' He tries to make a regular point of naming such community leaders in the Liturgy, whether in intercessions, in preaching or in notices. The British pastime of denigrating politicians and running down community leaders is a very damaging one. These are high callings; we need to encourage many more people to serve in these ways and to recognise the pressures faced by those who already do so.

If self help became increasingly possible in poorer families and community groupings, that would offer some resurrection signs now. The failure and the suffering will continue. We know that. It would make a difference if there were a new sense of acknowledging all round that the problems of poverty are *our* problems.

Taking a hard look at the realities of what society offers its poor is part of the way of the Incarnation. It will also recognise the potential for good in every community. And it will call each of us to enter into some of the failure and the suffering, and not to give up when faced with the complexities and cost of bringing about change in urban life.

CHAPTER TWELVE

Can the Church Bear Good News to the Poor?

This book has raised great and complex issues. The more the situation of the urban poor is understood, the more it becomes plain that questions are being asked about the whole of society. It may seem like an anticlimax to finish with a chapter about what the Church could be. Yet Christianity's claims have been that beginnings as insignificant as a mustard seed may come to influence the whole world.[1] The astonishing statement is made that through the Church the wisdom of God in all its varied forms might be made known to the rulers and authorities in the realms of heaven.[2] The Church is to be the place where signs of God's Kingdom can be seen, and where there are flickers of hope.

The poor have a deep instinct that Jesus is on their side, but they are not so sure about the Church. It is seen to be kindly, especially in serving the elderly and the children. But to the poor it seems to be primarily for the settled and successful, and unwilling to stand for justice on behalf of the poor if its own security might be threatened.

One deep question underlying this book is about the credibility of the love of God in a suffering world. This world is indeed a vale of tears. The poor do not demand that all those tears should be stopped before they will believe. They do expect to see some signs that validate the great promises about the coming of the Kingdom of God.

That was how it was in the Gospels. John the Baptist, lying in prison, desperately trying not to lose his faith, sent a message to Jesus, 'Are you the one who is to come, or are we to expect some other?' 'Go and tell John what you have seen and heard,' came Jesus's reply. 'How the blind recover their sight, the lame walk, the lepers are made clean, the deaf hear, the dead are raised to life, the poor are hearing the good news.'[3] No total victory yet swept all before it. But there were signs of God's Kingdom for those with eyes to see. Broken lives were being mended; those who had never counted before were hearing the good news.

Sometimes people took what they could get from Jesus, without seeing anything to make them stop and think. After the miracle of the feeding of the five thousand, a great crowd followed Him. He said, 'I know that you have not come looking for me because you saw signs, but because you ate the bread and your hunger was satisfied.'[4]

People will take God's servants for a ride today, satisfied to take what they can get from us, as they did from Jesus. What matters is whether those who have eyes to see are presented with authentic signs of God's Kingdom, when they are confronted by the Church. If that is to happen, we need to be the kind of Church, which

Stays present in the neediest areas and continues to believe and worship.

Recognises, develops and supports local ability within the Church and outside it.

Serves people where they are.

Tries to understand, and obey the word of God for both rich and poor.

A believing and worshipping presence

First we need to be the kind of Church which stays present in the neediest areas and continues to believe and worship. Sheer survival takes much courage in areas where the rate of collapse of community projects is extremely high. Often a small remnant clings on doggedly to the activities which have been handed down. Sometimes they keep the busy round of services and meetings, clubs and sales of work without asking what their purpose is.

It also takes a great deal of resilience for clergy and their families to survive. It is not easy to guard the vision. Yet without a vision of the living Lord, active and loving in that place, we give people a stone when they ask for bread.

When we realise that all is not as it should be, we are frequently tempted to look in the direction of reorganisation; we want to make the Church an efficient, problem-solving organisation. Looking at the confusing and destructive forces of great cities means facing more than a series of problems. Here are mysteries—the mystery of evil, which is so deeply embedded both in individuals and in society, and the marvellous mystery that the crucified and risen Lord continues to be present. We want to reduce the mysteries to a series of problems, which we can then pronounce solved or explained. It is true that there are problems which are within our grasp; we must be willing to spend ourselves in solving them. But as we try to serve people, we know we become out of our depth. We are still confronted with mystery, something bigger than ourselves.

One of the important contributions the Charismatic Renewal Movement has brought into all the main historic Churches is a spirit of expectancy in worship. There is a danger that this leads worshippers to shop around places of worship in search of excitement and entertainment. Sometimes they withdraw into motor-car distance fellowship made up of 'our kind of people', often also of the same age group. That is a withdrawal from God's call to Christians to serve those who may not fit in with our ways, to be a Church for all the people. The historic Churches need to be open to the longings of many young people like this. For they will slumber on until death, without the enthusiasm and the excitement of young Christians who believe that Jesus is alive and His spirit is with them.[5] Alan Ecclestone writes that the root sin is indolence of heart.[6] We are to come to worship single-mindedly, expecting to catch the vision of God. There is a balance to be held in our worship between the transcendence and the immanence of God. God is both beyond all our imaginings and He is near, intimately involved in our world. Some attempts to meet young people's needs have brought a casual familiarity which has lost the wonder and the greatness of God. But poor people in urban life are much more likely to believe that God is infinitely distant from them and all their doings.

If we ask what will call them to worship, we know it will no longer be fear. For many people, it is the sense that He comes to us through the life we live every day. He values and notices the actions and attitudes which affect many lives. In prayers, preaching, notices in Church services there should be frequent mentions of experiences, events and people in the local community. It is the 'feel' that Christ has to do with this world, as much as precise words, that is needed. When we lift up our hearts, it is to the Lord who has triumphed and triumphs still in this world by self-sacrifice, by making the first move, by enduring through suffering. When He does this through the daily lives of His people, we see acts which transcend our materialist, calculating world. We can't explain the selfless act which risks a person's reputation or their profit. We can only wonder, and believe that God is at work.

Worship gives us eyes to see. It should not all be words. We must learn to involve people in acting out a story or in dance or perhaps in a family bringing forward the bread and wine. Different gifts of the artist, the technician, the musician, the singer, the dancer, the flower arranger, the planner may involve many people beyond the clergy. Music, colour and silence should be part of worship as well as words. Involving members in planning and preparation means that clergy and lay people have to give worship a higher priority in their time.

On holiday my wife and I worshipped two Sundays running in two small villages. The service was Holy Communion from the Book of Common Prayer, 1662. There were no hymns and no address. No one took any vocal part except the vicar. It set me wondering what it is that has made this service so much loved in some churches. The most striking characteristic seemed to be that it is a very private service. No one need intrude on your personal devotions. All the more modern rites of every Church need the worshipper to enter into a corporate act. If he's unwilling to do so, the service will fall flat on its face. But the Eucharist was a corporate act in the earliest days, and this has rightly been restored. Certainly in urban working-class areas where the corporate sense of belonging is very strong, it is all gain to use forms of worship which encourage as many as possible to participate.

The Church is called both to be a sign of the coming Kingdom of God and to draw attention to signs of God's presence.
We have often limited the places where we have looked for
such signs to Church activities. In doing so we have helped to
blind people to the God who is already present in the midst of
the city. It is as though we have been aiming the frame of our
camera only at the piety which involves churchgoing or at the
morality we have always linked with Church people. In doing
so we have failed to see that the living God is already active
among other people in other ways. It makes all the difference
for those who find it hard to keep on believing to be able to see
signs. Here are some signs of God's presence which are to be
seen in the most disadvantaged areas of Merseyside:

A community's ability to catch up spontaneous moments in
celebration at a festival.

Self-sacrifice and the sheer will to survive of a mother,
insisting on values for her children, when other parents have
given up.

A youth leader being repeatedly let down, but always coming
back for more.

Church people and other volunteers regularly visiting the
elderly and handicapped, whether they are thanked or not.

Breaking down of old barriers between Protestant and
Catholic, so that congregations as well as clergy start to
know each other and join hands in a project.

Indignation and persistence of community leaders when
people's real needs are ignored.

Willingness of local government officers to hear angry
criticisms and their determination to make bureaucracy
serve the real interests of people.

A teacher's imagination and refusal to accept failure.

Fairmindedness under extreme pressure of a good policeman.

Reconcilers who bear the anger from both sides in a dispute
without giving up.

Generosity of time and cash in helping a family which faces
tragedy and giving to the poor in another area or country.

Resilience and wit of those who have refused to allow repeated disappointments to sour their minds.

Growing ability to live with mystery instead of insisting on clear-cut answers to everything.

There is plenty to make pessimists of us all in urban priority areas; but such signs can be seen every day. They bring the flickers of hope we need. A television interviewer was talking to the Rector of Kirkby, who had been speaking of hope. 'You are optimistic then?' asked the interviewer. 'I didn't say that,' said the Rector. 'I said that I am full of hope.'

Clergy and Church lay workers are the only professional people who are required today to live in the area which they serve. This gives them great opportunities of understanding how people feel. It also puts heavy strains on them and on married partners and families. In a number of corporation estate parishes it is not safe to leave the vicarage empty for one night. In some it is not possible to leave it empty for an hour in the daytime.

The Church owes them the very best support it can offer. I am not here setting out to write a Handbook for the Church in Urban Priority Areas; a summary of the kind of practical support which should be offered is all that is appropriate here.

The Urban Priorities Areas working party in Liverpool Diocese recommended that clergy ought not to serve in such parishes alone. They should be in team or group ministries.[7] Most of our team ministries have found help in the appointment of two consultants, one priest, one lay person. They offer at least one review day each year for members of the District Church Councils within the team parish and another review day for the team.

Clergy should take a regular day off and six weeks' holiday a year, including breaks at Christmas and Easter. This works out at decisively less time off than three weeks' annual holiday for those who work a five-day week; in addition they should take some sort of sabbatical leave for some months after a period like seven years. The clergyman's wife should also be helped to have the kind of longer break by which she would benefit.

I encourage all our clergy to have a joint work consultation each year with their rural dean or another consultant when they can review how their work is going. Accountability is always the other side of the coin of support; to set some objectives and assess them with someone else involved near to their work takes away some of the isolation which many clergy feel. One senior priest in the diocese said that a joint work consultation bridges the gap between indifference and interference.

In-service training is a vital link in the chain which helps clergy and lay workers stay fresh. Some kinds of course will enrich the individual in his own particular interests; other courses will help him appraise his ministry, do some theological reflection on what he is doing and make some plans for the task to which he is called.

At the time of the Toxteth riots a non-stipendiary priest met with some of his colleagues teaching in a college of further education. Together they offered to stay for some nights in vicarages, in order to give Toxteth clergy and families the chance to go away for a break. Such support from other parishes could make it possible for some of these breathers to take place.

The pay and working expenses of clergy and lay workers in these areas should not be allowed to fall behind that of their colleagues who work in parishes where professional people, who are used to claiming expenses, are members of Church councils.

Money is a major issue when we talk of needs of support. It is an expression of being 'members one of another' in Christ's body that all parishes in a diocese should pay an apportionment towards a general stipends fund and not simply towards their own clergy. The overseas Partners in Mission consultants, who took a loving and sharp look at the Church of England in 1981, issued a challenge that every parish should become independent of the Church Commissioners' money from past endowments by 1995.[8] They recommended that money should be made available for new mission projects in disadvantaged areas and overseas. The Church of England has committed itself up to the hilt to maintain its presence in every area in the country, whether there is sufficient membership to be self-supporting or not. The challenge of our Partners in Mission is a healthy one for parishes who have leaned too comfortably on past endowments and who have the potential to give much more. Mission projects which they should support could properly include maintaining a parish presence in mission areas as well as funding programmes or new mission projects.

I described the way in which we support the parish of Kirkby to a vestry of an Episcopal Church in a small town in Virginia, USA. Kirkby is a Team Ministry parish with a population of about 60,000. It has four Churches. Normally nine clergy serve there. There is a lively work in the Churches there, but Church attendance is not large. Church members give generously, but could never hope to support the staff which pastoral needs call for. Members of the parish vestry in Virginia were used to every parish having to be self-supporting. One small businessman immediately extolled the virtues of self-reliance and attacked the crippling effects of Socialism. The effects of our policy do not bear out that criticism. In Liverpool Diocese we have dis covered that the largest giving per head comes from Church members in priority area parishes, where a comparatively small number have to bear all the responsibilities. We are trying to find the best way to establish priority area parishes and links between those with strong membership in more affluent areas, so that there can be mutual giving and receiving.

Recognition of local ability

Secondly, authentic signs of God's Kingdom are shown by the kind of Church which recognises, develops and supports local ability within the Church and outside it. In urban working-class communities clergy and other professional people still frequently assume that there are no leaders to be found, despite all the evidence to be seen through community development and trade unions. My experience has been that everywhere there is intelligence and ability; but in areas where all those who have achieved well in school have moved out of the district, those who remain are likely to lack the self-confidence to accept responsibility.

Confidence building may happen in talking groups and

action groups. Such action groups may take on the running of a club for the elderly or form a working party, which will redecorate or do odd jobs for those who are shut in. As they use manual skills about which they already feel confident, they often feel more at ease in saying what they feel in the Church circle. At the Mayflower Family Centre we encouraged adults and teenagers to join small groups where they could talk about issues of life. We always began on subjects which were within people's experience. No one was made to feel silly or ignorant. On that sort of basis some confidence building can begin. Other inner city parishes tell me that they do a lot of story-telling. People who would sit silently while abstract ideas were being discussed grow in confidence when they are asked to tell their story, and when their story is clearly valued. It should be of the nature of the Church, in which the wisdom of God in all its varied forms is shown, that we give a hearing to the many different stories our members, and those around the edges of our company, have to tell.

It has been an accepted ideal to talk about such groups in Church life for many years. Yet there is a disappointing number of parishes in which such groups actually meet. When it is said that such groups will not work in a particular parish, it often means no more than that a notice was given out in Church, or a letter sent through the post, or that one invitation was given. Bringing a group together might mean spending a whole evening with two people, ending by agreeing two more names. That might need to be followed by an evening with the four, leading to a third evening when a group of eight might meet for the first time, each personally invited by a friend. Parishes in every kind of district have developed such groups.

Clergy and those lay people who have been the decision-makers in a Church for years, sometimes fear the development of house groups lest they get out of control. If we want local leadership to develop, we must take the risk that new groups of local Christians will develop their own self-confidence. That was the strength of the Methodist Class meeting. We must then be glad if, as from the Class meetings, some take their new-found self-confidence to a leading role in the secular community rather than in Church life.

I have written elsewhere about the way in which so much Church youth work turns out to be for those who achieve well at school.[9] Bible classes and uniformed organisations are likely to emphasise reading skills, regular attendance and good behaviour. This is very likely to restrict Church attendance to a predictable group of youngsters by the time they are fourteen. That group is made up of those who are most likely to move away from priority areas when they marry.

Churches need to have a policy about what kind of youth work they run. It only adds to young people's sense of being let down, if two or three enthusiasts open a youth club, only for it to be closed within a year because it made too much noise or damaged the Church property. Those who are willing to run youth work will only receive the support they need if others in the Church are firmly behind them. That must be more than voting a minimum budget because 'we must do something for young people'. A Church council or congregational planning day might tackle first three basic questions.

1. What are the real needs of young people, both those who are already in touch with the Church, and those who are not?
2. What are the aims of the Parish in all its work, and therefore what are the aims of its work with young people?
3. What resources in buildings, money and above all people are available, and what priority does youth work have in using them?[10]

Understanding what young people feel their needs to be involves careful listening. We need to review at regular intervals whether youth clubs and organisations are serving the present generation in their neighbourhood, or whether they are continuing to provide what the present leaders enjoyed when they were young. A generation in youth work probably lasts no more than three or four years. There is no one method, because there is not one group of young people. For example, some stay at school till eighteen years of age, have demanding homework and go on to higher education. They are likely to want very different provision from those who did little home-work, left school at sixteen and face unemployment after twelve months on the Youth Training Scheme.

In general there is not a lot of evidence that there is a youth culture in rebellion against the nature of society itself. Youth culture has changed along with the consumer boom, the emphasis on leisure and the sexual revolution which have affected society at large. MORI Opinion Research did an in-depth survey of attitudes and behaviour of a cross-section of fifteen-to twenty-four-year-olds in 1979. It concluded that young people in Britain might be termed 'The Complacent Generation'. They were happy with the life they were leading, optimistic about their future and felt they understood their parents well and were understood in return.[11] A British Council of Churches survey of opinions of young people who attend Lancashire Churches came to similar conclusions.[12]

In contrast the milieu of the inner city or of corporation estates with large-scale unemployment produces a deep sense of alienation from such a society among both black and white youth. Violence there does not seem to have a coherent goal. It is perhaps an angry and destructive reaction against a society which raises materialistic expectations through advertising, but appears unconcerned that these expectations cannot be fulfilled for so many young people.

Detached youth work offers the right opportunities for some youngsters. A variety of clubs and organisations appeal to different young people. They will serve them better if they take note of other youth organisations in their neighbourhood; it disappoints me that many Churches in the same district may be making very similar provision for very similar groups of young people. One of the reasons why many neighbouring Churches offer similar youth provision is that none of them feels that it has sufficient resources to offer something to the less conforming young people. Some could offer more if they joined hands with other Churches and shared resources. Others rightly encourage some of their members to help in secular youth projects.

It is likely to be the more purposeful minority which looks for positive alternatives to society's materialistic ways. When it comes to bringing young people to more definite Christian commitment, two main kinds of youth work seem to have particular appeal. On the one hand there are Christian movements which make a very decisive and clear-cut appeal to commitment. These may be Charismatic groups or those which have very definite teaching. On the other hand there are Christian groups which invite young people to tackle some of the great human problems of today; that might be in the Campaign for Nuclear Disarmament, or a work camp or in attempts to break down barriers, as in Corrymeela in Northern Ireland or Taizé in France. The passionate commitment to belief or causes, in which young people are sure that they are right, runs big risks of a reaction. It is important that older groups of Christians, who believe there are more questions to be asked, should keep strong contacts with such youth movements. The enthusiasm and the questioning need each other. It is valuable that Churches have activities which allow those who have cooled off from great enthusiasm to keep in contact with the Christian body without explicit Christian commitment having to be expressed.

Neither of these kinds of movements will easily appeal to the alienated urban youngsters. They come from a background which has often not known any religious practice for generations. They mistrust all institutions. They do not feel they have experienced the goodness of God. There are no short cuts to establishing positive links between young people like this and the Christian Church in any of its forms. Yet such links are established. Full-time and voluntary youth leaders are prepared to give time to being with young people for as long as they are wanted. It is a costly piece of Christian service, not least because so many Church people do not understand what such youth leaders are trying to do.

In one detached youth work project the leaders found that the role of acting as a bridge between aggressive young people and respectable citizens gave the leaders a rather schizophrenic feeling at times. 'They could be part of the swirling, blasting discotheque one night, and chatting up a Rotary Club or Quaker meeting the next.' They found they could explain the needs and attitudes of the skinheads to the straight, law-abiding, citizens and the reverse too. It often came as a surprising experience for one of the 'boot boys' to discover that a policeman or youth employment officer actually turned out to be a good bloke.[13] The skinhead group proved that they were able to plan their activities, to run and control discos. As in much detached youth work the progress was erratic and came to a hurtful end.

Many Christians measure a project like that as a failure because it produces no steady and continuing response. But it is of the nature of the urban experience of poverty that promising pieces of work often collapse. That does not mean that there was never any genuine response; if it was ever there, it was known to God. In a real sense nothing can take that away. Reliability is another thing. It sometimes takes generations to build into a community. Before it is achieved there will be flashes of insight, erratic initiatives and occasional loving acts; they need to be recognised as true responses to God's goodness and love. Often local people will feel enough confidence to step forward on an occasional basis; it may be at a community festival. It may be in the few weeks when a protest is being mounted. It will often be as one of a group rather than as a designated leader. Much enrichment will come to the community if local insights and initiatives of this occasional kind are encouraged.

As soon as the question comes up of designating a man or a woman as a teacher in the Church, a different yardstick appears. This not only concerns ordination to the priesthood; it is the same for Readers and accredited lay ministry. Readers are scarcely to be found in urban working-class parishes. Assumptions have been made that we would not expect men or women to come forward for selection as a reader, unless they have certain academic qualifications. I do not want dull people to be our preachers. But there are men and women who did not achieve well in school, who have keen intelligence and the ability to be the natural leaders in their local Church.

The Church's insistence on particular styles of training and qualifications has prevented some much-needed gifts from being used in God's service. This wastes the gifts of some who could help to bridge the long-standing gap between urban working-class people and the Church. And it is desirable that we should restore a certain localness to the Church's ordained ministry. These are the factors which make me support the idea of local ordained ministry. It has nothing to do with possible smaller numbers of stipendiary clergy. If there is any further substantial reduction in number, the urban mission areas must not be the parishes from which we withdraw stipendiary clergy. Strong congregations may have to learn to minister to themselves, and encourage non-stipendiary ministers to come forward to help in that ministry.

The Church has been forced to ask questions about local ordained ministry in rural areas, in order to maintain a ministry which has been known and expected for centuries. We need to ask whether local ordained ministry could provide a ministry which has not before been known in urban priority areas. In a vast urban parish of 25,000 people there will very likely be four or five communities—whether these are described geographically, or by ethnic or interest groups. A local ordained minister would need to be not simply a pastor to the congregation. He should have an understanding of mission which reaches beyond Church life, and a call to it. His ministry would not be measured primarily by what he did in Church services. He might work out his calling in leadership of house groups, in serving particular blocks of flats or an estate, and in relation to some community groups.

Anxiety has been expressed about standards. There needs to be appropriate rather than identical training. There might need to be a more local tutor at the beginning, who would help people over the hump of self-confidence. Training should not be only within the home parish, though the vicar could helpfully play a part in the course. The course should be one which candidates can follow, while continuing to live at home. Ways should be explored of making it possible for them to take time off work to do one or more terms of full-time study.[14]

In the Roman Catholic Archdiocese of Liverpool, as in a number of other dioceses in different countries, the permanent Diaconate has been revived. These men remain in their regular occupation after ordination. The majority of the twenty or more in Liverpool (some 300 in Chicago) come from the professional classes, but some are manual workers. They are recruited eight at a time, and are trained in groups of eight. There is a continuing period of training, which goes on beyond the two years which was originally laid down.[15] As with some Anglican training for reader ministry, essays and exams are not insisted on. A well kept notebook with illustrations or tape recordings of conversations with a tutor can provide proper ways in which men are pressed to articulate what they have been learning.

The factor which has made me hesitate most about going ahead with a scheme for the ordination of local ordained ministers in Liverpool is the question of what pressures this would bring on the man and his family. The factor may be described as great expectations. Whatever the bishop and the local ordained minister may believe he is called to do, there is a heavy expectation both among Church people and public that he should be like the clergyman they have known before. Those who have been ordained in this way in East London have described the switch off of support systems after they had been ordained. Instead of being the focus of attention and pioneers, they were in parish situations where people expected them to behave like other clergy.

Those support systems need to be prepared carefully. In particular a parish in which a local ordained minister is to be ordained needs to think through very carefully what their attitude should be to one of their members when he becomes a priest. He should always be part of a team and not the one assistant to a stipendiary vicar. If, side by side with the encouragement of local ordained ministry, recruitment of Readers is stimulated from the same parishes, they may share in training and in exercising their ministries.

The decisive issue in deciding whether to go ahead in this way is whether the existence of local ordained ministry would promote or inhibit other indigenous leadership. It has been argued that it would inhibit by reinforcing ideas that all leadership should be in the hands of ordained men; further that it might prevent some young men from accepting the discipline of training for stipendiary priesthood. I would not want to accept men for local ordained ministry before they were thirty years of age. My judgment is that it would promote, not inhibit, the development of other indigenous leadership. People could well say, 'If my friend can be a priest, perhaps I could be a leader, a play group leader, a Boys' Brigade officer, a churchwarden.'

A joint working party, set up by the Bishop of Manchester and myself, recommended in 1982 that we should ask the Advisory Council for the Church's Ministry and the House of Bishops to agree a scheme for local ordained ministry in Manchester and Liverpool.[16] It argued strongly for a bold experiment in discovering indigenous ministries, some of which might appropriately be marked by ordination to the priesthood. It would be a firm statement that we are the kind of Church which recognises, develops and supports local abilities both within the Church and in the wider community.

Serving people where they are

Thirdly, we need to be the kind of Church which serves people where they are. It is the style of life of the Church community which will decide for many people whether they will join or not. A black rector in Detroit said that people need to see a Church community that is open to different kinds of groupings. Every local Church likes to believe that it has a welcome for everyone. But many onlookers have concluded from what they have seen that there is a welcome only provided they fit in with our ways. They see a like-minded group, not one where the wisdom of God in all its varied forms is to be found.

This takes us back to a tension which we have noticed earlier in trying to understand how the poor see the Churches. On the one side is the wish for the Church to offer a sense of identity to those who belong to it; the tension is between that and the kind of Church in which those who have grown up altogether outside its ranks could feel that this Church is for them and could hear the Gospel of God's grace. It is true that the Church often provides a haven for those who are lonely and hurt. That is to its credit; we cannot expect such people to develop out-going personalities in a moment. Yet a Christian fellowship must learn to be open to 'the others'.

A young congregation in a modern corporation estate, where there is a lot of mental illness and depression, offers strong mutual support. The Church fellowship there supports each other on a more consistent level than the spontaneous coming to the rescue of neighbours at a time of family crisis. As soon as the Church fellowship develops strong friendships within its in-group, the danger of rejecting new people begins.

A Church community should feel sympathy for the community in which it is placed. It should also be a centre of resistance equally against the values of the consumer society and against the anarchic despair of a destructive society. These centres of resistance should encourage their members to commit themselves in faith and hope to the community which is not yet a reality. This is especially true in new Corporation estates. Too often Christians travel back to Church in their former district. They persuade themselves that there is no one to take their place in the Church where they used to live. Often they are shrinking from committing themselves to the 'not yet' community. At the same time they are denying their former Church the chance of having local leadership. This is a hard saying. But it needs to be heard if Churches are to be rooted in their community. If new areas are to be places of hope, people need to commit their future to them, rather than hope they may move on in two or three years. Establishing a warm community is the essence of whether a city is a place of life or death. Christians should be among the prime movers in working for a new community where human beings can feel that they belong.

A Puerto Rican community worker in the South Bronx, New York, told me that the Church there was a backbone to the people. That was not simply paying a compliment to a gifted rector. For example, when some youngsters from the parish had to appear in court, two lay people from the parish rather than the rector went to appear for them. They spoke up in court, and pursued contacts to try to obtain employment for the young men.

In the Church of England hard questions have had to be asked about Church social work. Mother and baby homes are not needed in the way they once were. A handful of Church social workers cannot hope to cover the ground of human needs. The greatest resource the Church has to offer is its army of lay people, who are willing to serve those in special need. A shift of Church resources to employ qualified social workers to inspire, train and support Church members in such service could release great resources.

A black American told me he had left the black parish in Harlem where he grew up as a choirboy. He felt that Church was for the self-improving, a Church *for* the neighbourhood rather than a Church *of* the neighbourhood. He came back to the Church as an adult in another district of New York. It was the time when the Black Panthers' movement was strong. They approached the rector and the vestry of an Episcopalian parish. They said that the children of the area were going to school without any proper food in their bellies. They wanted to use the church hall for a breakfast programme, and to give some political indoctrination. The vestry agreed. After a few months those who were running the programme grew tired of it. The breakfast programme would have come to an end. Members of his not very strong parish took up the responsibility for providing the breakfast themselves. For one black American this brought hard evidence that the Church was truly wanting to serve the community.

The tension remains between being a Church of the area and being a Church which is different from the area in the right kind of way; believing and worshipping Christians will want to share what is to them the best news in the world with their neighbours. Effective evangelism includes naming the name of Christ. The right moment for that may be ten years down the road, when neighbours have had the chance to see signs in the life of the Christian community. At that right moment Christians should be ready to give their witness by lip as well as by life. Some have reacted against the charge that Christians 'ram religion down people's throats', by determining never to mention the name of Jesus Christ. This is to misunderstand what is wrong with ramming religion down people's throats. That lesson we should learn is to respect people. It is not respecting my friend or colleague if I show that I am much interested in what makes him tick, but determine that in no circumstances will I ever try to explain what motivates me.

An international and ecumenical team of Christians in their report 'As Others See Us' on their visit to the North East of England challenged this embarrassment of English Christians about speaking of their faith. They said that Christianity is becoming less self-evident to the people of England; Christians must be prepared to explain what and why they believe. 'If you never discuss the Christian faith openly, people may think you're a good guy, but how will they learn what Christians believe?'[17]

In Easterhouse, Glasgow, a Church of Scotland minister told me of someone who described herself as an atheist, yet wears an Iona Cross. She is involved in every good project on the estate often in close partnership with Christians. During a community holiday on Iona she went to the Abbey every day. But she will never join the Church, though her daughter has done so. There were deep reasons inside her why she could not bring herself to believe, or to join the Church.

It is impossible to exaggerate the gap between very large numbers of urban working-class people and the organised Church. If that gap is to be bridged, there need to be many stepping stones, events, groups, projects in which those outside the Church can meet with members of the Christian community. This is not to deny our calling to name the name of Christ. We may need to understand that the gap is so great that for some people it will take a generation to bridge it. Meanwhile God understands what is possible for each individual and what is not.

It follows from the need for stepping stones that the Church should welcome rather than reject folk religion. Understandably some clergy and congregations want to withdraw from this often frustrating and ambiguous encounter, for example in baptisms. The English people have been encouraged for centuries to bring their children to be baptised. The desire for a clear-cut understanding of Christian commitment leads some clergy to lay down demanding conditions to prove the willingness of parents to come to Church before baptising their babies. They do not give much account to the place a believing grandmother may have in a family, or to the inarticulate longings after God of many who cannot think of themselves as churchgoers. Many poor people have to make humiliating requests to officials; if the Church insists on parents' fitting in to its institutional life before baptising their children, it will make them feel that yet again they are being told to fit in with form-filling, behave-like-us institutions. Instead, it can be a helpful stepping stone which brings a family nearer to the Christian experience and to the Christian fellowship.

We have already noticed the impatience which many feel with institutions. It is not surprising that the same impatience is felt with the Church as an institution. As with other institutions we need to do what we can to reconcile it to God's purpose before we consider shaking the dust off our feet against it. Institutions stand for continuity. People know they are there, when they need them. If the institution of the Church is to be called back to God's purpose for it, we must work to see that it serves people where they are. Sometimes Church organisations are still meeting a need which they were founded to deal with two generations ago, even though that need has long since been met by someone else.

Any debate on the Church in old inner city areas is bound to come round to the subject of church buildings. Many forward-looking clergy would dearly love to be rid of their burden. Yet local people inside and outside the Church would frequently see the closure of a church building, which has been one of their landmarks, as a withdrawal of the Church from their community.

There is no more painful matter in Church life than pastoral reorganisation which involves closing churches. The building where you were baptised and married and from which your parents were buried has many emotions attached to its stones. We cannot say in one breath that we have to take care about not trampling on folk religion, and in the next ignore the feelings people have about their Church. Yet it is right to go through the painful processes of making some churches redundant in areas where the population has drastically reduced. The reason is that the way the Church is organised affects the kind of Christians we are. If we keep too many church buildings, we trap small congregations into putting all their energies into maintaining the buildings and justifying their existence by running Church organisations to use them. It is not surprising if such a congregation has no contacts with the community. Its 'same few' members are too busy running Church activities to be serving people where they are.

Understanding the Word of God for rich and poor

Fourthly, we need to be the kind of Church which tries to understand and obey the word of God for both rich and poor. This book is not simply about what the Church should do in the inner city. It is about the attitudes, beliefs and priorities of the whole Church. Obeying the Word of God, which includes a bias to the poor, presents some costly choices for the whole Church in countries like Britain and the USA.

Bishop Colin Winter called on the Church to break its long association with the rich.[18] For years the Church has been seen to accompany and protect the established order. When we claim that we want to accompany the poor, and listen to them, there must be a shift of priorities. Church leaders have often been encouraged to keep good personal relationships with those in power, so that they may use their influence behind the scenes to bring about change. The discreet word will sometimes be the right way; but it may reflect 'an aristocratic lack of interest' in keeping the rest of the Church and the public informed.[19] If this is the main route by which we hope to influence the course of events, we have a most optimistic view of the powers that be. The poor want to see some demonstration of the power and truth of the Gospel—not necessarily of its success. So it will sometimes be right for the Church openly to argue for the cause of the poor, including the unpopular poor, and perhaps be seen to fail.

Any shift of priorities by Church leaders is likely to be taken amiss by those who have traditionally expected them to come to their meetings. When I came to Liverpool, I set myself an objective that, out of the time I set apart for meeting people and groups in secular life, I should try to spend an equal amount of time with those who are outside the circles of

power as with those who are within those circles. I try to log
that time each year; it is extraordinarily difficult to achieve the
balance. Those outside the circles of of power are not used to
meeting Church leaders, and may not want to, unless they feel
we might be allies in some issue of the moment. The bishop is
not on their traditional list of speakers. Yet my attempt to keep
such a balance, together with making public stands about
some controversial issues, has led to remarks like, 'The bishop
doesn't want to attend dinners', or in a newspaper profile,
'Unless you're poor, black and unemployed, he doesn't want
to know you!' and in the business news in a newspaper,
'Perhaps the bishop's views did not help to encourage city
businessmen to support the Diocesan Centenary Appeal'.

The Church is called to discover the Word of God for today
in those areas of life which most affect the poor. We must be
willing to go beyond issuing broad statements of principle.
We cannot assume that both sides have equally valid positions.
If we enter the confusing area of corporate ethics, we must be
ready, after arming ourselves with the best advice we can find,
to step forward along some controversial paths. For the Church
to hear the cry of the poor will mean losing its innocence on
social and political matters. There will be occasions when we
must get off the fence, and take sides.

The question is frequently asked, 'Isn't the Gospel for the
rich too?' Certainly it is. In response to the Gospel Jesus called
for repentance, a change of heart. He often spoke a different
word to the rich and to the poor. The consequences of sinful
materialism have hit the urban poor; the actions of the better
off cause and perpetuate much of that suffering, by protecting
their own opportunities and self-interest. Often the affluent
and influential recognise that they too are caught in the trap of
a divided society. It would be good news indeed to see a way
out of our corporate suffering.

Making people feel guilty at being affluent is not very helpful. Many who are well off would like to see ways in which
they could help change the course of events in favour of the
poor. Here are six areas in which the relatively influential could
reflect a bias to the poor:

The first is to do with their job. Many who travel into a city from its suburbs and surrounds are the gatekeepers to loans, training and jobs for many people. Helping those who start at a disadvantage to find a valued place may involve making some costly stands in someone's business or profession.

Secondly, there is voluntary service. One big firm in Liverpool has a long-standing tradition of service to the city. Every director seems to have a commitment to at least one voluntary organisation in the city. Some will help in Christian organisations. Many offer their skills to projects within the Youth Training Scheme. Such a firm is not going lightly to make decisions to disinvest from the city. Becoming aware of how people feel in poorer parts of the city affects policies of companies and attitudes in suburban communities.

Thirdly, there are needy people within their own community. Consciousness of the needs of poorer areas has often opened people's eyes to needs nearer home. The loneliness of elderly people can be intense, if they come from a background where a stigma is attached to asking for help from any sort of social or welfare service. There are sensitive skills to learn in offering help to the lonely or handicapped in a more affluent community.

Fourthly, they can influence attitudes. Conversations in drawing rooms or pubs, commuter trains or family parties change the attitudes of many who are the gatekeepers of opportunities for the poor.

Fifthly, there is political pressure—in national and local government, within political parties and in pressure groups. Some of the changes this book argues for will be to the material disadvantage of the more affluent areas. They will be passionately resisted in the name of individual freedom and the wealth of the nation. There is a great need for well-informed and committed voices in all the conversations which shape public opinion.

Sixthly, there are Church politics. The more affluent parishes are asked to play an increasingly unselfish part in a missionary-minded Church. It is one thing to raise money for a curate in your own parish. It is another to raise it for a stipends fund which will pay for a curate in the areas where Church membership is weaker. Strong lay voices from suburban

Churches have the greatest influence in arguing for policies which will reflect being 'members one of another', rather than 'Every congregation for itself'.

As we have seen, liberation theology insists that a commitment to action on behalf of the poor is the necessary point of entry into the circle of interpretation. In its way this expresses a very old Christian truth; you cannot expect to understand, unless you are willing to obey, once you do understand.

If we want to find the Word of God for today, we must learn how to hold side by side our experience of life with the revelation of God in the Scriptures. Theological enquiry does not take place in an intellectual vacuum of pure, disinterested reasoning, but in a context in which the way we think is powerfully conditioned by social, economic and cultural factors.[20] If we urgently want to discover God's way forward in a situation where we are ourselves involved, we may turn to an extended piece of study, perhaps as a group, using a tool such as the circle of interpretation used in the chapter 'Jews and Gentiles'. We shall then be digging deep in the Bible, not because we think Romans ought to be studied, but because we have to discover and obey the Word of God for today. To discover this we need to be increasingly competent theologically and competent in the milieu of the city in which we experience life.

That raises questions about complicated tools and arguments. Is it possible to expect working-class people to tackle a circle of interpretation? Lurking behind the question is some kind of assumption like 'Working-class people like things simple'. That is a dangerous assumption, for it is a short step to the lie which says, 'Working-class people are simple'. When confidence has been built up, working-class people are well able to handle ideas. This would be especially true when they speak from their own experience in helping a group understand the milieu of industrial and urban life. A good model which has been tested down the years is the See, Judge, Act, method of the Young Christian Workers. A Gospel enquiry is followed by an industrial enquiry, and in turn by social enquiry.

The retreat from the complicated is a temptation to which all of us are prone. But the issues of urban life are complicated.

The demand of Christian love is that we should reject snappy catch answers and slogans, and refuse to withdraw when the subject becomes difficult. We must stay with it until we do understand, as best we can, what are the causes of a particular situation and what are the options for a way out.

It is all too easy to study the Bible with an eye for pegs on which to hang our previously-settled ideas. There is advantage in thinking of the method of interpretation we have used as a circle. We keep coming round to each part of the circle, including that in which we let the text speak back to the questions we bring to it. It should also encourage us to enter the circle at different points, not always at the point of commitment to the poor today. Andrew Kirk argues that our attempts at interpretation should keep moving between two poles; these are our experience in the contemporary situation, with the best analysis we can make of it, and the Biblical message, read in the light of the Kingdom of God.[21]

Part of the circle of interpretation is to see how Christians view the same question or doctrine from their different economic and social experiences. In the Bible there is an interplay between the wilderness and the vineyard experiences of the people of God. The wilderness is the place of vision; the Law is given. There are no ifs or buts. There are no grey areas. Right and wrong are utterly clear. God leads in a pillar of cloud by day and a pillar of fire by night. Then the people of God are to go into the land; the symbol of Israel is the vineyard. They are to stop wandering, settle down and build a civilisation. A vineyard is a place of organisations and structures; its success is measured by its productivity. The settled life of Israel in the vineyard brings with it complicated structures, choices between two evils. But the vineyard people are to listen to the wilderness people, whom God keeps sending to remind them of that clear vision.

Today many of us are called to be vineyard people; to take a more complex society than ever, and make it work for the good of people and to the glory of God. Wilderness people are very important to us. They sit loose to the materialist demands, which seem so important to us. They may be young people looking for alternative styles of life, or the elderly holding on to values which have been tested through generations. They may be members of religious orders or Christians who sit very loose to Church structures. They may be those who are specially vulnerable to mental stress, who see some truths with blinding clarity. They may be the poor and powerless, who can see society and its values very differently from the way it appears to vineyard people.

In the Bible wilderness people like Amos or John the Baptist come into the vineyard with a word of judgment or questioning. Vineyard people are inclined to act like King Josiah in the Old Testament. He reorganised religious life in his day to establish a more efficient organisation. When people raise fundamental questions, we say, 'What you mean is we should do other things in addition to our regular commitments.' Then we add new reforms, new rules. Or we say to these disturbers of the peace, 'You must be free to pursue your ideas.' What we are unwilling to do is to ask what it is that the wilderness people with their heightened consciousness can see that we can't see. For, if we ask that, we may start to see things differently; we may all need to change our ways.

We live in a very polarised society. In the same city people have widely different experiences, and see the same events through very different eyes. The Church is one of the few bridges which can reach across to different sides of that polarised society. It is part of our reconciling task to help different groups to listen to what the others perceive to be happening.

If we can put ourselves in the shoes of the poor and disadvantaged, we may see how matters appear to their consciousness—not just inner city matters, but matters which affect the whole of our society. These are not side issues for some to pursue on the margins of the life of Church and society. Nor are they the result of a political preference. They are to do with the righteousness of God which has a persistent tendency to favour those at a disadvantage. They are to do with God taking flesh in the person of Jesus, living out His life in a special relation to the poor.

Notes

Chapter One—The Divine Bias (pp. 9–18)

1. David Sheppard, *Built as a City* (Hodder and Stoughton, 1974) pp. 32–40.
   See John H. Goldthorpe, David Lockwood, Frank Bechofer, Jennifer Platt: *The Affluent Worker in the Class Structure* (Cambridge University Press, 1969) pp. 1–30 and 163f.
2. A group of young black people from New Cross in South East London invited some Church leaders to meet with them to think through their experience as black people in November 1980. Some fifteen of us in all spent just under twenty-four hours away together. This was sponsored by the Moonshoot Club and the Community and Race Relations Unit of the British Council of Churches.
3. The Rev. Paul Washington, Rector, Episcopal Church of the Advocate, Philadelphia, USA, during a consultation on Urban Theology promoted by the Trinity Institute, New York. Some twenty-five Episcopalians came together from most of the major cities in the USA. I was present as a consultant.
4. Luke 1[51–3].
5. A. H. Halsey, 'Change in British Society, The Reith Lectures', *The Listener*, 2 February 1978.
6. Matthew 5[3]. But cf. Matthew 11[5], Mark 10[25], Luke 4[18], Luke 6[20,24].
7. Luke 12[48].
8. *To Hear and to Heed: The Episcopal Church Listens and Acts in the City*. Published for the Urban Bishops' Coalition by the Forward Movement, Cincinnati, Ohio, 1978.
9. Ruben F. W. Nelson, *Illusions of Urban Man* (The Ministry of State for Urban Affairs, Canada, 1976) p. 50.
10. Don Bullen in a seminar following 'The Divine Bias for the Losers'; four lectures given in the Extra Mural Studies Department of Liverpool University, November 1979. The lectures

were given in an earlier form as 'the William Barclay Lectures' in Glasgow, November 1978. They formed first steps towards the present book.

11. *Built as a City*, op cit., pp. 42ff.

Chapter Two—Losers in the Urban Race (pp. 19–36)

1. Merseyside County Council Planning Department.
2. 'Churches in Urban Priority Areas.' The report of a working party set up by Liverpool Diocesan Synod, 1982.
3. David Eversley, lecture in Liverpool University Extra Mural Studies 1977.
4. F. F. Ridley, 'View from a Disaster Area', *The Political Quarterly*, January 1981.
5. J. F. Hart, 'Some statistics of social contrast in Liverpool from the 1971 Census' (Liverpool Council for Voluntary Service, 14 Castle Street, Liverpool L2) p. 21.
6. *Change or Decay: Final Report of the Liverpool Inner Areas Study* (Her Majesty's Stationery Office, 1977) p. 57. The study was of District D, mainly Liverpool 7, partly Liverpool 8.
7. E. S. P. Evans, City Planning Officer, 'Economy 1982'. *Liverpool Planning Information Digest*. Chief Planning Officer, 'Employment in Liverpool', 1981.
8. Margaret Simey, quoted in Rosemary Righter: *Save Our Cities* (Calouste Gulbenkian Foundation, 1977) p. 14.
9. Bill Cox, a detached youth leader speaking at the Review Day of the Merseyside and Cheshire Special Programmes Board of the Manpower Services Commission, 1980.
10. Louis Burghes, *Living from Hand to Mouth* (Published jointly FSU, 207 Old Marylebone Road, London NW1 and CPAG, 1 Macklin Street, London WC2, 1980) p. 71.
11. M. E. Fletcher, 'Report on an investigation into the Colour Problem in Liverpool and other Ports' (Liverpool Association for the Welfare of Half-Caste Children, 1930) pp. 8, 11.
12. *The Economic Status of Coloured Families in the Port of Liverpool* (The University Press of Liverpool, 1940) pp. 12, 15.
13. Wally Brown in 'Under-achievement in School among Black and Ethnic Minority Pupils' (National Association for Multi-racial Education, Liverpool, 1980) p. 3.
14. Ralph Ellison, *Invisible Man* (Penguin Modern Classics, 1965) p. 462. First published in USA 1952.

Chapter Three—How Liverpool's Poor See the Church (pp. 37–57)

1. I am grateful to many friends for information and ideas quoted in this and the previous chapter; in particular Father Brendan Alger, Bishop Augustine Harris, Sister Mary McAleese, Monsignor Jim Dunn, Father Austin Smith OP, Father Ralph Woodhalls, the Rev. Neville Black, Rev. Christopher Smith, Rev. Michael Plunkett, Rev. Colin Oxenforth, Canon Neil Humphreys and Sister Norma Nelson, CA, who did some considerable research for me.
2. Isaiah 11[1-9].
3. Jürgen Moltmann, *The Theology of Hope* (SCM Press, 1967) p. 224.
4. Don Bullen in 'Passionist Inner City Mission' (Liverpool, 1974).
5. Jim Hart, 'The Protestant Churches of Toxteth' (Liverpool, 1974).
6. E. R. Norman, *Church and Society in England, 1770–1970* (Clarendon Press, 1976) p. 159.
7. Owen Chadwick, *The Secularization of the European Mind in the Nineteenth Century* (Cambridge University Press, 1975) p. 111.
8. I wrote about the early Methodists and the working classes in *Built as a City*, op cit., pp. 126–33.
   See R. F. Wearmouth, *Methodism and the Common People of the Eighteenth Century* (Epworth, 1945) and *Methodism 1800–1850* (Epworth).
9. Austin Smith OP, *Passion for the Inner City* (1982).

Chapter Four—Black Is Vulnerable (pp. 58–78)

1. Rennie Webb, Director, The Melting Pot Foundation, Brixton, in *Journal of the Evangelical Race Relations Group* (Editor, Maurice Hobbs, 269 Rotton Park Road, Birmingham B16 OLD), Vol. I No. 4, January 1976, p. 3.
2. Ralph Weeks, Member Shiloh Pentecostal Church, Dalston. Joint Editor Church To-day and Pentecostal Times, op. cit., p. 6.
3. Morris Stuart, Evangelist, op. cit., p. 9.
4. Candley George, Chairman, West Indian Welfare Association, joint Editor Church To-day and Pentecostal Times, op. cit., p. 4.
5. Monty Edwards, op. cit., p. 6.
6. Shedman Graham, Member Pentecostal Church in Willesden, op. cit., p. 7.

7. *The New Black Presence in Britain*, a statement by the British Council of Churches Working Party on Britain as a Multi-Racial Society (Community and Race Relations Unit of the British Council of Churches, 1976) p. 24.

8. John Root on *The New Black Presence in Britain* (Evangelical Race Relations Group paper, 1976).

9. *The Brixton Disorders 10–12 April 1981*, Report of an Inquiry by the Rt. Hon. Lord Scarman (HMSO, 1981).

10. John Alderson, *Policing Freedom* (Macdonald and Evans, 1979) p. 69.

11. *The Brixton Disorders*, op. cit., p. 67.

12. James McClure, *Spike Island, Portrait of a Police Division* (Macmillan, 1980) p. 53.

13. *The Toxteth Survey*, Tables (Liverpool City Council, February 1982), Table 27.

14. *Looking for Work* (Commission for Racial Equality, 1978).

15. *Racial Disadvantage in Employment* (PEP, The Social Science Institute, London, 1974).

16. *Half a Chance?* A report on job discrimination against young blacks in Nottingham. (Published by Commission for Racial Equality, Elliot House, 10–12 Allington Street, London W1, in association with Nottingham and District Community Relations Council. 37 Mansfield Road, Nottingham, 1980) p. 12.

17. *Urban Deprivation in Multi-Racial Areas* (Methodist Church Division of Social Responsibility, 1977) p. 3.

18. Norman Snaith, *Distinctive Ideas of the Old Testament* (London, 1944) pp. 76ff.

19. C. H. Dodd, *The Epistle of Paul to the Romans* (Moffatt New Testament Commentary, 1932; reprinted Fontana Books, 1959) p. 162.

20. Michigan Employment Security Commission, quoted by H. Coleman McGehee, Jr., Bishop of Michigan.

21. Frances Fox Piven, Professor of Political Science, Boston University, *The Witness*, January 1979, p. 8.

22. George W. Webber, *To-day's Church. A Community of Exiles and Pilgrims* (Abingdon, 1979) p. 84.

23. Robert Kennedy, *The Federal Role in Urban Affairs*, 1966. Quoted in Arthur Schlesinger, *Robert Kennedy and his Times* (André Deutsch, 1978) pp. 784ff.

24. *Blending into the Life: an Oral history* (Community Documentation Workshop, St Mark's Church in the Bowery, 10th Street and 2nd Avenue, New York City).

25. David Gracie, *Signs of the Kingdom* (St Barnabas Episcopal Church, Philadelphia, 1979).
26. *The Times*, 20 and 22 May 1981.
27. Wilfred Wood, then deacon of Southwark. Wilfred Wood has been good enough to share many of his feelings from within the black community with me down the last eleven years.

Chapter Five—Solidarity (pp. 79–90)

1. Ephesians 2^{15}.
2. Jorge Lara-Braud, National Council of Churches, USA.
3. Morris Stuart, *The Black Mirror* (Community and Race Relations Unit of the British Council of Churches, 1976) p. 14.
4. *The New Black Presence in Britain*, op. cit., p. 25.
5. Clergy Report: Communication among the priests of the Roman Catholic Archdiocese of New York, March 1977.
6. Don Cupitt, *The Leap of Reason* (Sheldon Press, 1976) p. 140.
7. Bhikhu Parekh, Senior Lecturer in Politics at the University of Hull: 'Problem or Opportunity?' in *Five Views of Multi-Racial Britain*. (Commission for Racial Equality, Elliot House, 10–12 Allington Street, London SW1, 1978) pp. 40ff. A Talk broadcast by BBC Television.
8. Bhikhu Parekh: op. cit., p. 44.
9. Taylor: *The Half Way Generation*.
10. See David Brown, *A New Threshold, Guidelines for the Churches in their relations with Muslim Communities* (British Council of Churches, 1976) p. 18.
11. Lesslie Newbigin, *Christian Witness in a Plural Society* (British Council of Churches) p. 20.
12. See *Britain as a Multi-Racial and Multi-Cultural Society*, Report by the Church of England Board for Social Responsibility. (Church Information Office, 1977) p. 6.
13. Joseph K. Donahue: Puerto Ricans and the Church. (Clergy Report, March 1977, op. cit.).
14. Ben Cunningham, General Secretary, Afro-Caribbean Council of Churches and Public Relations Officer. New Testament Church of God in England and Wales (interviewed in *Christian Action Journal*, Summer 1978).
15. Ermal Kirby, Pilgrim Holiness minister, 'Young, Christian and Black' (*Christian Action Journal*, Summer 1978).
16. Jeremiah McIntyre, overseer New Testament Church of God

for England and Wales at a conference on 'Integration in Church', January 1974.
17. John Root, review in *Evangelical Race Relations Group*, Vol. 3, No.1, March 1978.
18. Joseph Owen, *Dread: The Rastafarians of Jamaica* (Sangster. Available from Bogie L'Overture Publications, 5a Chignell Place, London W13) p. 47.
19. C. Peter Wagner, *Our Kind of People, The Ethical Dimensions of Church Growth in America* (John Knox Press, 1979).
20. Tom Nees, 'Evangelism without the Gospel' (*Sojourners*, 1309, L Street NW, Washington DC 20005, USA).
21. Paul Moore, Jr, 'Dilemmas in Bishoping, The Life or Death of City Churches' (papers for the Urban Coalition of Bishops, 1980).

Chapter Six—Jews and Gentiles (pp. 91–111)

1. Acts 10.
2. Acts 15.
3. Mark 7[24-30].
4. Vincent Taylor, *The Gospel according to St. Mark* (Macmillan, 1959) p. 347.
5. Stuart Blanch, *The Christian Militant* (SPCK, 1978) p. 28.
6. Ephesians 3[1-11].
7. Jean Russell, *God's Lost Cause* (SCM Press, 1968) pp. 131, 139.
8. Bernard Nicholls: *Dear Mary* . . . (Church Missionary Society, 157 Waterloo Road, London SE1, 1980) pp. 1ff.
9. Caroline Adams, *They sell Cheaper and they Live Very Odd* (Community and Race Relations Unit of the British Council of Churches, 1976).
10. Alan Ecclestone, *The Night Sky of the Lord* (Darton, Longman and Todd, 1980) p. 50.
11. Hosea 2[23].
12. John Hick, *Christianity and Race in Britain Today* (AFFOR, 1 Finch Road, Lozells, Birmingham B19 1HS, 1979) p. 6.
13. Catholic Commission for Racial Justice: Notes and Reports, March 1981.
14. George W. Webber, op. cit., p. 95.
15. The Rev. R. Collett in *Evangelical Race Relations Group Journal*, 1973.
16. G. R. Selby, 'Study of Innovative Theological Enterprises in the U.S.A. and Central America', 1976.

17. George W. Webber, op. cit. pp. 150–4.
18. I owe the phrase 'Let the text speak back to the questions we bring to it' to a chapter by Tony Thistleton, 'Understanding God's Word today' in *Obeying Christ in a Changing World* (Collins, Fountain Books, 1977) pp. 99–106.
19. 1 Corinthians 16.
20. Matthew 11[19].
21. John 8[48].
22. Alan Ecclestone, *Yes to God* (Darton, Longman and Todd, 1975) p. 75.
23. Hugh Montefiore, 'Glory in the Inner City.' An unpublished paper, 1979.

Chapter Seven—The Future of Work (pp. 112–128)

1. Bob Houlton, 'Syndicalism and Labour on Merseyside, 1906–14' in *Building the Union*, ed. Harold R. Hikins (Toulouse Press, 1973) pp. 122–9.
2. Huw Beynon, *Working for Ford* (Allen Lane and Penguin Education, 1973) cf. pp. 70–7 and 89ff.
3. 'No one from Liverpool 8 Need Apply.' A report on the employment situation of young people in South Inner Liverpool on behalf of The Inner Areas Study, 1975, p.11.
4. John Plamenatz, *Karl Marx's Philosophy of Man* (Clarendon Press, 1975) pp. 388, 392.
5. Len Murray, *Guardian*, 27 February 1979.
6. Ivor Clemitson and George Rodgers, *A Life to Live—Beyond Full Employment* (Junction Books, 1981) p. 26.
7. 'Chips with Everything—or Technology with a Human Face': a report of the panel established by the Merseyside Enterprise Forum to consider the social implications of advanced technology, 1980, p. 8.
8. David Bleakley, *In Place of Work . . . The Sufficient Society*, (SCM Press, 1981) p. 42.
9. *Sunday Telegraph*, 20 March 1979.
10. Professor Tom Stonier, Department of Science and Society, Bradford University: paper delivered to the Middlesex Science and Technology Education Centre, 1979.
11. E. R. Wickham, *Introduction to Work and the Future*: a report from the Industrial Committee of the Church of England Board for Social Responsibility (Church Information Office, 1979).
12. Consultative Document on Education in Schools, 1977.

13. Audrey Lees, then Chief Planning Officer for Merseyside at a Conference, The Future of Work on Merseyside, 1979.
14. Dr Joan Mitchell, Reader in Economics, Nottingham University, *Socialist Commentary*, February 1978.
15. James Robertson, 'Breakdown or Breakthrough', *The Ecologist*, November 1977.
16. The Rev. Professor Charles Elliott addressing the Lambeth Conference of Anglican Bishops at Canterbury, 1978.
17. David Bleakley, op. cit., p. 64.

Chapter Eight—A Crisis for Capitalism (pp. 129–144)

1. T. E. Utley, 'Capitalism—The Moral Case' (Conservative Research Department Paper, 1980) p. 267.
2. Daniel Jenkins, *Christian Maturity and the Theology of Success* SCM, 1976) p. 49.
3. Ecclesiastes 3^{1-11}.
4. Gerhard Von Rad, *Wisdom in Israel* (SCM Press, 1972) p. 232.
5. Proverbs 2^{10-20}.
6. Proverbs 1^{20} and 8^1f.
7. Gerhard Von Rad, op. cit., p. 158.
8. A. W. Coats ed., *The Classical Economists and Economic Policy* (Methuen, 1971) p. 9.
9. Ruben Nelson, *The Illusions of Urban Man*, op. cit., pp. 57, 59.
10. Irving Kristol, Values and Contemporary Society; a seminar sponsored by the Rockefeller Foundation, March 1974.
11. E. F. Schumacher, *Good Work* (Cape, 1979) p. 27.
12. Fred Hirsch, *Social Limits to Growth* (Routledge and Kegan Paul, 1977) pp. 102ff.
13. Friedrich Hayek, *The Constitution of Liberty* (Routledge and Kegan Paul, 1960) pp. 40ff.
14. Michael Young and Peter Willmott, *The Symmetrical Family* (Routledge and Kegan Paul, 1973) p. 20.
15. *Trinity Wall Street Newsletter*, July 1979.
16. Professor Brian Griffiths: Lecture at St George's House, Windsor, 1974.
17. T. E. Utley, op. cit., p. 274.
18. J. K. Galbraith, *The Affluent Society* (Hamish Hamilton, 1958) cf. pp. 196ff.
19. Frank Field, 'The Tories and the Poor in Thatcherism', The Jubilee Lent Lectures, ed. Kenneth Leech 1980.

20. John Plamenatz, op. cit., p. 407.
21. T. E. Utley, op. cit., pp. 271–4.
22. Richard H. Luecke, a paper, 'The Present Unemployment and the Future of Work', 1978, pp. 13–16; and see Pierre de Vise, 'The Suburbanisation of Jobs and Minority Employment', *Economic Geography*, October 1976.
23. Professor R. E. Pahl, 'Modern Pressures and Social Community': a lecture given in Canterbury Cathedral, 1972.
24. *The Times*, 30 July 1980.
25. *Daily Telegraph*, 31 July 1980.
26. David Sheppard, op. cit., pp. 183–97.
27. A. H. Halsey, A. F. Heath and J. M. Ridge, *Origins and Destinations; Family, Class and Education in Modern Britain* (Clarendon Press, 1980) p. 213; and Richard Hoggart in the *Observer*, 13 January 1980.
28. Matthew 5: [46ff].
29. See Fred Hirsch, op. cit., p. 178.

Chapter Nine—Liberation Theology (pp. 145–158)

1. Gustavo Gutierrez, *A Theology of Liberation* (Maryknoll; Orbis Books, 1973) p. 30.
2. Alfredo Fierro, *The Militant Gospel* (SCM Press, 1977) p. 80.
3. Juan Luis Segundo, 'Is Christendom a Utopia?' *Mimeografica Luz*, Montevideo, 1964, Vol. I, p. 66. Quoted by Kenneth Leech, Liberating Theology; the thought of Juan Luis Segundo (*Theology*, July 1981).
4. Jose Miguez Bonino, *Revolutionary Theology comes of age* (SPCK, 1975) pp. 68ff.
5. Gustavo Gutierrez, op. cit., p. 11.
6. Jon Sobrino, SJ, 'The Significance of Puebla for the Catholic Church in Latin America' in *Reflections on Puebla* (Catholic Institute for International Relations, 1980) pp. 39ff.
7. *Reflections on Puebla*, op. cit., p. 31.
8. e.g. Psalm 15[5] on usury; Titus 2[9]; Philemon 12 on slavery; Leviticus 25[23] on freehold land.
9. Gustavo Gutierrez, op. cit., p. 11.
10. Julian Filochowski in *Reflections on Puebla*, op. cit., pp. 13, 10.
11. Pope John Paul II, speech made at a General Audience on 21 February 1979. (Text from *L'Osservatore Romano*, 26 February 1979, included in full in *Reflections on Puebla*, op. cit., pp., 44–6).

12. *Puebla: Evangelization at present and in the future of Latin America: Conclusions.* Official English Edition (St Paul Publications, 1980) pp. 49, 178.
13. A. H. Halsey, 'Change in British Society, The Reith Lectures', *The Listener*, 16 February 1978.
14. A. H. Halsey, A. F. Heath and J. M. Ridge, *Origins and Destinations*, op. cit., pp. 62f, 71.
15. See Paul Lakeland, 'Responding to Liberation Theology' in the English Jesuit Journal, *The Month*, January 1980.
16. Metropolitan Anthony Bloom in a Bible Reading to the Lambeth Conference, 1978.
17. Philippians 2[8].
18. Jürgen Moltmann, *The Crucified God* (SCM, 1974) pp. 136ff, 143ff, 317ff, 328ff.
19. Juan Luis Segundo, *The Liberation of Theology* (Gill and Macmillan, 1977) p. 186.
20. James A. Joseph 'Towards an Urban Theology', *The Witness*, January 1979.
21. Samuel Escobar, 'Evangelism and Man's search for freedom, justice and fulfilment', in *Let the World hear His Voice*, the collected papers of the Lausanne Conference, ed. J. D. Douglas (1974) p. 304.
22. Gustavo Gutierrez, op. cit., p. 37.
23. Amos 9[7].
24. Mark 7[21].
25. John Plamenatz, op. cit., p. 168.
26. Alfredo Fierro, op. cit., p. 386
27. John Plamenatz, op. cit., p. 195.
28. cf. Deuteronomy 5[15].
29. Matthew 5[44], 6[12].
30. Matthew 7[3f].
31. Giles Ecclestone, 'The Church of England and Politics': report by the Board for Social Responsibility (General Synod Paper, 1980) pp. 116ff.
32. E. R. Wickham in *Priests and Workers*, ed. David Edwards (SCM, 1961) p. 125.

Chapter Ten—Human Hearts and Social Structures (pp. 159–173)

1. *Daily Telegraph*, 5 March 1981.
2. William Temple, *Christianity and Social Order* (first published

Penguin Books, 1942, republished Shepheard-Walwyn and SPCK, 1976) p. 32.
3. E. R. Norman, op. cit., e.g. pp. 279–84.
4. E. R. Norman, op. cit., e.g. p. 123.
5. E. R. Norman, *Christianity and the World Order* (Oxford University Press, 1979) pp. 14, 77.
6. John 1[9].
7. Alan Ecclestone, *Yes to God*, op. cit., p. 17.
8. Margaret Kane, *Theology in an Industrial Society* (SCM, 1975) p. 67.
9. Edward Schillebeeckx, *The Understanding of Faith* (Sheed and Ward, 1974) pp. 145ff.
10. Bernard Häring, *Sin in the Secular Age* (St Paul Publications, 1974) pp. 90, 102. See also pp. 13ff.
11. John Plamenatz, op. cit., p. 142.
12. Matthew 10[14].
13. 2 Corinthians 5[19f].
14. Colossians 1[15–20].
15. On 'the powers' see Hendrick Berkhof, *Christ and the Powers* (Herald Press, Mennonite Publishing House, Scottdale, Pennsylvania, 1962, 1977).
I am also grateful for a letter from Dr Wesley Carr, who has written a thesis on this subject.
16. Colossians 2[15].
17. Luke 23[9].
18. John 19[10].
19. Professor C. F. D. Moule in a study group.
20. The Rev. Robert A. Bennett Jr., Episcopal Divinity School, at a consultation in New York on Urban Theology, convened by the Trinity Institute, May 1979.
21. Ephesians 2[14,16].

Chapter Eleven—Attitudes to the Poor (pp. 174–199)

1. 'The Perception of Poverty in Europe': report on a public opinion survey carried out in the member countries of the European Community as part of the programme of pilot projects to combat poverty. (Commission of the European Communities, Rue de la Loi, 1049 Brussels, March 1977) pp. 70, 82, 88.
2. Luke 12[48].
3. Robert Holman, 'Poverty; Consensus and Alternatives', *British Journal of Social Work* 1973/4, p. 434.

4. Louis Burghes, *Living from Hand to Mouth*, op. cit., p. 15.
5. David Sheppard, *Built as a City*, op. cit., pp. 106ff.
6. Quoted by Philip Collins in the *New Statesman*, 15 December 1978.
7. 1 Corinthians 12[25ff].
8. Sir Keith Joseph in a speech to the Pre-School Playgroups Association, 29 June 1972.
9. Oscar Lewis, *La Vida: A Puerto Rican Family in the Culture of Poverty* (Panther Books, 1968).
10. Peter Townsend, *Poverty in the United Kingdom; A Survey of Household Resources and Standards of Living* (Penguin Books, 1979) pp. 69f.
11. Joan Higgins, *The Poverty Business, Britain and America* (Basil Blackwell, Martin Robertson, 1978) pp. 107f.
12. David Donnison, *The Politics of Poverty* (Martin Robertson, Oxford, 1982) p. 226.
13. Peter Townsend, op. cit., pp. 562ff.
14. *The Times*, 30 June 1981.
15. Sar Levitan, *The Great Society's Poor Law* (John Hopkins Press, Baltimore, 1969) quoted in Joan Higgins, op. cit., pp. 31f.
16. Ben Whitaker, *Participation and Poverty* (Fabian Research Series, 1968) quoted in Joan Higgins, op. cit., p. 126.
17. Joan Higgins, op. cit., p. 141.
18. *Change and Decay*: Final Report of the Liverpool Inner Areas Study (HMSO, 1977) pp. 168ff.
19. Richard Titmuss, *Commitment to Welfare* (George Allen and Unwin, 1968) quoted in Joan Higgins, op. cit., pp. 38f.
20. Richard Farnell, 'Urban Deprivation—Any Sign of Progress?' *Christians in Industrial Areas*, Autumn 1980.
21. Julian Charley in *Christians in Industrial Areas*, Autumn 1980.
22. Jack Dominian, *Marriage, Faith and Love* (Darton, Longman and Todd, 1981) pp. 58ff, 68ff.
23. Joan Higgins, op. cit., p. 122.
24. T. R. Batten, *The Non-Directive Approach in Group and Community Work* (Oxford University Press, 1967) p. 47.
25. Sister Norma Nelson, Church Army, 'Community Development in Britain', an essay for the University of Liverpool DASS Course 1976–7) p. 9.
26. 'Churches in Urban Priority Areas', op. cit.
27. Dr Ian Fraser, Dean of Mission, Selly Oak Colleges, Birmingham, in a letter to me.
28. Ephesians 4[11].

29. 'The Toxteth Survey: Technical Report' (Liverpool City Council, 1982) 2.1.
30. Jim Hart, 'Five Years at the Top', an account of five years living at the top of a block of flats in Inner City Liverpool, which includes a sensitive account of the pressures on community leaders, *Christians in Industrial Areas*, May 1978.
31. A. H. Halsey ed., *Educational Priority—E.P.A. Problems and Policies* (HMSO, 1972) pp. 117f.
32. Paulo Freire, *Pedagogy of the Oppressed* (Penguin Edition, 1972) p. 92.
33. Saul Alinsky, *Rules for Radicals* (Vintage Books, New York, 1972).

Chapter Twelve—Can the Church Bear Good News to the Poor? (pp. 200–225)

1. Luke 13[19].
2. Ephesians 3[10].
3. Luke 7[18-23].
4. John 6[26].
5. Garth Hewitt and Mike Paget-Wilkes, 'Be Free to Praise' in *Inside Out, a Handbook for Youth Leaders*, ed. Michael Eastman (Falcon Books, 1976), p. 115.
6. Alan Ecclestone, *The Night Sky of the Lord*, op. cit., p. 142.
7. Report of the Urban Priority Areas Working Party, op. cit.
8. 'To a Rebellious House?' Report of the Partners in Mission Consultation.
9. David Sheppard, op. cit., pp. 66–70.
10. *Young People and the Church*, the report of a working party set up by the British Council of Churches Youth Unit (BCC, 1981), pp. 71, 93.
11. *NOW!* magazine inaugural issue, September 1979.
12. *Young People and the Church*, op. cit., p. 57.
13. Dave Watts and Richard Longman, 'Youth on the Loose'. The story of one limited project with an unattached group. In *Inside Out*, op. cit., p. 49.
14. Stepney Action Research Team (START) recommends that candidates for local ordained ministry should be paid to take a year off work for full-time study during their period of training. START Report; 'Building an Indigenous Church in East London. The Development of a Local Ministry,' June 1980, pp. 34f.

15. I am indebted to Bishop John Rawsthorne for an account of the scheme for a permanent Diaconate in the Archdiocese of Liverpool.
16. 'Local Ordained Ministry', report of Joint Working Party set up by the Bishop of Liverpool and the Bishop of Manchester, 1982.
17. 'As Others See Us', report of an international ecumenical team visit to the North East of England, 1979, pp. 4, 8.
18. Colin Winter, *The Breaking Process* (SCM Press, 1981).
19. Giles Ecclestone, op. cit., p. 130.
20. Professor Ronald Preston in *Theology*, March 1981.
21. Professor Andrew Kirk, *Liberation Theology, An Evangelical View from the Third World* (Marshalls Theological Library, 1979) p. 193.

Index

Compiled by Robert Urwin

241

European Economic Communities
(E.E.C.), survey on attitudes to
the poor, 174–5, 177, 237n
Evangelical Race Relations Group,
conference (1975), 58–60
Journal of, 229n, 230n, 232n
Evans, E. S. P., 228n
Eversley, David, 27, 228n

Family Service Units, study of
(1980), 30
Farnell, Richard, 238n
Federal Role in Urban Affairs, 1966
(Robert Kennedy), 230n
Field, Frank, 235n
Fierro, Alfredo, 145, 156
The Militant Gospel, 235n, 236n
Filochowski, Julian, 235n
Five Years of Multi-Racial Britain
(Commission for Racial
Equality), 231n
Fletcher, M. E., 228n
Ford Foundation, 179
Ford Motor Company, 116, 117,
233n
Fraser, Ian, 191, 239n
Freire, Paulo (*Pedagogy of the
Oppressed*), 239n
Fuller Seminary (Church Growth
school), Pasadena, 89

Galbraith, J. K. (*The Affluent Society*),
135, 234n
George, Candley, 229n
God's Lost Chance (Jean Russell), 232n
Goldthorpe, John H., 227n
Good Work (E. F. Schumacher), 234n
Goss, Bishop, 53
Gracie, David (*Signs of the Kingdom*),
231n
Graham, Shedman, 229n
Grease, local school production of, 25
Great Britain (*see also* Liverpool):
analyses of classes in, 11–12, 42,
150

Great Britain (*contd.*):
Asians in Britain, 81–4
attitudes to the poor, 179, 182–6
anti-poverty programmes, 179,
182–5
E.E.C. survey report, 174–5,
176, 177
black group solidarity in, 79–81
deprivation of black people, 10, 176
the 'black experience', 58–68
ethnic Churches in, 86–7, 88
housing policies in, 50–1
industrial democracy and trade
unions, 117–20
Jewish immigration into, 98–9
Parliamentary Select Committee
on Employment, 121
police/community relations, 20,
60–8, 170
poverty in major cities, 9–10, 183
Inner Areas Study, 183
problem families and community
development, 186–99
proportion of coloured immigrants, 100–1
racialism in, 83, 84, 95–102, 103–
104, 127
unemployment and under-
employment in, 69–72
discrimination against black
people (examples), 69–70,
71, 76–7, 86–7, 142
violence in society, 13
West Indians'/Asians' educational
achievements, 76–7
Winter of Discontent, 119, 138
trade union selfishness, 138
1968 Immigration Act, 101
Great Society's Poor Law, The (Sar
Levitan), 238n
Green Revolution, 127
Griffiths, Professor Brian, 234n
Guardian, The, 233n
Gulbenkian Foundation, 228n
Gutierrez, Gustavo, 145, 154
A Theology of Liberation, 235n,
236n

INDEX

Sheppard, David (Bishop of Liverpool):
background, 12, 13, 16–17
Bishop of Woolwich (1969–75), 142, 164
Bishop of Liverpool (from 1975), 12, 220–1
Built as a City, 17, 141, 159, 227n, 228n, 229n, 235n, 238n, 239n
chairman of Area Board (Merseyside & Cheshire), Manpower Services Commission, 25, 126
leads pilgrimage to Taizé, 12
Shiloh Pentecostal Church, Dalston, 229n
Shriver, Sargent, 73, 181
Signs of the Kingdom (David Gracie), 231n
Simey, Lord, 1966 speech on colour prejudice, 33
Simey, Margaret, 228n
Sin in the Secular Age (Bernard Häring), 237n
Smith, Adam, 132
Smith, Father Austin, 56, 229n
Smith, Rev. Christopher, 229n
Snaith, Norman (Distinctive Ideas of the Old Testament), 230n
Sobrino, Jon, 146, 235n
Social Limits to Growth (Fred Hirsch), 234n
Sojourners (Washington, D.C.), 232n
Spike Island, Portrait of a Police Division (James McClure), 230n
Stepney Action Research Team (START), 239–40n
Stevedores' Union, 113
Stonier, Professor Tom, 121–2, 233n
Stuart, Morris (The Black Mirror), 229n, 231n
Sunday Times, The, series on inner city areas, 31
Symmetrical Family, The (Michael Young and Peter Willmott), 234n

Taizé, Ecumenical Community at, 12
Tate & Lyle factory, Liverpool, 29
Taylor, Vincent (Gospel According to St Mark), 232n
Tebbit, Norman, 119
Telegraph, Daily, 141, 159, 233n, 235n, 236n
Temple, Archbishop William, 39, 48, 49, 159, 160
Christianity and Social Order, 236n
Thatcher, Mrs Margaret, 14, 100, 159–60
Theology in an Industrial Society (Margaret Kane), 237n, 240n
Theology of Liberation, A (Gustavo Gutierrez), 235n
Third World, 9, 28, 121, 127
attitudes of richer countries to, 9–10
Liberal Capitalism, ideas for development of, 129–30, 135–6
unemployment / underemployment in, 126
Thistleton, Tony, 233n
Times, The, 100, 141, 231n, 235n, 238n
Titmuss, Richard, 184
Commitment to Welfare, 238n
To Hear and to Heed, Urban Bishops' Coalition (U.S.) publication, 227n
Today's Church. A Community of Exiles and Pilgrims (George W. Webber), 230n
Townsend, Peter (Poverty in the United Kingdom: Survey), 238n
Toxteth (see also Liverpool and Merseyside):
British Council of Churches gift to Liverpool, 8
Defence Committee, 65–6, 103
Government attempts to revive Industry, 68
Inner Areas Study, 183
Riots (1981), 13, 32, 34, 41, 61, 65–7, 113, 183, 184, 193, 206

250